New Interpretations of Beckett in the Twenty-first Century

Series Editor: Jennifer M. Jeffers

As the leading literary figure to emerge from post–World War II Europe, Samuel Beckett's texts and his literary and intellectual legacy have yet to be fully appreciated by critics and scholars. The goal of *New Interpretations of Beckett in the Twenty-first Century* is to stimulate new approaches and develop fresh perspectives on Beckett, his texts, and his legacy. The series will provide a forum for original and interdisciplinary interpretations concerning any aspect of Beckett's work or his influence upon subsequent writers, artists, and thinkers.

Jennifer M. Jeffers is Professor of English, Associate Dean, and Ombudsperson for the College of Graduate Studies at Cleveland State University. In addition to numerous articles, she is the author of *The Irish Novel at the End of the Twentieth Century: Gender, Bodies, and Power*; *Britain Colonized: Hollywood's Appropriation of British Literature; Uncharted Space: The End of Narrative*; the editor of *Samuel Beckett;* and coeditor of *Contextualizing Aesthetics: From Plato to Lyotard.*

Also in the Series:

Samuel Beckett: History, Memory, Archive
edited by Seán Kennedy and Katherine Weiss

Beckett's Masculinity
by Jennifer M. Jeffers

Sex and Aesthetics in Samuel Beckett's Work
by Paul Stewart

Previous Publications

Zone of Evaporation: Samuel Beckett's Disjunctions. 2006.

Sex and Aesthetics in Samuel Beckett's Work

Paul Stewart

First published in 2011 by
PALGRAVE MACMILLAN®
in the United States—a division of St. Martin's Press LLC,
175 Fifth Avenue, New York, NY 10010.

Where this book is distributed in the UK, Europe and the rest of the world,
this is by Palgrave Macmillan, a division of Macmillan Publishers Limited,
registered in England, company number 785998, of Houndmills,
Basingstoke, Hampshire RG21 6XS.

Palgrave Macmillan is the global academic imprint of the above companies
and has companies and representatives throughout the world.

Palgrave® and Macmillan® are registered trademarks in the United States,
the United Kingdom, Europe and other countries.

ISBN: 978–0–230–10881–3

Library of Congress Cataloging-in-Publication Data

Stewart, Paul, 1971–
       Sex and aesthetics in Samuel Beckett's work / Paul Stewart.
          p. cm.—(New interpretations of Beckett in the twenty-first century)
       Includes bibliographical references.
       ISBN 978–0–230–10881–3
          1. Beckett, Samuel, 1906–1989—Criticism and interpretation. 2. Sex
    in literature. I. Title. II. Series.

PR6003.E282Z8354 2011
848'.91409—dc22   2011005471

A catalogue record of the book is available from the British Library.

Design by Newgen Imaging Systems (P) Ltd., Chennai, India.

First edition: August 2011

10 9 8 7 6 5 4 3 2 1

Printed and bound in Great Britain by
CPI Antony Rowe , Chippenham and Eastbourne

Contents

Acknowledgments

I would like to thank the University of Nicosia for granting me a sabbatical and research time release, without which this book could not have been finished. My colleagues, Drs. Terzieva-Artemis, Kogetsidis, and Mackay, were very generous in covering for me during the sabbatical period. I would also like to thank Christina Papageorgiou of the University of Nicosia Library for her invaluable aid in overcoming the difficulties of conducting research in Cyprus. I would also like to thank Jill McDonald for her patient efforts at unpacking my prose and checking for howling errors.

I have enjoyed wonderful support from the wider Beckett community. I would like to thank Mark Nixon, Ronan McDonald, Matthew Feldman, Erik Tonning, John Pilling, and Sean Kennedy, in particular, for their assistance in accessing archive material, organizing conferences at which I was able to develop the arguments of this volume, and for their insightful and helpful suggestions. My thanks also go to Laura Salisbury, Ulrika Maude, and Elizabeth Barry.

Certain sections of this volume have appeared in different forms in journals and edited collections. I would like, therefore, to note with appreciation that a version of Chapter 1 first appeared in "All Sturm and no Drang": Beckett and Romanticism/Beckett at Reading 2006: Samuel Beckett Today/Aujourd'hui 18, edited by Dirk van Hulle and Mark Nixon. Aspects of Chapter 5 appeared as "Sterile Reproduction: Beckett's Death of the Species and Fictional Regeneration" in Beckett and Death, edited by Steven Barfield, Matthew Feldman, and Philip Tew (London: Continuum, 2009). My thanks to all these editors. The section of Chapter 5 entitled "The Art of Reproduction: Malone and Schopenhauer" is a revised version of "Sexual and Aesthetic Reproduction in Malone Dies," in Samuel Beckett: Debts and Legacies, Samuel Beckett Today/Aujourd'hui 22 (2010), edited by Erik Tonning, Matthew Feldman, Matthijs Engelberts, and Dirk van Hulle. Again, thanks to those editors.

I would also like to acknowledge the diligence and dedication of the Palgrave team, especially the series editor Jennifer M. Jeffers, my editor Brigitte Shull, and the editorial assistants Joanna Roberts and Lee Norton. They have guided me expertly through the whole process.

Finally, I am deeply indebted to the patience of Katy, Sam, and Joe Stewart, whose collective light darkened and deepened my understanding of Beckett.

Introduction

Sex, Procreation, and Suffering

Estragon: What about hanging ourselves?
Vladimir: Hmm. It would give us an erection!
Estragon: [*Highly excited.*] An erection!
Vladimir: With all that follows.[1]

Vladimir and Estragon are waiting for Godot, of course, as they briefly entertain the possibility of hanging themselves and arguably thereby taking control of their situation and ending the pause in which they seem to live. There are other benefits to hanging oneself, as Vladimir points out. This spilling of semen as one expires through asphyxiation might be taken as an ironic comment on the very sexlessness of these two old men; the only hope of erection and ejaculation for this jaded, beleaguered couple is in the act of suicide. Such an ironic reading, as shall be seen, would suit the more general treatment of sex and sexuality within Beckett's works, which often views matters of sexuality as an early concern that is rigorously excised from the novels and plays as Beckett succeeds in focusing on the more universal, less temporal themes with which his work has become associated. Such a reading would ignore the "highly excited" reaction of Estragon at the mere possibility of an erection. Didi and Gogo are still excited by the prospect of physical sexual expression and not (as a thoroughly Cartesian reading might suggest) horrified by a body seemingly acting beyond the control of the mind. It is certainly true that the opportunities for sexual expression have dwindled to almost nothing for Didi and Gogo, but this does not mean that the possibility of sexual expression, nor the desire for it, has disappeared. Didi's and Gogo's excitement over an erection may be a ruined remnant of "normal" sexuality, but the fact that it is entertained at the point of death speaks to the tenacity of that remnant.

The matter, however, would not be closed with death and ejaculation. Vladimir's "all that follows" goes beyond the spilling of semen: "Where it falls mandrakes grow. That's why they shriek when you pull them up" (18). The myth of the mandrake as a by-product of a suicide's semen is an old and varied one. Beckett activates two key components of the myth—that the mandrake is a human-vegetable (the Greeks referred to it as *anthropomorphon,* and the Romans as *semihominus*[2]) and that when pulled up the plant shrieks as if in pain. In some accounts, the shriek is fatal to humans, as Shakespeare relates in Henry VI, Part 2: "Could curses kill, as doth the mandrake's groan."[3] The mandrake has a paradoxical set of associations surrounding it, best described by Hugo Rahner in *Greek Myths and Christian Mastery*: "The mandrake [can] be the herb of life or of death, symbol of both sensual love, the bringer of death, or of divine love, the restorer of life."[4] The mandrake was used as an aid to fertility, and yet also hedged about with dire warnings for those who would pick it. The association of life and death with this single semi-human vegetable is precisely what Beckett gains by the allusion. Vladimir's comment points to the cycle of birth, suffering, and death, which is a consistent motif in Beckett's work, and he also points to the danger inherent within sexual activity; even semen spilled on the ground at a suicide's feet might not be safely spent but might rather perpetuate the chain of events that guarantees pain.

The mandrake association of sex, suffering, and death forms a key part of this volume, for it is through sex that death and suffering are perpetuated. This association, as expressed by such figures as Mani, Augustine, and, most importantly for Beckett, Schopenhauer, has been a constant if somewhat submerged current throughout Western thought. In his persuasive and almost encyclopedic work, *Death, Desire and Loss in Western Culture*, Jonathan Dollimore effectively catalogues the tone of much early Christian thought concerning reproduction and death. In a comment that might cast a new perspective on Beckett's use of "Death and the Maiden" as a musical introduction to *All That Fall*, Gregory of Nyssa, as recorded by Dollimore, writes:

> the bodily procreation of children [. . .] is more an embarking upon death than upon life. [. . .] Corruption has its beginning in birth and those who refrain from procreation through virginity themselves bring about a cancellation of death by preventing it from advancing further because of them. [. . .] they keep death from going forward [. . .] Virginity is stronger than death. [. . .] The unceasing succession of destruction and

dying [. . .] is interrupted. Death, you see, was never able to be idle while human birth was going on in marriage.[5]

The maiden, in other words, proves fatal to death inasmuch as she breaks life's progression into death by refusing to provide fresh life. "In the Gospel of the Egyptians," writes Dollimore, "is the same idea that to procreate is to nourish death. To abstain from procreation is to hasten the end of the world and so defeat death."[6]

Beckett was not necessarily versed in the Egyptian gospels or the works of Gregory of Nyssa, but the concepts they forcefully present are also present in those works with which Beckett was familiar, not least in the works of St. Augustine. Beckett took copious notes from Augustine's *Confessions* in preparation for writing *Dream of Fair to Middling Women*—citing, for example, Augustine's estimation of the pious as becoming "eunuchs for the kingdom of heaven's sake"[7]—and seems to have been drawn to much of the Saint's thinking concerning sexuality and spirituality. Toward the end of his life, when the sins of the flesh were but a memory, Augustine returned to the spiritual/sexual dichotomy. In *The City of God*, Augustine is faced with the apparent paradox that while mankind is enjoined to multiply, the lust that necessarily precedes procreation is itself shameful. Augustine would prefer the prelapsarian form of generation (an option that logically would have been available to Adam and Eve but was prevented from occurring by the intervention of the first sin) in which the sexual organs are under the governance of the conscious will, in similar fashion to one's hands or feet, leading to "impregnation and conception by an act of will" thus making procreation a "gift of marriage."[8] Unfortunately, the first sin, the punishment for which is death, also results in lust taking control of the sexual organs against the will. Lust is then a fitting punishment for the sin of disobedience, for the sexual organs are now disobedient to the man's or woman's will. In lust, lapsed sexuality itself involves a form of death as so "intense is the pleasure that when it reaches its climax there is an almost total extinction of mental alertness; the intellectual sentries, as it were, are overwhelmed."[9] This death of the will in lust finds its more spiritual counterpart in the "death" of the first parents insomuch as their souls were severed from the Divine: "For in that unruly disturbance that arose in the flesh of the unruly soul, which caused our first parents to cover their *pudenda*, there was experienced one death, the death in which God forsook the soul."[10]

For Augustine, sin, procreation, and death form a complex of bidirectional causalities. Sin opened the way for both death and lust to enter the human condition, and death and sin are in turn generated by lust. Hence, "death is perpetuated by propagation from the first man, and is without doubt the penalty of all who are born,"[11] and "lust in opposition to the spirit [...] is the conflict that attends us from our birth. We bring with us, at our birth, the beginning of our death," thus "mankind is led from that original perversion, a kind of corruption at the root, right up to the disaster of the second death." Through lust-driven reproduction "everyone is in death from the moment that he begins his bodily existence."[12] Such unsparing logico-theological strictures might be felt to underpin much of Beckett's "birth-astride-the-grave" thinking, and, more specifically, Augustine's struggle with the concept of when one is *in* death might account for Beckett's odd phraseology in *Malone Dies*: "given birth to into death."[13] Specific resonances aside, while not condemning procreation in its totality—after all, God has ordained the number of citizens who will inhabit the City of God, and these souls have to be generated—Augustine shares with his less well-known brethren of the early Church a supreme suspicion of the generative capacities of sexuality and is certain that sexual intercourse, itself shamed by sin, is the means by which the punishment for sin, death, is continued.

Augustine does not recommend abstinence as a method of defeating sin and death as Gregory of Nyssa does, partly one suspects because of the heretical Manichaean doctrines with which he was so familiar. (Augustine was a "listener" within Manichaeism for several years before his final conversion to Christianity.) The extreme dualism of Manichaeism, in which this world is a creation of the demi-urge designed to imprison the "true light" of the spirit that would rejoin the pleroma, or fullness, upon death, was not as forcefully rejected by Beckett as it was by Augustine. As James Knowlson has shown, Manichaeism (which Knowlson associates with Gnosticism[14]) can be seen to underpin Beckett's use of light and dark throughout the oeuvre and in particular in *Krapp's Last Tape*. In the Schiller Theatre workbooks of *Krapp* written in 1969, Beckett makes explicit reference to one of Mani's three laws of renunciation: of animal food and strong drink (*signaculum oris*), of property and the secular world (*signaculum manuum*), and of sexual reproduction and marriage (*signaculum sinus*). Demonstrating a working knowledge of Manichaeism, Beckett writes:

> Separation of light from darkness [...] man created by Satan. Cain and Abel sons not of Adam but of Satan and Eve.
>
> Ascetic ethics, particularly abstinence from sexual enjoyment. Sexual desire, marriage, forbidden (signaculum sinus).[15]

Here Beckett focuses on the Manichaean prohibition of marriage and sexual reproduction, at least for those "perfected" within the community.

The logic of such a ban is simple: birth is an act of imprisonment of the "true light" of the spirit and abstinence from sex will prevent this from occurring. The Manichaean "seal" of the prohibition of marriage, and therefore sex, in order to prevent the entrapment of the true light might suggest grounds for Krapp's renunciation of his love; the girl on the punt. Rather than pursuing a relationship of sexual gratification (as the image of the undulating punt certainly suggests), Krapp renounces the flesh in order to live an ascetic existence focused on the channeling of his spirit toward his art. However, Krapp remains dependent on the more material aspects of this world also, not least on the "bony old ghost of a whore" (*CDW* 222), Fanny, for sexual gratification. It may be that this only underlines Krapp's personal weakness, that he is unable to devote himself fully to art. Yet, as a more nuanced reading of Manichaeism in Chapter 5 suggests, it may also lead to the recognition of a certain skepticism on Beckett's part concerning the ability of art to transcend the gross, material world from which it derives. It may be that sex cannot be divorced from aesthetics quite as easily as might be wished.

Nevertheless, if, as in Manichaean thought, the greatest boon really is to have never been born, this concept, via Beckett's *Proust*, leads on to its expression in the works of Schopenhauer,[16] which may well lie behind much of Beckett's thinking on sexual reproduction and death. Beckett claims the true Proustian tragedy is the necessary expiation of "...the original and eternal sin of him and all his 'socii malorum', the sin of having been born."[17] Beckett concludes the section of the essay by quoting approvingly from Calderón de la Barca:

Pues el delito mayor
Del hombre es habier nacido[18]

Beckett is here borrowing both the content and the structure of the expression from Schopenhauer's *World as Will and Representation*. Before quoting this exact passage from Calderón, Schopenhauer writes that the "true sense of the tragedy is the deeper insight that what the hero atones for is not his particular sins, but original sin, in other words, the guilt of existence itself."[19] In this one passage from *Proust*, Schopenhauer, Calderón, and, it can be argued, the Augustinian notion of original sin are joined into a compelling argument against the calamity of birth, which elsewhere Schopenhauer puts in stark terms: "human desires [...] must be originally and in their essence sinful and reprehensible, and the entire will to live itself reprehensible."[20] The reprehensible will-to-live, according to Schopenhauer, duly finds its utmost expression in sexual reproduction. In *The World as Will and Representation,* he writes that "[sexual desire] is the kernel of the will-to-live, and consequently the concentration of all willing"[21] and that with the

> affirmation [of the will-to-live] beyond one's own body to the production
> of a new body, suffering and death, as belonging to the phenomenon
> of life, are also affirmed anew, and the possibility of salvation, brought
> about by the most complete faculty of knowledge, is for this time declared
> to be fruitless.[22]

For Schopenhauer, it therefore follows that in order to gain salvation, in order to renounce the will-to-live, with its concomitant desires and inevitable sufferings, there must be a renunciation of procreation:

> If the act of procreation were neither the outcome of a desire nor accompanied by feelings of pleasure, but a matter to be decided on the basis
> of purely rational considerations, is it likely the human race would still
> exist? Would each of us not rather have felt so much pity for the coming generation as to prefer to spare it the burden of existence, or at least
> not wish to take upon himself to impose that burden upon it in cold
> blood?[23]

The abhorrence of procreation partly accounts for the often virulent misogyny to be found in both Schopenhauer and Beckett's early works. This misogyny is reinforced in Beckett by an oft-expressed hatred of the child, or misopedia, which again is rooted in an understanding of the inherent dangers of procreation and indeed of existence as such. Both misogyny and misopedia—two of the more unpalatable aspects of Beckett's oeuvre—are an integral part of his reaction against the results of heteronormative, penetrative sex. The turn away from procreation also entails the exploration of what are, in the terms of *Mercier and Camier,* "other channels" (*MC* 59), be it other orifices or different genders.

Sex and Aesthetics

Schopenhauer, with whom Beckett was so familiar, provides the necessary link between the abhorrence of procreative sex and the supposed joys of aesthetic contemplation. As we have seen, Schopenhauer identified sex as the locus of the will, and it was precisely the will-to-live that he wished to overcome. As laid out in *The World as Will and Representation,* the will can be overcome or ablated (and life made thereby at least somewhat bearable) in three ways: through aesthetic contemplation, compassion, and resignation. Gottfried Büttner has argued that "Beckett followed all three of Schopenhauer's recommendations against unhappiness, although with different intensity: in the practice of his art; in his compassion towards his fellow beings; and, to a certain extent, in the resignation he exercised..."[24] It might be tempting to pattern Beckett's life and art on Schopenhauer's philosophy, but as shall be seen there is good reason to believe that Beckett followed Schopenhauer only up to a certain point, and that he was especially deeply ambivalent about the "mysticism" with which Schopenhauer associated resignation that had the ability to "free its owner from all care and anxiety for ever."[25]

Schopenhauer's palliative system begins with aesthetic contemplation:

> What might be otherwise called the finest part of life, its purest joy, just because it lifts us out of real existence, and transforms us into disinterested spectators of it, is pure knowledge which remains foreign to all willing, pleasure in the beautiful, genuine delight in art.[26]

To be lifted out of "real existence" is to free oneself from the dictates of the will-in-time. The aesthetic object elicits a disinterested contemplation in which the viewer's individual will is suspended, along with the separation of object and subject. The viewer and viewed in effect merge and "we are no longer able to separate the perceiver from the perception, but the two have become one, since the entire consciousness is filled and occupied by a single image of perception."[27] The result of such an experience of the sublime is the *momentary* suspension of the ravages of the will; we are no longer driven by lack (and hence pain) into a yet further round of pyrrhic desire, but removed both from want and time. Instead, "knowledge can withdraw from this subjection [to the will], throw off its yoke, and, free from all the aims of the will, exist purely for itself, simply as a clear mirror of the world..."[28]

Such a throwing off of the yoke of the will through aesthetic contemplation is incompatible with sexual activity and procreation. Schopenhauer asserts that the body is an objectification of the ever-desiring will and that the ultimate aim of the preservation of the body is the continuation of the race and, therefore, of the will as thing-in-itself beyond its objectification in the body of the individual. He argues that "the fundamental theme of all the many different acts of will is the satisfaction of the needs inseparable from the body's existence in health; they have their expression in it, and can be reduced to the maintenance of the individual and the propagation of the race."[29] Individuals are therefore born into an existence of suffering as mere momentary phenomena of the perpetual, timeless will. Abstinence from sexual activity would not only assist the quieting of the individual will but would strike a blow against the will itself and, hopefully, break the cycle of sex, birth, and suffering. Indeed Schopenhauer, alongside offering aesthetic contemplation as a momentary respite from the will, advocates asceticism and abstinence and yet admits that the overcoming of sexual desire "is a difficult and painful self-conquest."[30] The difficulty of abandoning sexual activity in all its forms might in part explain why even Didi and Gogo get "highly excited" at the thought of an erection, and the very tenacity of sexual expression in Beckett's work might itself point to a divergence from Schopenhauer's philosophy of salvation.

Schopenhauer's brand of sublime optimism—wherein access to the sublime can palliate suffering engendered by the will—gives one possible solution to the problem of a suffering existence, which can be seen to have concerned Beckett. As will be seen, his anti-procreative stance certainly bears comparison to that of Schopenhauer. However, Beckett was not only engaged in aesthetic contemplation but also in aesthetic creation. As far as the artist is concerned, Schopenhauer's philosophy is perhaps less optimistic. Initially, the artist is one in whom the genius for pure perception is most pronounced and who has "the capacity to remain in the state of pure perception, to lose oneself in perception, to remove from the service of the will the knowledge which originally existed only for this service."[31] Creation then begins in an act of aesthetic contemplation, with all the momentary benefits that this entails. For Schopenhauer (and Beckett follows him closely on this point in *Proust*), this capacity is then translated into the work of art that is subsequently created whereby the "artist lets us peer into the world through their eyes. That he has these eyes, that he knows the essential in things which lies outside all relations, is the gift of genius and is inborn; but that he is able to lend us this gift, to let us see with his eyes, is acquired, and is the technical side of art."[32] Although the artist enjoys the initial joy of pure perception, he does not feel the benefits for long as "he himself bears the cost of producing that play; in other words, he himself is the will objectifying itself and remaining in constant suffering."[33]

Schopenhauer may pass over this "technical side of art," but as a working artist, it is precisely this question of the technical that would continue to concern Beckett. The diversity and development of Beckett's oeuvre speaks of a constant struggle to fashion the necessary technical tools that Schopenhauer assumes are but the secondary part of artistic creation. For the present volume, the creation of art is viewed in the light of Beckett's Schopenhauer-affirmed view of sexual procreation. The question for Beckett that this volume proposes is whether or not a form of aesthetic creation can be attained without recourse to paradigms of sexual procreation. If procreation is an absolute expression of the will and perpetuates suffering, can artistic creation avoid such unfortunate results? To put this as an ethical problem; if it is ethically wrong to create further life, can it be ethically correct to create fictional life? Can the creation of an existence be free from the consequences of actual procreation?

Defining Sex

Is Didi's and Gogo's excitement at the thought of an erection and "all that follows" actually sexual in nature? Common sense might suggest that any emission of semen accompanied by high excitement should qualify as at least some form of sexual expression. Yet defining what sex is has proved a difficult task in contemporary philosophical circles.

Alan Goldman's definition of what should be included within sexual activity and sexual desire, for example, would exclude Vladimir's and Estragon's erections from being sexual at all. He writes that: "Sexual desire is desire for the contact with another person's body and for the pleasure which such contact produces; sexual activity is activity which tends to fulfill such desire of the agent."[34] Of course, hanging oneself from a tree does not entail, nor does it even imagine, "contact with another person's body." However, desire is present, although the sexual element of ejaculation is uncomfortably merged with the desire for death in a manner not dissimilar to auto-erotic asphyxiation. It might be argued that this is a deviant form of sexual expression, but it is undoubtedly sexual in nature and intent.

Robert Solomon's view of human sexuality, in a drive to distinguish between animal and human forms, again necessitates the presence of at least one other person, as human sexuality is "a means of communication, it is [...] *essentially* an activity performed with other people."[35] No such communication is envisaged by Didi and Gogo, nor, one suspects, would any such communication be actually welcomed. Similarly, when considering arousal, desire and love in sexual mores, Roger Scruton contends "that all are human phenomena, or rather, that they belong to that realm of reciprocal response which is mediated by the concept of the person, and which is available only to beings who possess and are motivated by that concept."[36] The stress on reciprocity in Scruton's account again excludes Didi's and Gogo's imagined act from the realms of "proper" sexual desire and action: their actions are solitary. One might argue, then, that Estragon's "high excitement" is only indicative of a deviant sexual desire that cannot, or will not, find the necessary reciprocal accompaniment.

Given these accounts of sexual desire and activity, perhaps the erection-through-suicide model espoused by Didi and Gogo is simply beyond the pale of sexual activity. However, according to Scruton's, Solomon's, and

Goldman's definitions, masturbation—which most people would admit is a sexual act whether or not it is morally acceptable—would similarly be disqualified, as Alan Soble has pointed out.[37] Such an outcome seems unjustified. As Christopher Hamilton has suggested, any philosophically rigorous definition of sex "end[s] up ruling out some desire or act which, in the absence of the definition, we should have no difficultly in regarding as sexual."[38] With the case in point—suicidal autoerotic asphyxiation—some might feel more difficulty in regarding it as sexual, yet that does not thereby disqualify it as a form of sexual expression.

"Sexual desire," argues Hamilton, "is a huge, sprawling phenomenon, which casts its shadow over almost every aspect of our inner life and can find expression in a fantastic variety of acts."[39] Beckett's works display just such a "fantastic variety," from heterosexual vaginal penetration to masturbation, homo- and/or heterosexual anal penetration, sadomasochism, fellatio through to hints of bestiality. Following Hamilton, it could be argued that what binds this disparate group of activities together is a form of "family resemblance" as described by Wittgenstein in connection with games. Individual games, such as football, poker, and chess need not necessarily share a common feature, but may be bound together by "a complicated network of similarities overlapping and criss-crossing: sometimes overall similarities, sometimes similarities of detail."[40] This allows for the inclusion of sexual activities that do not include shared characteristics. For example, if one were to take penetration as a defining characteristic, then masturbation and autoerotic asphyxiation would be excluded, or, by contrast, these two categories of activity would also be excluded if a partner (let alone reciprocity) were the *sine qua non* of sexual expression.

Such a working definition might seem to elide any consideration of what constitutes sexual desire and sexual expression in Beckett's work, and also hedge the question of the nature of the intention behind the sexual activities which are described. However, it does recognize that desire and intention might change depending on the act itself and the circumstances surrounding it. In the case of Didi and Gogo, they would not hang themselves with the intention of gaining sexual pleasure, but that pleasure would be a welcome by-product of the intention to kill themselves. The changing nature of intention, desire, and sexual activity is captured in *How It Is* as the protagonist recalls his sexual history from his "life in the light":

Pam Prim we made love every day then every third then the Saturday then just the odd time to get rid of it tried to revive it through the arse too late she fell from the window or jumped broken column[41]

The details here are schematic, but the trajectory of decline in and the variety of sexual activity attests to the changing nature of intention and desire. Newlyweds expressing reciprocal love and attraction give way to a feeling of conjugal obligation, which is in turn replaced by a mechanical need to "get rid of it" until the final effort to enliven the relationship through anal sex is attempted. In each case, the intention is different without excluding the individual acts from the "family" of sexual activity.

Given the variety of sexual acts and intentions within Beckett's work, a prescriptive definition of sex has been avoided in what follows. In its stead, individual sex acts—real or imagined—are viewed through those philosophical and/or psychological concepts that are either invited by the text through contextualizing allusion or that offer perspectives on the nature or significance of those acts. The nature of the sexual desire expressed and the means of its expression are often precisely at issue.

* * *

This volume follows an approximately chronological order, beginning with the dense, punning prose of *Dream of Fair to Middling Women* and ending with the theatrical austerity of *What Where*. This arrangement is intended to show the development of Beckett's thinking on sexual matters and how issues of sex, and the concept of aesthetic reproduction to which they gave rise, were deployed across the range of his career in different genres that, in turn, occasioned different artistic difficulties. Chapter 1 acts as a form of case study in which the sexual stimulation Belacqua feels at the sight of a defecating horse on page one of *Dream* opens up key associations (via Freud's case of "Little Hans") between sex, birth, and excrement. This is then traced in Molloy's narrative and *All That Fall*—in which Maddy Rooney has a "lifelong preoccupation with horses' buttocks," (*CDW* 195)—to suggest that Beckett reacts against reproductive forms of sexuality and seems to be advocating sterility, or the exploration of non-reproductive forms of sexual expression.

Chapter 2, "The Horror of Sex," begins by arguing against a Cartesian reading of Beckett's works that has assumed that the body (and, therefore, sex) was viewed by Beckett as something that needed to be denigrated and hopefully transcended. In contrast, the chapter demonstrates how masturbation, which necessarily plays across the mind/body divide, is integral to *Dream* and intimately related to the process of aesthetic creation. Belacqua's apparent revulsion to sex is undermined by the persistence of sexual expression across *Dream* and the stories of *More Pricks than Kicks*, and *Murphy* continues in a similar vein but also demonstrates the protagonist's resistance to "normal" reproductive sexual forms. Finally, the prose of the 1930s is contextualized by outlining the debates surrounding birth control within the Irish Free State in particular and Europe more generally. Beckett's interventions in this debate, "Che Sciagura" (1929) and "Censorship in Saorstat" (1935), are examined and seen to mark a clear difference between Beckett and those with a nationalist and/or natalist agenda. Indeed, the horror of sex is amply demonstrated to be a horror of reproduction through the satirical attack on the Free State's contraceptive ban in the shape of the Bando story of *Watt*, and the absurdly fertile Lynch family, who, precisely because of such fertility, condemn generations to suffering and submission to Schopenhauer's will-to-live.

Chapter 3 develops Beckett's reaction against reproductive sexuality more deeply through a reading of the short story "First Love." This text is considered through the prism of Otto Rank's theory of the trauma of birth (with which Beckett became acquainted in the mid 1930s), Freud's "Wolf-man" case, and the already established birth/excrement nexus. It is argued that the protagonist recoils from sex with Lulu/Anna and rejects the subsequent child due to a wish to return fully to a womb-like state, the expulsion from which is meant to be assuaged by heterosexual sex, according to Rank. This recoil and rejection is then manifested through Beckett's misogyny and misopedia. Of the former, the often virulent hatred of women in the texts is argued to stem from the wish never to have been born and a fear of the fertility of the female. Yet, Beckett's characters are repeatedly drawn toward women, suggesting a need to once again approach the womb through sexual intercourse. That this is unsuccessful then accounts for the pattern of repeated flight and return to woman that so many of Beckett's male characters display. Beckett's misopedia is viewed as a necessary corollary for the misogyny of the texts. "The Expelled," *Watt*, and *All That Fall* demonstrate the importance and pervasiveness of misopedia within the works. These are considered in the light of St. Augustine's theory of original sin, and Schopenhauer's will-to-live, both of which assert that suffering and death are brought into being by birth itself. The child is then viewed as a regrettable guarantor of future suffering, thus somewhat justifying Dan Rooney's desire to murder a small child. Yet, many of Beckett's characters still wish to find some form of continuation. This is examined in the light of the Cronus myth in *Malone Dies*, and the father and son relations of Moran and Jacques Jr. in *Molloy*, which display the paradox of wanting a child to replicate oneself and precisely fearing the child because it *is* a successful replication. All these elements suggest a deep suspicion of what might be termed the "tyranny of the child," a tyranny that is undermined by Beckett's repeated recourse to forms of impotent sexuality, such as the geriatric relations of Molloy and Ruth/Edith, or those of Macmann and Moll. In these cases, the *telos* of sexual relations, reproduction, has been removed, allowing Beckett to focus on the grotesque nature of sexual congress and the absurdity of notions of romantic love as a form of ideological justification for the creation of further suffering beings.

As Beckett repeatedly turns away from reproductive forms of sex, it is logical that nonheteronormative forms of sexual expression should be featured in his work, and Chapter 4, "Alternating and Alternative Sexualities," charts the deployment of homosexual and homosocial possibilities within the oeuvre. Mercier's and Camier's sexual acts are first examined, and these, it is argued, suggest that the boundaries between male and female, the homosexual and the heterosexual, are of a porous nature that calls into question the association of sexual preference with identity. This thematic is then explored as Beckett makes strategic use of homosexual acts or characters as forces that are disruptive of heteronormal identities. Yet, through the relation of Molloy and Ruth/Edith, in which the exact gender of the "woman" is uncertain and so the nature of the sex equally so, it is argued that Beckett also does not allow the nonheteronormative possibilities to coalesce into an alternative identity based on sexual preference. With reference to the work of Leo Bersani and Lee Edelman, Beckett's characters of the 1940s prose are shown to be indifferent to sexual difference and their refusal to be contained within the homo-heterosexual dyad suggests a fluidity that will not be dammed by established social identities, no matter how transgressive or marginalized such identities might appear to be. The possibility that the "queer" might offer new forms of social relation and connectedness, as Bersani has suggested, is finally questioned through the anally fixated sadism of *How It Is*. It is argued, though, that (following Deleuze) the sadism displayed within the novel does not allow for any form of reciprocation or give access, as Foucault has claimed for S/M, to any form of jouissance. However, with the focus on the anus as a site of possible connectivity, it is finally argued that the anus/vagina conflation within Beckett's work might lead one to question the desirability of a new form of relation based on a shared experience of being born as excrement into an excremental world.

Chapter 5 begins by considering the theme of sterility within such plays as *Happy Days* and *All That Fall*, which, nevertheless, demonstrate the tenacity of sexual desire and the difficulty of averting Schopenhauer's will-to-live. *All That Fall*, in particular, is seen to capture the imperative to bring procreation to a halt—an imperative that is harshly laid out by Dr. Piouk in *Eleutheria*. The desire to embrace sterility is, however, mitigated by the desire for continuation, and, in this respect, Hamm in *Endgame* is exemplary as he searches for means of continuance (such as adoption and the creation of characters for his narrative) that are not implicated in the regrettable consequences of sexual reproduction. Hamm's narrative and the fact that Beckett has created the sterile world of *All That Fall* out of the literal nothing that precedes the radio play suggest an adoption of forms of aesthetic reproduction as a replacement of sexual reproduction. This sex and aesthetics relation is characterized through *Krapp's Last Tape*. In-line with Manichaean thought, a form of masturbatory aesthetics is revealed within the play in which the gross world is distilled through the aesthetic process into a pure art form that is meant to transcend its baser origins. However, the success of Krapp's aesthetics, which are related to those of Joyce's *A Portrait of the Artist as a Young Man*, are uncertain and suggest a pessimism on Beckett's part as to the possibility of the transcendental, consolatory role of art. This pessimism is then further examined through a detailed analysis of the "play" and "earnestness" dichotomy within *Malone Dies*, which is related to the aesthetics of Schiller and Schopenhauer. The chapter demonstrates how Malone attempts to free himself from time and the will through pure aesthetic reproduction, but that this is compromised by this purity becoming conceptually infected by paradigms drawn from sexual reproduction. In such a way, Beckett shows himself to be skeptical of the supposed benefits of Romantic aesthetics, and Beckett's art is seen to be a failure in terms of the aesthetic attitude as espoused by Schiller and Schopenhauer.

The final chapter traces forms of aesthetic reproduction across Beckett's later prose and drama. As the works become increasingly abstract, moments of overt sexual expression are replaced by a thematic and structural awareness of the manner in which aesthetic creation is infected by implications more normally associated with procreation. *Texts for Nothing* and *How It Is* are both seen to depend on a constant process of recommencement, which is cast in procreative terms, and both texts display an uncomfortable awareness of the ethical problems concerning the creation of suffering being. With the rotunda stories of the 1960s, especially "All Strange Away," Beckett, it is argued, reverses the process of civilization through art, which Otto Rank saw as the progressive move away from forms of maternal dependence toward an art of human agency and autonomy. Beckett, though, takes his figures back into the womb-like spaces of the rotunda, as if to compensate for the trauma of an initial expulsion. Yet again, though, it is seen that art fails to compensate for such a trauma precisely because aesthetic creation entails the creation of bodily form. Finally, aesthetic reproduction and the ethical problems it implies are brought on to the stage in Beckett's late drama. The question of who or what is responsible for the creation and concomitant suffering within the plays is explored with reference to the "voice" that is often displaced from the dismembered body on the stage itself. Through *Not I*, *Footfalls*, *A Piece of Monologue,* and the late radio plays *Cascando* and *Rough for Radio II*, the section argues for a consistent attempt to displace creative authority—an authority that is closely associated with the torturing of a suffering being into speech. Throughout these late works for the stage and the page, Beckett sought to find a form of art and expression that would not reproduce the regrettable consequences of sexual reproduction, yet in each new form and with each increase in abstraction, the perennial problem of art giving birth to a suffering being persisted. In this sense, Beckett's attempts to create an art of impotence continually struggled against the very potency inherent within artistic creation; he failed to fail enough.

CHAPTER 1

A Rump Sexuality: The Recurrence of Defecating Horses in Beckett's Oeuvre

A s the Introduction noted, remnants of sexuality, in a variety of expressions, can be found throughout Beckett's works, albeit often in nonnormative, distorted, or oblique forms. The prevalence of sex and its use as a motif in the works can best be traced to the origins of Beckett's oeuvre, the aborted novel *Dream of Fair to Middling Women*. This exuberant, if not entirely successful, work was cannibalized to form the backbone of the collection *More Pricks than Kicks,* although important differences pertain between the two works. Beckett consistently refused to publish this first novel, describing it as the "chest into which [he] threw [his] wild thoughts,"[1] and only the author's death finally permitted its publication. Yet this chest proves to be a treasure trove in terms of the attitudes expressed toward, and the uses made of, sexuality. It might be argued that Beckett's attempt to distance himself from *Dream of Fair to Middling Women* implies that what might be there to uncover would have little or no bearing on his more mature works. However, such an assertion is undermined by the consistent deployment of sexual motifs across the decades and genres of the oeuvre, which are first found in *Dream of Fair to Middling Women*. A case in point is the bizarre sexual stimulation occasioned by the sight of a defecating horse.

If one were in any doubt about the prevalence of sexuality within the novel, then the sheer number of quotations—either in altered form or buried within the fabric of the text—from two obscure works on sexuality reveals the extent to which the motif is woven into the fabric of the novel. Beckett, somewhat in the manner of James Joyce, took a magpie approach to writing, noting down a host of phrases and images from a wide range of works that were then incorporated into the novel itself to form a tapestry of quotations and allusions. In the notebook for *Dream,* William M. Cooper's *Flagellation and Flagellants* has 71 entries and Pierre Garnier's *Onanisme seul et à deux sous toutes ses formes et leurs conséquences* is noted some 50 times.[2] Indeed, Beckett's novelistic career might be said to begin within, and to grow from, adolescent sexuality. The first chapter of *Dream of Fair to Middling Women* charts the modes of Belacqua's sexual awakening—modes that include the first of Beckett's defecating horses:

> Behold Belacqua an overfed child pedalling, faster and faster, his mouth ajar and his nostrils dilated, down a frieze of hawthorn after Findlater's van, faster and faster till he cruise alongside of the hoss, the black fat wet rump of the hoss. Whiphim up, vanman, flickem, flapem, collop-wallop fat Sambo. Stiffly, like a perturbation of feathers, the tail arches for a gush of mard. Ah...![3]

Before dealing with the defecating horse as sexual stimulus, this passage will also serve to illustrate the nature of the critical discourse as regards the sexual elements within Beckett. As Bel cycles past the hawthorn, two modes of sexuality meet: the literary and the physical. The hawthorn, as John Pilling in *A Companion to Dream of Fair to Middling Women*[4] has pointed out, alludes to the young Marcel of Marcel Proust's *Swann's Way,* who was entranced by the hawthorn on the altar in the church at Combray. The vision of this hawthorn itself is not innocent of sexual undertones. Marcel, in order to process the beauty of the flowers, transforms them into the image of a young girl. The first encounter with Gilberte, in which Marcel wishes to "reach, touch, capture, bear off in triumph the body"[5] at which his gaze is directed, is also presaged by a return of the hawthorn motif.[6]

While this might be a slight point, a more thorough critical privileging of the mind over the body can be glimpsed through the first reference to a bicycle in Beckett's works. The bicycle is an integral part of Bel's adolescent sexual experience. It offers immediate physical stimulation as the motion of the legs rising and falling provide the necessary friction elsewhere offered by sliding down ropes in the gymnasium. Of course, bikes in Beckett have received some critical scrutiny, yet a sexualized perspective on these apparently Cartesian machines has not formed part of that inquiry. Molloy's regard for his bike occasions one of the few quasi-romantic apostrophes in Beckett's work: "Dear bicycle, I shall not call you bike, you were green, like so many of your generation."[7] Why is Molloy so attached to his bike? One is more accustomed to seeing the bicycle as a Cartesian mind/body amalgam, a "product of the pure intelligence." Hugh Kenner describes the experience of riding a bicycle as "the mind set on survival, mastery, and the contemplation of immutable relativities [...], the body [is] a reduction to uncluttered terms of the quintessential machine," without which the "Cartesian man [...] is a mere intelligence fastened to a dying animal."[8] No doubt due to the verve of Kenner's arguments, the bicycle as a symbol of the intellect's independence from the demands of the accursed body has become a mainstay of critical reactions. Although the bicycle might be a product of the pure intelligence, one cannot go on to assert, as Kenner does, that now the pure intelligence "dominates it in function."[9] While the cerebral may pertain here, the critical maneuver is to emphasize that aspect at the cost of a sexualized perspective, which stubbornly asserts that the body is a crucial factor of Molloy's love of his bike. First, the one thing to remain of the bicycle is the horn; a horn, moreover, described in sexually charged terms. To blow it, was, for Molloy "a real pleasure, almost a vice," and he goes further to declare that "if I were obliged to record, in a roll of honour, those activities which in my interminable existence have given me only a mild pain in the balls, the blowing of a rubber horn—toot—would figure among the first" (*M* 12–13). The masturbatory undertones of Molloy's fixation on the horn over and above his supposed love of his bike need not be underlined. Certainly, once the prism of sexuality has been inserted, a pattern far from Cartesian dualism emerges.[10]

As Molloy derives pleasure from his bike, so Moran from his autocycle. When considering which form of transportation to use for his pursuit of Molloy, Moran gives in to "the fatal pleasure principle" (*M* 102) and chooses the autocycle—a pleasure which might well be enriched by the feeling of a throbbing machine between one's thighs. To complete this foray into the sexuality of bikes, one need only consider the sad fate of the bicycle in *Mercier and Camier*:

Of it there remains, said Mercier, securely chained to the railing, as much as may reasonably remain, after a week's incessant rain, of a bicycle relieved of both the wheels, the saddle, the bell and the carrier. And the tail-light.[11]

Janet Menzies, in her article "Beckett's Bicycles," chooses to gloss this passage as an occasion for the interrogation of bike *qua* bike, stating: "All this leads to a much closer examination of the bicycle: what is its most important feature, what is it that makes a bicycle a bicycle?"[12] She notes that the bicycle pump mysteriously remains, but the pump does not feature in her thinking:

her focus is the cerebral appreciation of and the intellectual discourse surrounding the bicycle. But the pump does remain. Just as Molloy's bike is reduced to the phallic horn, so Mercier's and Camier's bike is reduced to the phallic remainder of the pump, reminiscent of the "demented hydraulic" (*Dream* 41) of Belacqua's sexual appetite.

Reacting in part against the cerebral discourse of Janet Menzies, Jake Kennedy, in his article "Modernist (Im)mobilities: Marcel Duchamp, Samuel Beckett and the Avant-Garde Bike," gestures toward a sexualized reading of the bike in "Fingal" in *More Pricks than Kicks*. Belacqua, out for a romantic clinch with Winnie, finds a bicycle near the Portrane Lunatic Asylum. He is strangely drawn to the bicycle, in a manner that Janet Menzies finds "faintly disturbing."[13] Kennedy suggests that what disturbs Menzies is the erotic suggestiveness of the bicycle: "Belacqua's interest in the bicycle is described in relation to his desire: he could, on no account, 'resist' a bicycle. In this way, too, the bicycle is the clear, if wry substitution of or for Winnie and, indeed, the scene mimics the encounter just previously in which the lovers had been lying on the grass."[14] This observation is not pursued by Kennedy, but, if one were to do so, an interesting paradigm emerges: Bel (quite literally) flees from a "proper" sexuality with Winnie in favor of a solitary, bike-led sexuality. But why?

Deleuze and Guatarri in *Anti-Oedipus* also suggest what might be at stake in the question of the sexualised bike, although they do so in the form of a tantalizing question. They note the proximity of Molloy's rhapsodies on his bike to his less-than-rhapsodic account of his birth. The text of *Molloy* reads:

What a rest to speak of bicycles and horns. Unfortunately it is not of them I have to speak, but of her who brought me into this world, through the hole in her arse if my memory is correct. First taste of the shit (*M* 13).

Deleuze and Guattari ask, "What relationship does the bicycle-horn machine have with the mother-anus machine?"[15] In a manner, that question will be answered by addressing the horse-anus-excrement machine.

Once again John Pilling provides a valuable, if slightly misleading, hint in his annotations to *Dream*: "A fascination with horses excreting is the neurosis of 'little Hans' in Freud's classic study."[16] This comment is valuable in that it correctly offers little Hans as an analogue to, if not a direct allusive source for, Bel's fascination with horses' posteriors. It is misleading in that little Hans's neurosis is not quite a "fascination with horses excreting," but rather a phobia concerning horses (especially getting bitten by one, or one falling while pulling a bus or heavily loaded cart) is accompanied by a fascination for, and repulsion by, defecation. Pilling's characterization of the little Hans case certainly provides striking and troubling parallels with Bel's adolescent excitement.

When Hans was less than five years old, his initial neurotic symptom was a phobia of horses that was so extreme as to make him housebound. The psychoanalysis of Hans by his father in consultation with Freud revealed that the fear of being bitten by a horse was more a fear of the horse falling and possibly dying. Freud summarized the result of the analysis thus far:

> Behind the fear to which Hans gave first expression, the fear of a horse biting him, we had discovered a more deeply seated fear, the fear of horses falling down; and both kinds of horses [...] had been shown to represent his father, who was going to punish him for the evil wishes he was nourishing against him.[17]

At this Oedipal stage, scatological concerns come to the fore as Hans started to show disgust at things that reminded him of excretion, among which was the color black. Freud again takes up the story:

> [His father] recognized that there was an analogy between a heavily loaded cart and a body load of faeces, between the way in which a cart drives through a gateway and the way in which the faeces leave the body...[18]

Properly deciphered through analysis, the loaded carts were symbolic of his mother's pregnancy (his sister had been born some 18 months prior) leading to one of Freud's more famous theories of infant sexuality: the theory of anal birth. According to Freud, the belief in anal birth was an inevitable consequence of a gap in physical knowledge since "the boy would be bound to approach the subject of childbirth by way of the excretory complex."[19] The horses of which Hans was so scared are, of course, overdetermined: on the one hand, they represent the father whom the child wishes to replace in order to have children with his own mother; on the other, they are representations of the childhood theory of procreation as anal birth, and so connected with the mother, for: "when a heavy or heavily loaded horse fell down he can have seen in it only one thing—a childbirth ['ein Niederkommen']. Thus the falling horse was not only his father dying but also his mother in childbirth."[20] Freud states this theory in his essay of 1908 "On Sexual Theories of Children":

> Their ignorance of the vagina also makes it possible for the children to believe in the second of their sexual theories. If the baby grows in the

mother's body and is then removed from it, this can only happen along the one possible pathway—the anal aperture. *The baby must be evacuated like a piece of excrement, like a stool...*[21]

One further strand needs to be added. In one phase of the analysis, little Hans admitted to a wish to beat horses. He is reported as saying: "It doesn't do the horses any harm when they're beaten. [...] Once I did it really. Once I had the whip, and whipped the horse, and it fell down and made a row with its feet."[22] This Freud took to be an obscure sadistic desire for the mother.

The parallels with the sequence in *Dream* are striking. First, the horse is pulling a delivery van for Findlater's grocery store. Second, the sadistic whipping of the horse is emphasized, as is the color black. Finally, excreta is an integral part of the experience. It would appear that Beckett is very closely following the story of little Hans, or at least activating the key representational factors of the boy's case history. One should note that Bel is described as "overfed," similar to little Hans, who had trouble with constipation and was seen by a doctor who was "of the opinion he was overfed, which was in fact the case..."[23] However alike the Freudian and Beckettian texts seem to be, one crucial element in Bel's excitement is nonetheless absent from the little Hans case study. The climactic moment for Bel is the horse raising its tail and defecating. In the Hans case, the fecal focus is parallel to, and then merges with, the neurosis he experiences, and a defecating horse as such does not feature in that neurosis. The importance of this difference cannot be overstressed, for it is precisely the same action, or the possibility of such an action, that the Unnamable, when armless and legless and thrust into a jar, hopes might mean the possibility of an orgasm: "With a yo heave ho, concentrating with all my might on a horse's rump, at the moment when the tail rises, who knows, I might not go altogether empty-handed away."[24]

What Bel and the Unnamable both possess, unlike little Hans, is a dual image. The defecating horse is at once an erotic image of penetration and, following Freud somewhat, an image of evacuation, or a shitting birth. In the first case, the feces of the horse acts as a representation of the penis entering into the vagina. In its appearance, the anus of a horse is reminiscent of the vagina, allowing for both the images of penetration and evacuation to work. To support this empirical observation, one need only consider the equine terms that are applied to some of the fair and middling women. The Frica, for example, is said to have a "mouth [that] champs an invisible bit..." (*Dream* 179). The Frica's mother had "curvetted smartly" as a "young mare," and the Frica herself is described as an ambling foal who whinnies after Belacqua (180). The Smeraldina-Rima is "a generous mare neighing after a great horse, caterwauling after a great stallion...." (23). This other side of the equine sexual equation, the stallion, is a repeated image of the sexually active male from which Bel carefully distinguishes himself in conversation with the Mandarin (100). Throughout the book, equine imagery is allied with heterosexual sexuality, and, as Bel recommends to the Mandarin to "get thee to a stud" (101), it is also allied with sexual reproduction. Yet for both Bel and the Unnamable, the symbolic penetration of the horse's anus is the occasion for the possibility of autoerotic satisfaction. Rather than the image acting as a signpost toward reproductive intercourse, it is a means of retaining sexuality while avoiding the chance of reproduction. Belacqua does not shun sexuality altogether, for while he recoils from intercourse with the Smeraldina, he persists in masturbating—a safe, nonreproductive expression of sexuality.

The sterile nature of the defecating horse as sexual stimulus is again evident in *The Unnamable*. While the Unnamable hopes that something can be "wrung" from his penis through "manstuprating" he explicitly states that whatever might occur will be "fruitless," that is, there might be no emission at all, or if there is any emission, he can rest safely in the knowledge that it will be issueless. This is reinforced by his speculations over his own fertility: "Does this mean they did not geld me? I could have sworn they had gelt me. But perhaps I am getting mixed up with other scrota." (*U* 45–6) To geld: to castrate, from the Old Norse for barren, and of course a gelding is a castrated animal, especially a male horse. If the Unnamable were not gelded, the only result of his erotic imaginings of the defecating horse would be the production of waste matter in the form of semen.

The second half of the defecating horse image suggests a basis for the horror at the thought of reproductive sexuality. The child's theory of anal birth, as set out by Freud, here comes into play, albeit with some twists of Beckett's own making. Freud posited that the belief in anal birth arises from the child's ignorance of female physiology. A similar ignorance, leading to comic confusions, is at play within Beckett's work, especially within the trilogy. Molloy, for example, is ignorant of female physiology: "She had a hole between her legs, oh not the bung hole I had always imagined, but a slit..." (*M* 56). This could account for his apparent belief in his own birth through his mother's "hole in her arse" (13) in accordance with Freud, but might also explain his confusion as to what intercourse actually entails:

I went in from behind. It was the only position she could bear because of her lumbago. It seemed all right to me, for I had seen dogs, and I was astonished when she confided that you could go about it differently. I wonder what she meant exactly. Perhaps after all she put me in her rectum. A matter of complete indifference to me, I needn't tell you. But is it true love, in the rectum? That's what bothers me sometimes (56).

Of course, Molloy then goes on to wonder if Ruth or Edith was in fact a man, which brings a homosexual element into the equation that will be fully considered in a subsequent chapter. For the present purposes, a number of aspects should be noted. First, throughout the whole discussion of sex with Ruth or Edith, the issue of reproduction is never once mentioned. Second, the confusion over orifices and genders increases the possibility of nonreproductive sex. Most importantly, Molloy's ignorance allows for the plausibility of anal birth. Returning to the defecating horse, a rather complex series of associations becomes apparent. The symbolic penetration of the horse's anus offers a doubly safe expression of sexuality: first, the stimulus is autoerotic, and second, the confusion of anus and vagina offers the safe possibility of anal sex. In addition to this, the Freudian possibility of anal birth creates an analogy between procreation and defecation that is itself suggestive of why reproductive sex is best avoided; not only does birth entail one's first taste of the shit but one is born as shit. Little Hans's case again here becomes apposite. His infantile theory of reproduction posits that all babies are essentially little shits, or, in his terms, *lumfs*. "All babies were lumfs and were born like lumfs," as Freud comments.[25] For Freud, this association is a positive one, for the child is close enough in time to the phase in his or her life when defecation was a source of pleasure. In the case of Hans, "[t]his child was still not so distant from his constitutional coprophilic inclinations. There was nothing degraded about coming into the world like a heap of faeces, which had not yet been condemned by feelings of disgust."[26] Indeed for Hans, the memory evoked by seeing his little sister being changed was one of the combined pleasures of defecation and being looked after, and he hopes in turn to be able to repeat these pleasures, both in the form of giving birth himself (pleasurable inasmuch as it is the same as excreting) and thereafter looking after his own children. As Freud puts it:

> He was able to imagine the act of giving birth as a pleasurable one by relating it to his own first feelings of pleasure in passing a stool; and he was thus able to find a double motive for wishing to have children of his own: the pleasure of giving birth to them and the pleasure (the compensatory pleasure, as it were) of looking after them. [27]

For Freud, particularly in the case of Hans, the anal birth is coprophilic in nature, and this coprophilia leads to a desire to take part in reproductive sexuality, in this case—with an overlay of Oedipal desire—with one's mother. For

Freud, the fecal waste is an incentive to procreation. In Beckett, the opposite would appear to be the case. Molloy's "first taste of the shit" is not an incentive to further the species; it is only a matter of utter regret, and his mother is only to be thanked in so far as "she did all she could not to have me, except of course the one thing, and if she never succeeded in getting me unstuck, it was that fate had earmarked me for less compassionate sewers" (15). Here, the fetus and the child that is Molloy are both waste material to be flushed away and both waste material that do not recommend repetition. Thus, Molloy credits his mother for not having another child, and Molloy takes something like proud satisfaction in at least being the "last of [his] foul brood" (15).

The association of the defecating horse with the figure of the mother is one that Beckett came back to again and again. The complex relation is again in evidence in a short poem of 1934, unpublished but included in a letter to Nuala Costello:

Mammon's[28] bottoms,
La Goulue's, mine, a cob's,
Whipt, caressed.
My mother's breast.
But God's
A goat's, an ass's,
Alien beauty,
The Divine Comedy.[29]

Beckett comments of his own poem that he doesn't "care for it much" but then defends it, saying "that it is a poem and not verse, that it is a prayer and not a collect, I have not the slightest doubt, not the slightest."[30] The elusive and allusive nature of the poem presents associations without presenting the comforting method of linkage. The bottoms of richness are listed and seem random, spanning that of the Moulin Rouge performer, Louise Webber, of Beckett himself, and of the "cob" or stout, short-legged horse.[31] Those elements of sexual stimulus that Belacqua reacted to in *Dream* are also given in condensed form with the whipping of the bottoms (a sadomasochism that will be explored in a later chapter) merging into the more normative pleasure of the caress. By including his own bottom in the list, Beckett could be seen as allying himself with the whipped rather than acting merely as a voyeur, as Belacqua and the Unnamable are represented in their adoration of horses' posteriors. Certainly, the violence implicit within the description forms an integral part of the sexualized experience.

Separated from the list by a definite end-stop, yet obviously somehow connected, is the mother's breast. The punctuation here is highly nuanced.

The full-stop allows for a degree of separation, and yet the breast is part of the thinking of the stanza. The period, therefore, acts as a bridge where no logical bridge is either possible or, perhaps more accurately, thinkable. The image of the mother's breast—the (unfortunate) nurturing coupled with an eroticism–arises from the images of the whipped bottoms even though the connection is not or cannot be stated. One is reminded of Molloy's attempts to keep images of his mother distinct from the images of women whom he has encountered sexually: "I once rubbed up against one [woman]. I don't mean my mother, I did more than rub up against her. And if you don't mind we'll leave my mother out of this" (55–6). The same merging and concern for separation occurs a few pages later: "And God forgive me to tell you the horrible truth, my mother's image sometimes mingles with theirs, which is literally unendurable, like being crucified, I don't know why and I don't want to" (58). This final clause perfectly captures the relation of the mother to the whipped horse in the poem of 1934—an illogical and unwelcome relation is felt, but best not be delved into too closely. In the poem, the period bears a great weight of the unsaid and the cannot-be-said.

The image of the defecating horse in both *Dream* and *The Unnamable*, coupled with the cloacal theory of birth as seen in *Molloy*, suggests a thorough turning aside from reproductive sexuality. This turning aside is not through the horror of being shackled to an accursed body nor through a horror of all forms of sexuality—masturbation remains as a conceivable, if fruitless, option—but precisely through a horror at the thought of reproduction itself, at the thought of the perpetuation of the species. The horror, as the poem of 1934 suggests, is inevitably connected with the figure of the mother. In these terms, one can answer Deleuze and Guatarri's question: "What relationship does the bicycle-horn machine have with the mother-anus machine?" Faced with the disgusting fact of one's own birth and of reproductive sexuality in general, the blowing of one's horn provides a safe, impotent remnant of sexuality—better the bicycle-horn machine than the mother-anus machine.

This cluster of associations surrounding defecating horses finds its fullest, if somewhat more opaque, expression in *All That Fall*, a play which is expressly concerned with the end of the possibility of reproduction. Despite Maddy Rooney's "lifelong preoccupation with horses' buttocks," (*CDW* 195) upon which the "mind" doctor can shed no light, there is no actual mention of a defecating horse within the radio-play. There is, however, and perhaps even more appropriately, a defecating hinny.[32] All the elements that marked the defecating horse of *Dream* are again present within *All That Fall*: the hinny defecates, the pseudo-sadistic beating of the animal is also present, from which arguably Maddy gains some sort of excitement, possibly of a sexual nature.

One element that receives a greater emphasis, however, is the identification of Maddy with the poor beast: "Well!" She says, "If someone was to do that for me I should not dally. [. . .] How she gazes at me, to be sure, with her moist clag-tormented eyes" (*CDW* 173). This identification between Maddy and the hinny does alter the dynamics of the image, but that alteration is dependent on the change in gender, for Maddy looking at a defecating hinny cannot be the same as the adolescent Bel looking at a defecating horse. Such an identification is also apparent in "Mammon's bottoms" where the cob and the speaker of the poem share a whipping caress. However, the result of the image—the denial of reproductive sexuality—remains unaltered. The hinny is a sterile hybrid as the offspring of a female donkey and a male horse. Through its defecation it may suggest birth, but actual birth is an impossibility. Maddy knows this, even if she asks Dan for confirmation: "Hinnies procreate. [*Silence*] You know, hinnies, or jinnies, aren't they barren or sterile, or whatever it is?" (*CDW* 197) The hinny isn't the only barren female in the play; Maddy herself is long past menopause and is now childless, her daughter Minnie having died at some unspecified age. In a form of double-safety reminiscent of that at work for Bel and the Unnamable, had Minnie been alive, she also would have been entering into menopause. Sterility haunts the play. Could this be the motive for Maddy's identification with the hinny? A recognition of a common, inevitable childlessness evoked and replaced by that wasteful bringing forth from the body—shitting? The shit, one might suggest, is all that Maddy and the hinny can bring into the world.

If there is a regret on Maddy's part for now being barren, one should not assume that she necessarily continues to wish for the continuation of the species. In the context of the defecating hinny, Maddy doesn't make any objection to the defecation itself, but does react strongly to the dung it produces: "Dung? What would we want with dung at our time of life?" (*CDW* 173). It is an odd response unless one considers the properties of dung as fertilizer. The waste—and here seems to be Beckett's new insight into the image that first caught his attention in *Dream*—is not safely waste; even dung holds forth the possibility of regeneration, of making fertile. It is the possibility that the waste itself might foster further life that provokes Maddy's seemingly exaggerated reaction. The fear is the same as Hamm's in *Endgame* where life might start again from a crab louse: "But humanity might start from there all over again! Catch him, for the love of God!" (*CDW* 108). It is the same fear that provokes Dan, as many have suggested, to push the small child—a potential procreator—under the wheels of the train.

Maddy Rooney, punished perhaps not so much for having been born but for desiring to give birth, says that Jesus entered Jerusalem on a hinny and

claims: "That must mean something" (*CDW* 197).[33] It could mean many
things. Like the hinny, Jesus is a hybrid with a divine father and a human
mother; like the hinny, he was condemned to childlessness; or is it that, ultimately, like the hinny, Jesus is sterile, as is the hope that he offers to all those
that "fall"? When Maddy and Dan are shaken by laughter by the biblical
phrase, "The Lord holdeth up all that fall and raiseth up all those that be
bowed down,"[34] it might be that they laugh because such has not been their
experience. But might they not also be mocking the Lord who will not let
the fallen remain fallen, who will not let humanity end as it should end—in
sterility?

Beckett was, of course, childless; a fact that one might interpret as a desire
to save at least one being from the suffering inevitable to life. Something of
a different order might be proposed. The image of the defecating horse,
bizarre and amusing in its details, might lead one to suspect that a more
far-reaching desire might be at work within the plays and novels; the desire
for the end of all reproduction save the literary and for the purely sterile—
one might say Beckettian—anal birth as opposed to the continuation of
humanity. If this is possible, then it would call for a realignment of where
our sympathies should lie, for it would mean not condemning but applaud-
ing Hamm in his condemnation of all humanity, and it would mean that we
should applaud Dan Rooney's appalling act and reassess it not as a killing
but as a far-sighted and necessary culling.

Yet sterility and the end of humanity are not all that arise from Beckett's
deployment of the defecating horse as sexual stimulus. The fixation on the
anal passage—and Molloy later claims that we "underestimate this little hole"
(80)—points to the possibility of "explor[ing] other channels" of sexuality,
to adopt the words of *Mercier and Camier* (59). The implications, as shall
be seen later, are not solely homosexual and rather gesture to a key facet of
Beckett's thinking on sex: sexual reproduction and sexual activity are not one
and the same thing and that a crucial line must be drawn between the two.
Sexual reproduction is reprehensible and should be avoided, while nonreproductive sexuality is acceptable and may even prove useful. This basic division
informs much of Beckett's use of sexuality and allows for the remnants of sex
to appear within the works in various forms. As has been seen, masturbation
remains an option, even when it would seem to be an impossibility, and it is
also closely allied to artistic creation. Anal sex, whether in the confused form
adopted by Molloy or in its sadistic incarnation in *How It Is*, also remains as a
safe, nonreproductive form of sexual expression, albeit an ultimately complex
one. Once the danger of issue has been removed, it seems Beckett does not
hesitate to explore whatever alternative sexual issues might arise.

CHAPTER 2

The Horror of Sex

It is in Beckett's early prose works, particularly *Dream of Fair to Middling Women, More Pricks than Kicks,* and *Murphy,* that reactions against certain forms of sexual activity are most pronounced. As the previous chapter suggested, however, a blanket horror of sexual activity does not allow for the many different forms of sexual expression that are available to the Beckettian character. A distinction must be drawn, therefore, between the acceptable and unacceptable forms of sexual expression. Certainly, as we shall see in these early texts, sex is very much at issue, but for too long the nature of this sexual activity—and the nuances within a variety of sexual expressions—has been obscured by the critical discourses that quickly grew up within Beckett studies, particularly the assumption that a Cartesian framework can best explain the works. In this chapter, it is necessary to question the Cartesianism that has so long been applied to an understanding of the early novels and stories through a consideration, at first, of the themes of masturbation and prostitution within *Dream of Fair to Middling Women.* It is also the case, however, that Beckett's attitudes toward sexual expression arose within a distinct milieu in the Irish Free State, in particular, and Europe, more generally. Beckett, as shall be seen, allied himself to certain aspects of contemporary social and political thinking regarding sex and rigorously defended himself and his art against others. This suggests that, even from the early stages, sex and aesthetic creation were closely connected and that from the fear of reproduction and the voyeuristic masturbation of Belacqua through to interventions in the censorship debate in the Irish Free State, sex was at the center of Beckett's art of the 1920s and 1930s.

Placing Dream of Fair to Middling Women *in the Oeuvre*

The critical discourse surrounding Beckett's novels traces an oddly philosophically chronological trajectory. While the later works, from *Molloy* on, have been the scene of a postmodern or postessentialist appreciation in recent years, the early prose has stayed mainly within the discursive field of Descartes, with occasional forays into related occasionalists such as Leibniz, alongside a Bergsonian concern for the mechanization and comic aesthetics of those works. *Dream* criticism until recently had been firmly within the discursive field policed by Descartes on the one hand and Bergson on the other. Both Cartesian and Bergsonian readings have approached the issue of Bel's sexuality; the former best summed up by Jeri L. Kroll's account of Bel's sexual activities in both *Dream* and *More Pricks than Kicks* as a failed attempt at living entirely within the mind: "Belacqua," she writes, "cannot deal with sexual experience because it reminds him that he is, in fact, a creature composed of two seemingly contradictory elements: mind and body."[1] A Bergsonian account of Bel's proclivities as offered by Yoshiki Tajiri takes the "teary ejaculation" on the occasion of the Smeraldina leaving for Europe as its starting point and notes that "it seems that Belacqua is trying to mechanically control his emotion after parting from his girlfriend, as well as the concomitant emission of tears. But in fact, what is really at stake is sexual drive rather than mind of emotion [...] Belacqua seems to be trying to regulate and control his sexual drive by mechanising it."[2]

There is no denying the Cartesian and Bergsonian possibilities of *Dream*, especially in the realm of sexuality. However, the extent to which one can rely on particularly Cartesian accounts must be questioned. As Matthew Feldman has demonstrated in *Beckett's Books*, Cartesian interpretations of the works dominated the first decade of Beckett's critical reception, beginning with Ruby Cohn's editorship of the *Perspective* Beckett issue of 1959, and still exert a strong influence that is largely unwarranted by the archival evidence. Feldman writes that Beckett's interest in Descartes "waned quickly" after completion of his first published poem, *Whoroscope,* and yet "the earliest scholarship in Beckett studies found this to be the dominant influence, positing virtually unanimously that Descartes underwrote Beckett's interest in and rejection of or artistic debt to Cartesianism. The effect of this reading continues to bedevil Beckett studies."[3] From a natural assumption of a knowledge of Descartes exhibited by *Whoroscope,* which includes elements of the life of the philosopher, critics quickly extended the shadow of Descartes over Beckett's work so that, for example, John Fletcher in *Samuel Beckett's Art* confidently asserted that "traces of Descartes' influence can be found [...] in nearly all his writings."[4] Whether the particular reading was pro- or anti-Cartesian, the dualistic framework assumed the mind/body dichotomy was active within Beckett's work and that it was the mind that should be the focus of concern. As sex is, of course, an affair of the body, albeit not exclusively, it was assumed therefore that it cannot be of much concern for a writer who denigrates the body to focus on the liberation, or struggle for liberation, of the mind. In these terms, Beckett's first major character, Belacqua, is seen as struggling to free the mind from the body and so banishes sexuality in the process. A clear critical trajectory is then established with successive protagonists retreating further into a perfect solipsism. This trajectory arguably reaches its end point with the Unnamable, who is denuded of a body and therefore of all forms of sexuality. Yet even the Unnamable, in his armless state as Mahood, thrust into a glass jar as a form of advertisement for a restaurant in the slaughterhouse district of a town, can still become sexually excited at the thought of a defecating horse, as we have seen.

It might be suggested that *Dream* cannot be safely packaged into a Cartesian or Bergsonian box when that box has been found wanting for the later works. For while *Dream,* particularly in terms of style, seems alien to the later works, certain images and passages reveal concerns not out of place in *Murphy* or *The Unnamable.*

The narrator of *Dream* despairs of, or does not care about, capturing the real Belacqua, for Belacqua will not settle into an adequate description. In terms similar to one instance in *The Unnamable,* the narrator of *Dream* writes : "*At his simplest trine,* we were at pains to say so, to save our bacon, save our face. He is no more satisfied by the three values, Apollo, Narcissus and the anonymous third person, than he would be by fifty values, or any number of values" (*Dream* 124). I shall return to this trine man in Apollo, Narcissus, and other modes later. For the moment, it is enough to register the similarity between this passage and the following: "At no moment do I know what I'm talking about, nor of whom, nor of where, nor how, nor why, but I could employ fifty wretches for this sinister operation and still be short of a fifty-first, to close the circuit, that I know, without knowing what it means" (*U* 52). Numerically similar, the passages are thematically all but identical; the continuous deferral of identity along a never-ending series of values assigned to the figure. Bel as the trine man provides further evidence of thematic consistency between 1932 and 1952. "At his simplest he was trine. Just think of that. A trine man! Centripetal, centrifugal and...not. Phoebus chasing Daphne, Narcissus flying from Echo and...neither. Is that neat or is it not?" (*Dream* 120). The passage continues to play one identity off against another, or to go through a process of "affirmations and negations invalidated as uttered" (*U* 1) with opposing terms cancelling each other out and implying a third term. In a manner that postessentialist accounts of the Trilogy have happily identified, the oppositions, through their negations, play across the divide of the neither/nor. The Unnamable briefly stated as a tympanum neatly captures this neither/nor state:

> ...perhaps that's what I feel, an outside and an inside and me in the middle, perhaps that's what I am, the thing that divides the world in two, on the one side the outside, on the other the inside, that can be as thin as foil, I'm neither one side nor the other, I'm in the middle, I'm the partition (*U* 100).

Belacqua as the trine man is also a foreshadowing of the more developed tripartite description of Murphy's mind as occurs in chapter six of that novel. The trine Belacqua, centrifugal, centripetal, and not, adheres to the same structure as Murphy's three zones of mind: "In the first were the forms with parallel [...] In the second were the forms without parallel [...] The third, the dark, was a flux of forms, a perpetual coming together and falling asunder of forms."[5] The gradations of interiority within Murphy's and Bel's three zones are also alike: mind directed outward to the world, inward to itself, and, as it were, further inward to beyond itself, in the "wombtomb" where Bel is "without identity" (*Dream* 121) and Murphy is not free "but a mote in the dark of absolute freedom" (*Murphy* 72). A Cartesian account of this trine man would have no difficulty with the first two stages delineated. They can be seen as a casting off of the body in favor of the mind. But the third zone is beyond such categorization, such an antithetical approach. Murphy's and Bel's progress, or regress, is not toward an indubitable "I" upon which to build but beyond any identification at all. Again, the structure first seen in *Dream* and more carefully developed in *Murphy* points toward, and can be thought alongside, the "being-less" state that seems to underpin the Trilogy, at least in a postessentialist reading of those novels. The tools brought to bear with such success on Beckett's later works can be applied to his earliest of novels.

Dream requires a nondualistic approach, not least as far as concerns the issue of sexuality. As the novel states: "nothing so simple as antithetical" (137). Bel's response to sexual intercourse can be seen as an antithetical reaction, a shrinking into the life of the mind away from the body in horror at the gross invasion of the person that sex entails. This, however, is far from being the whole story, for Bel never attains that state of perfect solipsism— self contained, alive within the mind, and dead to the world. We might charge him with being a failed Cartesian, but this would only beg the question as to why Beckett created a failed Cartesian leading man. Moreover, the boggling of his affair with the Smeraldina-Rima, which the novel squarely blames on the fact that they had sex, does not put an end to sexuality, rather it redirects the sexual drive into masturbation. If Bel has a primary sexual mode it is that of onanism, which, although it may be solitary, is far from being an affair of the mind alone. The relationship between sex, masturbation, and, as will later be demonstrated, creativity cannot be adequately explained as a recoil into the refuge of the mind against the impertinence of carnality.

Then Everything Went Kaputt

The first question to be entertained is: what is at stake in the boggling of the Smeraldina-Bel affair? The narrator is in no doubt about the dramatic nature of their unfortunate intercourse: "Until she raped him./Then everything went kaputt" (*Dream* 18). The initial coupling leads to a "gehenna of sweats and fiascos and tears and absence of all douceness" (19) based on the transgression of boundaries. For rather than remaining two identities separated by a form of tympanum that is styled by the narrator with obvious hymeneal overtones as the Platonic tissue, the "rape" forces together the two identities, leading to an inevitable recoil, at least on Bel's side of the affair.

However, the recoil from the physical is only part of the problem with sexual intercourse as far as Bel is concerned. Certainly, and with a great deal of misogyny, the sexual appetite of Smerry is styled as a gross, if inevitable, invasion: "...she would surge up at him, blithe and buxom and young and lusty, a lascivious petulant virgin, a generous mare neighing after a great horse, caterwauling after a great stallion, and amorously lay open the double-jug dugs. She could not hold it" (23). Bel would rather have her as a version of himself, as the reference to her as Dante's Belacqua seems to make clear: "So he would always have her be, rapt, like the spirit of a troubadour" (23). So it would seem that Bel eschews the crossing of the sexual divide in order to have better communion with a version of himself, with Smerry acting as a mirror image the better to contemplate himself. Such solipsism would fall neatly into a Cartesian framework, but it should be recognized that Bel is less engaged in seeking a comforting image of himself to contemplate in the vision of the rapt Smerry, as hoping for the dissolution of the identity of Smerry, and by extension, the dissolution of his own identity, such as it is. For, importantly, Smerry, when like the spirit of a troubadour, casts no shade and is herself shade. Bel's preferred Smerry is undefinable. Far from being a distinct individual separate from Bel, she is envisioned as losing all identity.

Therefore, the mere fact of preferred separation is not enough: what precisely is being separated by a shying away from sexual congress? Bel is not concerned with the preservation of his individuality, or with his identity within the life of the mind. Rather, he is concerned to preserve the possibility of the dissolution of identity:

> I, he thought, and she and the neighbour are cities bereft of light, where the citizen carries his torch. I shall separate myself and the neighbour from the moon, and the lurid place that he is from the lurid place that I am; then I need not go to the trouble of hating the neighbour. I shall extinguish also, by banning the torchlight procession in the city that is I, the fatiguing lust for self-emotion. (24)

The initial separation envisaged here is certainly a removal of the "I am" from the "she is"—one lurid place of an individual distinguished from another. The citizen with his or her torch, casting light on the denizens of the individual, is, I take it, a figuring of the light of personality and identity, and it is crucial that the light within Bel himself is extinguished, obviating the need to falter in the fatiguing solipsistic desire to contemplate the self. The ultimate goal of the separation from himself and another is not the better contemplation of the self, but the better dissolution of the self.

This account of what is at stake in Bel's desire for separation and his mistrust of sexual intercourse makes still more strange his continuing sexual activity in the form of masturbation. Are we to pass him off, as he passes himself off, as just a "dud mystic" (186) unable to reach or maintain the darkened "city that is I" and forever drawn back into the mire of sexuality?

On the shocking news that Bel doesn't go to Parisian brothels, the narrator states that "Love demands narcissism" (38). Is this form of narcissism the Narcissus in love with his own image or the Narcissus that flees from the attentions of Echo? Nevertheless, through narcissistic maneuvers, Bel avoids the brothel and attempts to have Smerry according to his god through the auspices of masturbation.

The significance of the brothel sequence is first the admission that the mind is not body tight. The inner man is not left entirely outside the whorehouse. Beatrice, we are told, "lurked in every brothel" (40). The "cabbage-stalks of sex" (41) infect the idealized image of the Smeraldina in an intolerable manner, obliterating the spiritual boon that Bel's mental version of Smerry confers upon him. For Bel, the "oneness" of Smerry is obliterated in the proliferation of whores demanded by the "demented hydraulic that was beyond his control," that is, his sexual appetite. This scheme at once admits a mind-body congruence while privileging the mental Smerry, who is "incorruptible, uninjurable, unchangeable" (41). The result of hauling his

Smerry into the brothel is that there "as one and as spirit, as spirit of his spirit, she was abolished" (43).

In "the mansion of him whose shoe was loosed," that is in masturbation, this process is reversed. By positing a Smerry of flesh, Bel acquires her in spirit: "...he forced her to play the whore, he exploited her unreal and arbitrary to the end that he might annex her real and unique..." (42). Masturbation, rooted in the physical, is the means of nullifying the physical, of denuding Smerry of her carnality, for "...when she was first glibly postulated as flesh, willfully distorted by him into the carnal detail, then she was conferred upon him in spirit, as spirit she was affirmed" (43). Again the physical is devalued in favor of the spiritual, and one might argue that yet again we have a Cartesian privileging of the mind over the body. However, this does not contradict my previous assertion that Bel seeks nonidentity and wishes to see Smerry mirror him in this state of statelessness, for the mental arena of Bel's masturbation is within the first two zones of his mind, not within the third dark zone, the "wombtomb," where he ceases to exist in identity. Bel as the trine man, in the terms of *Murphy*, redistributes the kicks of reality as to direction as the physical affront from Smerry is mentally reversed.[6] The flesh Smerry is thereby transformed into the spiritual through imagination and masturbation; the spiritual Smerry is infected by the fleshy reality of the Beatrice-like prostitute. The narrator later cryptically explains:

> Trine. Yessir. In cases of emergency, as when the Syra-Cusa became a saint or the Smeraldina-Daphne, that he might have her according to his God, a Smeraldina-Echo, the two first persons might sink their differences, the two main interests merge, the wings of flight to the centre be harnessed to flight thence." (120)

Masturbation is, then, a manipulation of the real and mental worlds within a confusion of cross-contaminations: the mind of the body, the body of the mind: "The same dirty confusion and neutralisation of needs when he wands her into a blue bird, wands whom, how the hell do we know, anybody, into a blue bird and lets fly a poem at her, immerging the better to emerge" (120).

The reader is explicitly told that all this "chiroplatonism" and avoidance of brothels is so that Bel can have Smerry "according to his God" (40). Earlier in the narrative, having Smerry according to his God entailed the possibility of literary creation: "...only when he sat down to himself in an approximate silence and had a vision on the strength of her or let fly a poem at her, anyhow felt some reality that somehow was she fidgeting in the catacombs of his spirit, that he had her truly and totally, according to his God" (25). As seen above in the Trine man description (where again "according to his God" is recorded), the "dirty confusion," which one could imagine might lead to orgasm through masturbation, can also lead to the creation of a poem. Masturbation and literary creation are allied or flow from the same situation. That Beckett was fully aware of this alliance is evidenced by a letter to Thomas McGreevy of 1931, which alludes to the completion of the two "Alba" poems. He writes that "they came together one on top of the other, a double-yoked orgasm in months of aspermatic days and nights."[7] Returning to the "love demands narcissism" dictum, one notes that it is only through the imagined manipulation of the real, of the flesh, that Bel "proved the spiritual intercourse." The flesh and blood Smerry and the physical encounter are themselves only postulated, they are acts of imagination, which are then manipulated to achieve the desired effect, be it an orgasm, or as in the case of Bel waving goodbye to Smerry from the pier, a curious mix of emotion and ejaculation, or a poem.

Placing artistic creation within the realm of masturbation (and the historian of masturbation Thomas W. Laqueur[8] has comprehensively demonstrated the thematic and cultural links between the supposed dangers of masturbation and those of literary output and consumption) must lead us to rethink the relationship between the physical and mental at work within *Dream*. Bel cannot turn his back on sexuality. Instead, that sexuality turns into an imaginative manipulation of sensory data, a reordering of the real followed by a process of distillation that results in the "spirit" or the "art" being achieved. The process is at once physical and not, mental and not. The stimulus is there in the physical world and yet is filtered through the imaginative faculty, and the spiritual is only achieved through the auspices of the physical, as masturbation nulls the physical and releases the essential and spiritual. One might wish to adapt Beckett here and suggest that just as "there is at least this to be said for mind, that it can dispel mind,"[9] so there is at least this to be said for physical, that it can dispel physical.

The process of sexuality here differs from Lawrence Harvey's reading of sexuality and literary creation in the reading of the poem "Dortmunder,"[10] which he conclusively proves to have intimate links with *Dream*. He writes of the poem that "with the satisfaction of physical desire [...] and music aiding, other worlds may be glimpsed in black eyes" in a form of spiritual, narcissistic vision.[11] He relates the poem to the brothel sequence in *Dream* saying that "the physical act nullifies both desire and the girl and makes possible the spiritual vision." In his reading of "Dortmunder," the sating of physical desire renders the poet null and allows him to achieve, again with the aid of music, an "aesthetic ataraxy."[12] No doubt, the relationship between physical desire and aesthetic creativity is profoundly difficult to untangle in *Dream*, yet Beckett insists in the novel that poetry is associated only with having Smerry according to his God; that is, when she has been mentally manipulated by Belacqua. This places the aesthetic activity not within the "null" of Bel's wombtombing but within his first two zones of mind. It is within these two zones that the "real" and "mental" meet, are confused and have issue, either in the form of orgasm, or of poetry.

An examination of the Bel's wombtomb zone should make apparent why the activity of poetry, and for that matter sexuality, would be unthinkable within that site.

> ...the limbo and the wombtomb alive with the unanxious spirits of quiet cerebration, where there was no conflict of flight and flow and Eros was as null as Anteros and Night had no daughters. He was bogged in indolence, without identity, impervious alike to its pull and goading. The cities and forests and beings were also without identity, they were shadows, they exerted neither pull nor goad. His third being was without axis or contour, its centre everywhere and periphery nowhere, an unsurveyed marsh of sloth. (121)

First, Bel is without identity within the wombtomb. While one could argue, following Harvey, that in the null mode of aesthetic ataraxy the poet's identity is lost, making him a cipher or nonintellectually engaged scribe of events within the null zone, still the fact remains that in *Dream* the aesthetic is allied with "flight and flow" of Eros. In the wombtomb, a site of neither the womb nor the tomb, both Eros and its opposite are cancelled out. It is this process of cancellation through the clash of opposites that precisely allows Bel to attain his blessed dark zone. The only alternative to this darkness without axis or contour is the "dreary fiasco of oscillation" between opposites, as partly embodied in Bel's sexual relations. Again, the description of him as a trine man is apt. Bel is described as

> Phoebus chasing Daphne, Narcissus flying from Echo and...neither. Is that neat or is it not? The chase to Vienna, the flight to Paris, the slouch to Fulda, the relapse into Dublin and...immunity like hell from journeys and cities. The hand to Lucien and Liebert and the Syra-Cusa tendered and withdrawn and again tendered and again withdrawn and...hands forgotten. The dots are nice don't you think?" (120)

David Green has captured the importance of this passage well, when he writes:

> Belacqua is split between the lure of an outward love and the peace of an inward love. Phoebus, or Apollo, is the active, extroverted god associated

with the enlightening powers of the sun and described by Ovid as the aggressive suitor of Daphne. Narcissus is the unattainable object of Echo's love. But lying an ellipses away, like a sting in the tail, is the negation of these personae.[13]

Bel then oscillates between the inner and outer, between the sexual chase and the flight into the mind. Importantly, not one of these opposites triumphs over the other, for Beckett makes plain (and makes sure we realize with reference to the dots on the page) that within the clash of the opposites a third state appears, that which has been previously characterized as the neither/nor, or which Bel would rather call the wombtomb.

Bel's ability to "let fly a poem" (25) at Smerry, and for that matter to masturbate on the strength of a vision of her, is dependent upon the oscillation between the inner and outer, carnal and spiritual, in which the imagined flesh releases spirit and the envisioned spirit is contaminated by the flesh. This oscillation may be dreary, and it may lead Bel into intolerable confusion, but it is the necessary play of opposites that gives rise to both aesthetic and carnal appreciation. A total recoil into the life of the mind, a Cartesian solipsistic ideal, would mean the end not only of masturbation but of also aesthetic creation. So, perhaps, Bel's own accusation that he is a "dud mystic" (186) is accurate, for the true mystic, safe within the wombtomb site, would not dwell within the oscillating grip of the inner and outer worlds. Similarly, Bel is also accurate in his estimation of himself as being a "borderman," (186) for he cannot inhabit the third zone but rather shuttles between oppositions, crossing and re-crossing the border that in turn makes one aware of the very existence of the third zone. Bel as masturbator and poet dwells on the cusp of the relation between the inner and outer worlds; he is neither all carnal, nor all cerebral; he is neither/nor.

Beckett seems to have been well aware that sex and its transgressions of boundaries, its dual nature as cerebral and physical, play across the divide of the inner and the outer. It suits his purposes, for the novel is almost obsessed with playing across divides, be it figured in Nemo who is always in-between the banks of a river, the dot, dot, dot, of the trine man description, or in the lesion of Platonic tissue with Smerry and the sexual complications and manipulations it gives rise to. However, one stated aim of the novel (if the narrator can be believed) is to use this crisscrossing to delineate the real subject:

The experience of my reader shall be between the phrases, in the silence, communicated by the intervals, not the terms, of the statement, between the flowers that cannot coexist, the antithetical (nothing so simple as antithetical) seasons of words, his experience shall be the menace, the miracle, the memory, of an unspeakable trajectory. (137)

Without dwelling too long on the German letter to Axel Kaun, which Beckett later described as bilge, the description just offered is akin to the aesthetic ambitions of using the word against the word that that letter hinges upon. However, within *Dream*, just as the wombtomb zone is the all but unattainable goal of Bel, so the silence and the unspeakable trajectory of which the narrator speaks are unattainable. It seems that the narrator is driving the reader to consider the state of separation between opposites, but, as David Green has again perceptibly shown, this leads to a "beautiful nothing," or "bel niente." Green argues that the "beautiful nothing [...] is a quietism free from the divisive illusions of the surface. It is also an obliteration of the handles by which we are accustomed to dealing with each other. In fact it is an obliteration of 'each other.' "[14]

However, even the description of this "beautiful nothing" is not free from masturbatory overtones:

Then you find when you come to the core and the kernel and the seat of the malady that behold it is a bel niente. Now there are few things more bel than a niente but considered as a premise, and be you Abbot himself, it presents certain difficulties in the manner of manipulation. So you draw your wand and strike from the air ad your own sweet lib whatever premises you fancy. You will have to live on them, you cannot get rid of them, so take much thought, tis a critical moment. Then proceed in the ordinary way. (161)

The images of masturbation permeate throughout this key passage. First, the "bel niente" cannot be manipulated, it is not open to the chiroplatonism or the narcissistic maneuvers with which Belacqua reordered the spirit/flesh dichotomies involved in his affair with Smerry. The bel neinte, being nothing, cannot manually be brought to issue. With the penis figured as a magic wand and the crucial element of "fancy" or the imagination introduced, the distinctions between masturbation and literary creation are blurred. As we have seen, Bel masturbated on the strength of his visions of Smerry where she was "first glibly postulated as flesh"; here again postulates, or premises, are created in a literary-masturbatory amalgam. We are back in the world of oscillations between the inner and outer, spirit and flesh, and, as with Smerry's expression of sexuality, the dreary oscillation is inevitable: "You will have to live on them."

Through its masturbatory and literary overtones this passage suggests that faced with the unspeakable trajectory of the "bel niente," the masturbator and artist retreats into the oscillating world, receives stimulus from the "real" and reorders it in an issuing forth of an excess, be it of literary creation or semen. The situation is similar to that in which the Unnamable is caught; he cannot speak of himself as he is, as he is nothing, so a series of creations, purportedly in the real world, are created to cover over the bel niente. And we should not forget Malone's almost joy when he remembers that he might be able to masturbate: "...I shall find myself abandoned, in the dark, without anything to play with. Then I shall play with myself. To have been able to conceive such a plan is encouraging" (*MD* 4). Rather than fall into the abyss of the dark, Malone, just as the narrator of *Dream*, might be able to conceive, albeit (and appropriately) fruitlessly, through the auspices of masturbation and literary creation.

In *Dream*, masturbation is at once the preferred method of negotiating the oscillation between the inner and outer worlds, and through such oscillation, the preferred method of suggesting the third dark, null, bel niente zone that underpins the novel. But also, through the novel's close alliance between onanism and literary creation, masturbation might also be the preferred method of keeping the novel going.

"Give me chastity, and continence, but not yet":[15] The Belacqua of More Pricks than Kicks

This focus on the sexual manipulations of Belacqua in *Dream* not only undermines an assumption of an underlying Cartesianism but also begs the question of the precise nature of the sexual activities against which Beckett's characters react. If, as we have seen, masturbation can perform a beneficial role for Belacqua, the problem does not lie with the concourse of the body and the mind. As Beckett adapts and develops Belacqua in *More Pricks than Kicks*, the problem becomes clearer as Belacqua flees procreative sexual intercourse.

Belacqua has relations with a host of women: Winnie ("pretty, hot and witty, in that order."[16]), the Smeraldina, the Alba, Ruby Tough (hoping that Belacqua "would so far forget himself as to take her in his arms" [82]), Lucy ("Truly there was no fault or flaw in the young woman" [99]), and Thelma bboggs. Of these women, Belacqua marries three: Lucy, the Smeraldina, and Thelma. He also has sexual intercourse with Winnie and Ruby. The text is necessarily discreet—although not discreet enough to pass the board of censorship of the Irish Free State—but it is clear that with Winnie and Ruby, at least, vaginally penetrative sexual intercourse is not Belacqua's preferred mode. His implied congress with Winnie leaves him a "very sad animal indeed" (17) (*post coitum omne animal triste est* is most often attributed to Galen or Aristotle), and he doesn't seek to repeat the experience, preferring to make his getaway on a more desirable bicycle (see Chapter 1). The intercourse with Ruby is no less a failure; a failure, not necessarily in the act itself, but inasmuch as Ruby and Belacqua had set out not to have sex but to kill themselves. After the revolver has discharged one of its balls prematurely, which Belacqua blames on the "digitus Dei...for once" (91), a "turmoil of life-blood sprang up in the breasts of our two young felons, so that they came together in inevitable nuptial." The inevitability of the act has no doubt been increased by the copious whiskey both have drunk and the fact that Ruby has had to remove her skirt. Importantly, the inevitability of the act is also felt by Belacqua to be a danger; he is not immune to the sexually provocative skirtless Ruby: "If you would put back your skirt [...] you would make things easier for me" he comments (88). Sexual desire, and the life-blood that preceded it, are not foreign to Belacqua, but they are unwanted, especially as the aim of the outing is death, the stilling of the life-blood itself. As was previously noted with reference to *Dream*, Belacqua's goal in "Love and Lethe" is not the quieting of the body to free the mind but the eternal quieting of both mind and body; rather than come alive within the mind or reveal his essential self as mind alone, he wants to get rid of mind entirely. The closing comments of the story try to put a brave face on his unfortunate failure:

> It will quite possibly be his boast in years to come, when Ruby is dead and he an old optimist, that at least on this occasion, if never before or since, he achieved what he set out to do; car, in the words of one competent to sing of the matter, *l'Amour et la Mort*—caesura—*n'est qu'une mesme chose.*
>
> May their night be full of music at all events. (91)

The deployment of one of Ronsard's *Sonnets to Helen* may not be entirely convincing, yet the association between death and "dying," itself a Romantic cliché, could also suggest the cycle of birth and suffering to which Augustine and Schopenhauer allude, albeit from different perspectives. However, if the aim is to cease being—both mentally and physically—then falling back into the greatest expression of the will-to-live, sexual intercourse, is a serious failing indeed, one which, as music, music music, Murphy will repeat with Celia.

Although Belacqua regrets coitus, he does not therefore forego all manner of sexual expression. As Belacqua of *Dream*, masturbation—but now with an added element of voyeurism—is a pleasure not only admitted but actively sought in "Walking Out." Belacqua is betrothed to Lucy, whose loveliness, "with its suggestion of the Nobel Yeats" (99), has not prevented him from making it plain that they should "establish their married life on [the] solid basis of a cuckoldry" (96). Again, the avoidance of coitus is paramount and ensured in his marriage with Lucy after she is disabled in the riding accident detailed in the story. When Lucy overtakes him on her horse while he is walking with his bitch, Belacqua tries to make his excuses by claiming he is "no fit company for anyone let alone lovely Lucy" (99) and that "...the best thing to do was to go to the wood for a little sursum corda" (100). Lucy realizes what this entails and is shocked to find her betrothed a "creepy-crawly" (101) and a "trite spy of the vilest description" (102). Belacqua's voyeuristic onanism is habitual, yet seems less than successful while he watches a young couple; nevertheless, he "rouse[s] himself finally" before being discovered and beaten by the "infuriated Tanzherr" (104). The question is, therefore, the degree to which continual sexual activity and a discontinuation of reproductive sex are compatible and an answer might be glimpsed in the role he wishes Lucy to adopt in the married life: "of her living with him like a music while being the wife in body of another" (101). The first half of this dream communion is precisely what Belacqua gets as, after the accident, they "sit up to all hours playing the gramophone, *An die Musik* is a great favourite with them both, he finds in her big eyes better worlds than this..." (105). The deployment of music in "Love and Lethe" and "Walking Out" appear to be at odds; in the former it describes sexual congress, and in the latter (perhaps again inspired by Schopenhauer) describes a form of more spiritual communion. The pull between the two possible poles of music is one, arguably, in which Murphy becomes caught and indicates an equally polarized viewed of women as the gateway to the spiritual or the gateway to the physical.

Jeri L. Kroll is right to focus her attentions when considering "Belacqua as Artist and Lover" on "What a Misfortune," a story replete with "innuendo and allusion."[17] The allusive nature of the title alone opens up a complex social, religious, and political context in which sex was embroiled in the early years of the Irish Free State—a complex that will be examined in more detail later. For the moment, it is enough to note that the *locus classicus* of "what a misfortune" is the end of chapter 11 of Voltaire's *Candide*. As a castrated male witnesses a young, naked, and distressed countess (she has been raped and is the sole survivor of a massacre), he opines, "che sciagura d'essere senza coglioni" ("Oh what a misfortune to be without balls!").[18] Belacqua's situation is somewhat the reverse; having balls, he wishes he had none. As Kroll suggests, the density of allusion and symbol at the climax of the story "create[s] a comprehensive picture of Belacqua's sexual prefer-ences and fears."[19] In keeping with his willingness to marry Lucy once the possibility of coitus would not arise, Belacqua hopes that his new marriage might also be sexless and certainly without issue, because Thelma "however much she left to be desired, was not a brood-maiden." (112) On the strength of this, perhaps, Belacqua rather tentatively introduces his desired model: the "babylan," or eunuch, which is reinforced by his vision of the beaver on a horse; beavers being supposed to remove their own testicles to appease hunters. Kroll's comprehensive exegesis is admirably attuned to the allusive possibilities, yet it needs to be emphasized that Belacqua's castration fantasy must be one that is just fantasy. The desire to express himself sexually, if only onanistically, would be curtailed by actual castration.

It is noteworthy that Belacqua exhibits two key Freudian traits in his recoil from reproductive sexuality: scopophilia (the love of looking, or voy-eurism) and castration. Of the first, Freud lists it among one of the "sexual aberrations" in the "Three Essays on Sexuality." He admits that pleasure in looking forms an important role in sexual pleasure in general, yet it can become "a perversion if (a) it is restricted exclusively to the genitals, or (b) if it is connected with the overriding of disgust (as in the case of *voyeurs* or people who look on at the excretory functions), or (c) if, instead of being *preparatory* to the normal sexual aim, it supplants it."[20] It is certainly the case with Belacqua that the "normal" sexual aim is supplanted by voyeuristic pleasures, although it may be the case that this is *willed* rather than a psychic aberration. His attraction to voyeurism—aside from the avoidance of the dangers inherent within coitus—might also ally him with a certain artistic ambition. Freud writes that scopophila can be

diverted ('sublimated') in the direction of art [...] It is usual for most normal people to linger to some extent over the intermediate sexual aim of a looking that has a sexual tinge to it; indeed, this offers them a pos-sibility of directing some proportion of their libido on to higher artistic aims.[21]

The continuum from artistic appreciation to aberrant sexual stimulation attests to a theme already discovered: the connection between the sexual and the aesthetic. Belacqua's failing at this stage seems to be that he overshoots the "higher plane" of the artistic to fall into the "perversion" of voyeurism. Yet the continuum also suggests that in order to achieve art some degree of scopophilia is required and, further, that a relation with a love object is also needed. Belacqua cannot, therefore, eschew the relation with the female altogether.

Belacqua's castration fantasy—one he shares with Molloy—would seem to be the opposite of Freud's castration anxiety. Belacqua seems to embrace the notion of castration, yet this is in contradiction with his voyeuristic pleasures. Instead of full castration, then, Belacqua wishes to behave as if he were castrated only in relation to an actual, sexual woman, such as Thelma or the Smeraldina.

The Business and Music of Murphy

To a great degree, sexual desire is the driving force of *Murphy*, for good or ill. Murphy desires to return to Celia and the music of sex. The secondary characters are all similarly motivated by sexual desire. Neary initially desires Miss Dwyer, then, after she has succumbed, switches his desires to Miss Counihan, who desires Murphy (both physically and, she hopes, fiscally); Wylie desires Counihan and to frisk Neary and/or Miss Counihan. In the latter two cases, sexual and financial desire are merged, pointing to sexual activity becoming a commodity. Although Neary and Wylie are perhaps more overtly motivated by the desire for physical possession, it would be misleading to draw too much of a distinction between their desires and those of Murphy. Even before Celia, Neary suggests that Murphy himself has been motivated purely by sexual desire in his affairs with various women: "He [Neary] recalled how Murphy had boasted of conducting his amours on the lines laid down by Fletcher's Sullen Shepherd" (*Murphy* 33). The shepherd in question is "one that lusts after every severall beauty,/But never yet has knowne to love or like."[22] Murphy is also claimed to hold the "*plaisir de rompre* [to be] the rationale of social contacts" (33); that is, the "pleasure of breaking" relationships once satisfaction has been gained, as in Jules Renard's play of the same title. These allusions, combined with the attractiveness of Murphy's (erroneously called) "surgical quality," (41) create an impression of a more sexually active, if not more sexually predatory, Murphy than his actions within the novel might suggest.

Nevertheless, there is no denying that Murphy seeks to flee from the "big world" to that of his own mind, yet equally the pull which Celia—the Irish-born prostitute—exerts over Murphy cannot be denied. Indeed, this pull is so great that it is only the intervention of a gas explosion that prevents him from returning to her at the end of the novel. Murphy casts his relations with Celia as an apparently either/or situation, as the "part of him that he hated craved for Celia, the part that he loved shrivelled up at the thought of her" (7). Celia, as prostitute and love object, perfectly chimes with the disdain Murphy displays for the mercantile world of London in which he attempts to find work. It is a world in which "the sense of time as money [...] was highly prized in business circles," (46) and Celia's mode of making money suggests the corrupting influence of a somewhat resurgent capitalism. (As Andrew Gibson points out, *Murphy* is set in the 1930s, and so one would imagine the Depression would have featured prominently, yet the precise date of 1936 coincides with a temporary economic bounce.[23]) Yet Murphy, rather than wishing Celia to stop working, delights in her ability to support them through the selling of sex:

> Surely between them they could contrive to earn a little. Murphy thought so, with a look of such filthy intelligence as left her [Celia], self-aghast, needing him still. Murphy's respect for the imponderables of personality was profound, he took the miscarriage of his tribute very nicely. If she felt she could not, why she could not, and that was all. (15)

This commoditization of sex makes it all the more likely that Murphy, who himself fears becoming a commodity in the job market, would shrink from coitus. The word "gehenna," which was applied to sexual activity in *Dream of Fair to Middling Women,* is now applied to business: the "gehenna of sweats and fiascos" (*Dream* 19) of sex has become "the mercantile gehenna" (27).

An apparently contrary strain to this association of sex and commerce in the novel is that of sex with music. On two occasions, Murphy's and Celia's nights together are described as "serenade, nocturne and albada" (*M* 49 and 157), and Murphy kisses Celia in a "Lydian mode" (89), which, as C. J. Ackerley reminds us, is "one of the modes in ancient Grecian music, characterized as soft and effeminate."[24] This association of sexual contact and music is not restricted to Murphy and Celia; Wylie and Miss Counihan (Murphy's previous amour and, possibly, another prostitute[25]) similarly enjoy a musical gloss on their physical pleasures:

> A kiss from Wylie was like a breve tied, in a long slow amorous phrase, over bars' times its equivalent in demi-semiquavers. Miss Counihan had never enjoyed anything quite so much as this slow-motion osmosis of love's spittle. (75)

The mixed tone of this description—from the raptures of music to the grossness of spit—demonstrates the rather ambiguous attitude toward sexual activity in the novel, as if Beckett could not quite decide which side of the moral divide sex should fall. Such a hesitation might suggest that sexual activity is not solely of the body, but also of the mind, as was certainly the case with Belacqua. Murphy might seek mental refuge in the three Ms of the Magdalen Mental Mercyseat, the lunatic asylum in which he finds work and where he hopes to retire into the "little world" he believes the inmates inhabit, yet the other three Ms of "music, MUSIC, MUSIC" (157), as in sex, Celia, and the "big world," finally prove more attractive. However, at the moment of this resolution, Beckett promptly blows up his hero, making issues of flesh and/or mind redundant. This dissolution of the hero might be suggestive of a punishment for Murphy failing to adhere to the mind, or a more ironic granting of Murphy's wish, now that it is no longer held, to be within "a perpetual coming together and falling asunder of forms [and] a mote in the dark of absolute freedom" (72). However, in the afterlife that is granted to Murphy as ashes, he is thrown back into the physical world as his remains mix with the detritus of a pub floor, with all the "sand, the beer, the butts, the glass, the matches, the spits, the vomit" (171).

The association of sexual activity and music appears to have been informed by Beckett's initial understanding of Schopenhauer and its immediate application in the *Proust* essay of 1931. Beckett focuses on the significance of music for Proust in the final paragraphs of the monograph and claims that the "influence of Schopenhauer [...] is unquestionable" (91). Beckett's reading of Schopenhauer claims that music is the greatest of the arts for the other forms "can produce only the Idea with its concomitant phenomena, whereas music is the Idea itself, unaware of the phenomena, existing ideally outside the universe, apprehended not in Space but in Time only, and consequently untouched by the teleological hypothesis" (92). Such an Idealistic art would seem to be ill-suited to describe sex within *Murphy,* which is precisely concerned with the phenomenon of physical possession. Neary, for example, may entertain his adoration for Miss Dwyer as a Gestalt moment in which the love-object becomes "the single, brilliant, organized compact blotch in the tumult of heterogeneous stimulation," yet such an adoration is mingled with a very physical sense of possession: "To gain the affections of Miss Dwyer," he said "even for one short hour, would benefit me no end," although he would settle for "[h]alf an hour" or the more clichéd, and less ambitious, "[f]ifteen minutes"(5). Neary may be more spiritually inclined than Wylie, but both find the physical phenomena of Celia disturbing as they all share a cab to visit the remains of Murphy. The seating arrangements allow for Neary to contemplate Celia's face while Wylie, seated next to Celia, enjoys the more physical aspects "when they came to a cobbled surface or turned a corner"(159). Yet Beckett persists throughout *Murphy* in describing carnality in musical terms. This apparent contradiction, or the conflation of the Idea with the world of phenomena, is perhaps explained through *Proust* when Beckett considers "the listener who, being an impure subject, insists on giving a figure to that which is ideal and invisible, on incarnating the Idea in what he conceives to be an appropriate paradigm"

(92). As John Pilling has pointed out, this description of the listener's effect on music is not to be found in Schopenhauer (nor is the concept that music is the "Idea itself," for Schopenhauer speaks only of music as a *"copy of the Will itself"* as opposed to other art forms that are a "copy of the Ideas"[26]) and suggests a merging of Proustian themes with what Beckett has remembered of Schopenhauer's "On The Metaphysics of Music." The shape of the idea, though, is particularly apt for the deployment of music as a metaphor for sexual activity in *Murphy* where the Idea (in Beckett's Schopenhauer-inspired terminology) is made physical as a spiritual appreciation gives way to a regard for physical phenomena. In the terms of *Murphy*, this means a turning away from the Idealistic music of the Magdalen Mental Mercyseat back to the incarnate music of life with Celia.

Beckett identifies the incarnation of music in *Proust* through the listener as a corruption and a distortion of the real aesthetic quality of music. In doing so, Beckett briefly pauses to attack opera,[27] which he sees as an intolerable adulteration. He writes that "opera is a hideous corruption of this most immaterial of all the arts" (92) precisely because of the attachment of impure words to the purest of forms. The language of the Fall—corruption, distortion and impurity—is dominant throughout this musical coda to *Proust,* and when Beckett comes to attach words to music in *Murphy,* this fall is again in evidence. Celia remembers two songs she was sung as a child by an inebriated, and worryingly lecherous, Willoughby Kelly:

Weep not, my wanton, smile upon my knee,
When thou art old, there's grief enough for thee.

And

Love is a prick, love is a sting,
Love is a pretty, pretty thing. (145)

In its original context of Robert Greene's *Menaphon* (1589), the first song is one from a mother to her child in distress and suits the overall pastoral theme.[28] In a drunken Kelly's mouth and delivered to an infant Celia, the "wanton" takes on harsher undertones and, given her life of prostitution, the song seems sadly prophetic. The second song, from *The Hunting of Cupid*[29](1591) by George Peele, is more overt in its sexual punning and is even more inappropriate to be directed at a child who is still in her cot. Ackerley finds that these two songs create "a poignant melancholy note,"[30] yet the sexual allusions within both (overt in the second, and more dependent on the context in *Murphy* in the first) suggest that a more carnal and less sentimental note is being struck. For the present purposes, it is perhaps enough to note that when music is degraded by words in the text, the words express the demands and dangers of sexual desire. The corporeality of sex can then be seen to corrupt the Idealism of music. It is just such an abuse of music that Beckett identifies in Proust's depiction of Swann who "identifies the 'little phrase' of the [Vinteuil] Sonata with Odette, spatialises what is extraspatial, establishes it as the national anthem of his love..." (93).

Swann's error casts a rather less positive perspective on Beckett's use of musical imagery to describe sexual acts. Murphy is not celebrating sex or raising it up to the spiritual standard of music, but misrepresenting music, "corrupting" it by sullying it with the corporeal. In this sense, music is tied down to both time and space through its association with sex, and the "teleological hypothesis" (92) is therefore once again raised as a question. It is the ending of Murphy himself that suggests that those involved in the pursuit of physical sexual gratification who consider music as an appropriate (if somewhat trite) metaphor for sex are mistaken. It is clear that the narrator does not make the same mistake. This distinction was also made by Beckett in connection with Proust. Swann may misuse music to characterize his love for Odette, but the Proustian narrator "sees in the red phrase of the Septour [...] the ideal and immaterial statement of the essence of a unique beauty, a unique world, [...] the 'invisible reality' that damns the life of the body on earth as a pensum and reveals the meaning of the word: 'defunctus.'" (93) Murphy wishes to return to "Celia, serenade, nocturne, albada" (157), but the underlying music of the novel asserts an immaterial quality that sees Murphy's body burnt almost beyond recognition and his ashes strewn on a pub floor. The immaterial music of the novel reveals Murphy himself to be defunct.

Yet Murphy's decision to return to Celia is also a decision to return to the big world he has sought to avoid. Logically, then, sex belongs to the business of that big world: the business of jobs, commerce, and taking one's place within an economic community. Jennifer M. Jeffers, drawing on the works of Adler whom Beckett read in the 1930s, interprets Murphy along just these lines, with Murphy's ascetic withdrawal motivated by an inferiority complex occasioned by the political and social emasculation of the Anglo-Irish male in the Irish Free State. This inferiority, masked as an intellectual superiority, is finally overcome as Murphy resolves to "become a man" and take on his "proper" social and sexual role.[31] However, Murphy, in disparaging Celia's cajoling to get him into gainful employment, implies that sex might not only be a matter of the "big world":

Women are all the same bloody same, you can't love, you can't stay the course, the only feeling you can stand is being felt, you can't love for five minutes without wanting it abolished in brats and house bloody wifery. My God, how I have the charVenus and her sausage and mash sex. (26)

Here Murphy very clearly suggests that sex need not be associated with the material, but with the spiritual "love." What he fears is that such a love will be obliterated by the business not only of living but of creating further life. Murphy has a touch of the petulant child about him—an only child who fears a rival. Sex, it should be noted, is not condemned as such; "sausage and mash sex" and "house bloody wifery" are, however, certainly condemned. This abolition of "love" through the engendering of brats is not merely evidence of a certain childish selfishness in Murphy; the language of sexual reproduction is also explicitly linked in the novel to the mercantile world from which Murphy flees for so long: "For what was all working for a living but a procuring and a pimping for the money-bags, one's lecherous tyrants the money bags, so that they might breed" (49). Two discourses are here being merged: the economic and the reproductive. Rather than place sex solely within the unit of the lovers themselves, or within a family relation, it is here used to characterize the wider world of capitalistic desire. The merging of these discourses points to yet another objection to procreation. Procreation is here shown decidedly not to be a matter only for the individual and his or her partner, but a matter for the state itself. As *Murphy* suggests, sex has been made into a commodity and its value has been pegged to the creation of further life to perpetuate economic health.

Banned, Bando, and the Irish Free State

The first ten years of Beckett's career, as we have seen, are marked by a particular concern for issues surrounding sex in social, economic, ontological, psychological, and artistic terms. Sex is not banished from the discourses of these works, but given a centrality for which a strictly Cartesian reading cannot account. As we have also seen, the problem that these texts address is not sexual activity as such but coitus with the aim of reproduction. Beckett is not unusual in this respect, for issues of sex, procreation, and their proper social role were very much at the fore both within Western thinking in general and the Irish Free State in particular. A cluster of texts around *More Pricks than Kicks* speak to a connection between the "misfortune" of Voltaire's castrati and the social and political debates in the Irish Free State concerning sex and censorship. In "Che Sciagura" (1929) and "Censorship in the Saorstat" (1935), the supposedly private realm of the sexual moves into the public and the artistic spheres.

Published anonymously in the Trinity College, Dublin Magazine *Miscellany*, "Che Sciagura" is a dense and, at times, obscure dialogue devoted to the question of birth control, or, more precisely, what manner of birth control was or was not morally acceptable in the Irish Free State. As David Hatch has pointed out, obscurity is perhaps a necessity if one is to "address issues that are sensitive politically and morally,"[32] and the obscurity was welcomed by the Editorial Subcommittee who thought only devotees of Joyce and Voltaire would get the point.[33] Although artificial contraception was not banned in the Free State until 1935, the Censorship Act of 1929 had clearly stated that any literature thought to promote the use of contraception would fall foul of the law, thus signaling an intent to curtail the use of contraception. It was this intent to which Beckett was reacting and would do so again in the (then unpublished) "Censorship in the Saorstat." In the dialogue, certain forms of birth control are debated: abstention from sexual contact ("spatial [elasticity]"), the use of condoms ("qualitative elasticity"), the rhythm method ("unexpressed clock-wisdom"), and the "uncompromising attitude as advocated by the Catholic Truth Society," which is no method of birth control whatsoever. The supposed sexual practices of the Theosophists—chastity buttressed by recourse to masturbation—is rejected from the dialogue by one speaker as being of no concern for the question of birth control as such, while his interlocutor persists in wishing to see masturbation and chastity as within the remit of their discussion:

> Can you not see that the most extreme and passionate form of any act whatsoever, more than actual participation, is an energetic, vehement, and self-conscious abstention?[34]

In other words, utter abstention from coitus must be the most effective form of birth control. Beckett here reveals, according to Hatch, that "the embargo on objects of contraception is hypocritical,"[35] yet the nature of the hypocrisy is greater, perhaps, than this allows, as Beckett is pointing to a fundamental contradiction within Christian thought: the contradictory desirability of children and celibacy, which Beckett rather neatly identifies in "Censorship in the Saorstat" as "[p]aradise peopled with virgins and the earth with decorticated multiparas" (*Disjecta* 87).

St. Paul, in his first letter to the Corinthians, is caught within the same dilemma: "It is good for a man not to touch a woman. Nevertheless, to avoid fornication, let every man have his own wife, and let every woman have her own husband."[36] Of course, fornication here alludes to sex outside of wedlock, but St. Paul unapologetically, if somewhat personally, places celibacy as morally preferable to "lawful" congress. The same contradiction exercised St. Augustine who, commenting on Paul, somewhat manages to square the circle by arguing that sexual congress within marriage, despite its unfortunate but necessary postlapsarian reliance on at least a degree of concupiscence, is acceptable as long as the couple "entertain the firm purpose of generating offspring to be regenerated—that the children who are born of them as 'children of the world' may be born again and become 'sons of God.'"[37] It is interesting to note that here Augustine elides the business of living; the child who is born in sin will be born again through death into the kingdom of heaven. For Augustine, it seems, birth and death are thought in the same instant. In his reaction to St. Paul, Augustine is able to argue that fornication can exist within marriage if the aim is not procreation, yet he is willing to allow a degree of toleration for "such embraces of husband and wife as have not procreation for their object, but serve an overbearing concupiscence [...] are [...] permitted, so far as to be within range of forgiveness..."[38] Despite such toleration of a degree of sexual desire for its own sake, Augustine is still in no doubt as to the moral hierarchy: celibacy, sex for procreation within marriage, sexual expression within marriage without the aim of procreation (venial sin), and the final mortal sin of sex accompanied by some form of interruptive birth control or abortion for such married couples have "not come together by wedlock but by debauchery."[39] Both Paul and Augustine emphasize that the choice between celibacy and "lawful" marriage is down to the individual and the nature of God's gift to him (not to her), yet celibacy—Beckett's "self-conscious abstention"—remains the preferred state. The very danger of sex, and the possibility of falling into sinful concupiscence, is amply demonstrated by the strictures and categorizations placed upon it. It is in this context, and directed at a cultural elite who know their Italian and their *Candide*, that the title functions to suggest that the best birth control is the utter abstention from procreative sex; a view at once in keeping with and contrary to Christian doctrine.

It might be tempting to adduce a simple opposition, here, along Catholic/ Protestant lines. Beckett's suggestion that complete abstention from all forms of sexual activity was the most effective form of birth control is one that is also to be found in the deliberations of the Anglican Lambeth Council of 1930. The council approved the use of contraception but only with a number of caveats attached:

Where there is clearly felt moral obligation to limit or avoid parenthood, the method must be decided on Christian principles. The primary and obvious method is complete abstinence from intercourse (as far as may be necessary) in a life of discipline and self-control lived in the power of the Holy Spirit. Nevertheless in those cases where there is such a clearly felt moral obligation to limit or avoid parenthood, and where there is a morally sound reason for avoiding complete abstinence, the Conference agrees that other methods may be used, provided that this is done in the light of the same Christian principles. The Conference records its strong condemnation of the use of any methods of conception control from motives of selfishness, luxury, or mere convenience.[40]

The text, here given in full, represents the Anglican, and therefore also the Church of Ireland's, official position on the use of contraception. While giving guarded permission for such use, the emphasis is not far removed from that of St. Paul and St. Augustine. The difference does not lie in the "moral obligation to limit or avoid parenthood," which is not specified, nor in the recommendation for complete abstinence, but only with the last resort of "other methods." A fear for modern moral laxity is evident in the concern that "luxury, or mere convenience" must not be considered valid motives for contraception.

That the Church of Ireland, along with the wider Anglican Church, adopted this limited acceptance of contraception in 1930—just one year after the censorship law came into effect—might suggest a doctrinal difference of opinion, with Beckett on the side of the Protestant minority. However, the arguments surrounding the censorship bill reveal a more nuanced set of attitudes concerning sex and reproduction, which played along and across Protestant and Catholic lines in terms of the political as much as the religious. It is certainly the case that many members of the Church of Ireland had no objection to the notion of banning dangerous books. As pro-censorship campaigners repeatedly emphasized, many other nations, some with large Protestant majorities, had censorship laws already in place. The examples of New Zealand, Canada, Australia, Germany, and the United States were often cited. In defense against the charge of sectarianism, the pro-censorship campaigner Fr. Richard Devane SJ pointed to the Protestant members of the Committee on Evil Literature. As Peter Martin has noted, the Church of Ireland, through its *Gazette*, initially remained indifferent and styled the proposed censorship law as addressing only the Roman Catholic majority.[41] There was even a prominent Protestant defender of the bill in the person of William F. Trench, Professor of English at Trinity College. However, Protestant disquiet grew quickly, particularly over the issue of the banning of works promoting contraception. As we have seen, there may have been a certain degree of official doctrinal congruence between Protestantism and Catholicism on the moral nature of contraception, yet the Lambeth Council Resolution also firmly indicates a role for the conscience of the individual in following "Christian principles." The

Protestant tradition was, therefore, opposed to the imposition of Catholic doctrine in law on a matter of personal conscience. There was particular disquiet about the proposed role of "recognized associations" in the working of the law. It was felt that this would inevitably mean the law in effect would follow the agendas of the more vigilant Catholic societies, such as the Catholic Truth Society of Ireland. Although this section of the proposed bill was amended and no "recognized associations" officially sanctioned under law, in practice the Censorship Board was dependent on such bodies for the works referred to them. It is a point to which Beckett, writing in 1935, was particularly keen to draw attention:

> ...any individual is now in theory entitled to lodge a complaint [about a publication] on his own bottom. But as this would entail his procuring five copies of the work for submission to the Board, he finds himself obliged, precisely as the original Bill intended, to cast around for some body whose interest in the public state of mind condones, more amply than his own, a small outlay. And behold the Catholic Truth Society, transformed into an angel of light, stands at his right hand. Precisely as the original Bill intended. (*Disjecta* 86)

The obvious unease here is further compounded in "Censorship in the Saorstat" by what Beckett senses to be a nationalist and natalist agenda within the Free State. When he turns to part four of the law which prohibits publications advocating contraception, Beckett writes that "France may commit race suicide, Erin will never. And should she be found at any time deficient in Cuchulains, at least it shall never be said that they were contraceived" (86–7). The reference to Cuchulain, the Irish hero of legend and defender of Ulster who was cultivated as a symbol of the new Ireland under the de Valera government (it is on the buttocks of the statue of Cuchulain in the General Post Office that Neary dashes his brains in *Murphy*), suggests a process of "Irish-ing" Ireland. As a member of the Irish Protestant minority, Beckett could hardly have welcomed such attempts to define Ireland in such a way. Perhaps just as importantly, as a member of a cultural elite defined in large part by English and European thought, such a race of heroes would suggest an equally unwelcome parochialism. It is important to note, however, that Beckett here reflects much of the pro-censorship discourses of the Free State. Devane, for example, called for the necessity to "legislate according to Irish Ideals and Catholic standards" and the Catholic Truth Society suggested that "decency" in the law might be defined as any publication "offending the cherished traditions of their [the committee's] and our Irish ancestors."[42]

Many of the arguments concerning "race suicide" and a nationalist, protectionist stance were voiced by Oliver St. John Gogarty:

> No one who has any care for a nation's welfare can for one moment countenance contraceptive practices which are a contradiction of a nation's life. In England, the condition of the miners and the unemployed is as it is because England has allowed its capital to go into yellow, brown and black labour, so that the government tolerates clinics for education in the practice of contraception.[43]

Certain key elements to the debate coalesce in Gogarty's thought. It is clear, here, that the health of a nation is dependent upon maintaining or increasing the birthrate. Beckett's comment that "France may commit race suicide, Erin will never" might appear factually inaccurate unless it is placed in a broader European pro-natalist context. In the context of the "Censorship in the Soarstat" essay, Beckett would appear to be contrasting the lax laws concerning contraception in France to the strict laws of the Free State. However, France had also banned any form of publication promoting contraception as early as 1920, in a law that was intended to address the long-term declining birthrate in France that had been exacerbated by the war. Mary Louise Roberts has described the law as "the most oppressive of its kind in Europe,"[44] so one would be mistaken to assume Ireland was entirely out of step with all European countries. Nevertheless, France was offered as an example of the dangers of depopulation. In 1929, the Justice Minister, Fitzgerald Kennedy, pointed to France as an example of "the decay of one of the greatest nations in the world. France cannot keep up its population [...] That is an evil we are not going to have in this country."[45] France's concern for maintaining or increasing its population was in large part inspired by economic and security concerns, which were made all the more pressing by the war. As Gogarty makes clear, similar concerns were at work in the Free State. The warning he adduces from England is that capital should be preserved within the state itself rather than globally diffused, and Gogarty's casual racism also suggests a sneer at the degeneration of England's once pure economic well-being. As was seen in *Murphy*, Beckett was also aware of this neo-Malthusian argument.

However, the "race suicide" argument in the interwar period was not only used by pro-natalists but also by the most vigorous advocates of birth control, who asserted that "only cheap contraceptives could prevent the "breeding of the unfit."[46] This position was adopted by George Bernard Shaw, who, at the invitation of AE (George Russell) denounced the censorship law in the Free State. (Interestingly, AE did not object to the portion of the law banning contraceptive promotion as such.) In the *Irish Statesman,* Shaw condemned the law as aimed at "the extermination of the Irish people," because it would mean the censorship of "any attempt to cultivate the vital passion of the Irish people or to instruct it in any function that is concerned with that passion."[47] In similar fashion to Beckett, Shaw approvingly refers to the birth-control activist, Marie Stopes, and argues that the inability to learn the "techniques of marriage" from such a source would mean "unnecessarily troubled and occasionally wrecked" home lives.[48] Shaw here allies himself with the arguments of Stopes and her American counterpart, Margaret Sanger, who, according to Angus McLaren, "developed the positive argument that contraception was not only compatible with pleasure but essential if the woman's passions were to be allowed full expression."[49] In order to make this more palatable politically, Sanger and Stopes both suggested that the quality of the race could be improved by making contraception available to the lower classes, thus, in effect, "breeding out" the weaknesses that might have been more properly identified as stemming from poor-living conditions and social inequalities. Shaw was not the only major writer to publicly condemn the Free State's censorship law. AE was the prime instigator of a rear-guard action against the bill and his stance was that censorship was not itself a bad thing if a law could be effective, which he claimed would be highly unlikely. He was little concerned with the contraception issue and then only inasmuch as it would mean the banning of English newspapers, where such issues were debated, more likely. Yeats, in one particularly rather high-handed intervention, made a case for the necessity of "sexual passion" within art that derived from a Thomist appreciation of the soul as manifested in the body. His argument, then, was that censorship based on issues of sexuality in art was profoundly un-Catholic.[50] Liam O'Flaherty, who suffered under the censorship law, did not choose to dwell on the contraception issue but rather argued that the "soutaned bullies of the Lord, fortressed in their dung-encrusted towns, hurl the accusation of sexual indecency at any book that might plant the desire for civilization and freedom in the breasts of their wretched victims."[51] These sentiments were echoed by Sean O'Faolain who saw the law as creating a "moronic mass to which [one] can make no intelligent appeal whatever."[52] The challenges to the censorship law were, therefore, wide ranging, from the highly aesthetic to the highly political. Yet it is in Beckett's essay that the strands of the political (the creation of Cuchulains), the sexual (the ban on mentioning contraception), and the aesthetic are most tightly woven together.

Beckett did not seek to intervene in this question of the Free State censorship law, nor, in the end did he publicly intervene, as *The Bookman* went into liquidation before the essay was published. However, once the opportunity presented itself, Beckett drew upon a mass of opinion—some of it contradictory—surrounding sexual reproduction in the interwar period. Some of this was not necessarily particular to the Ireland of the Free State: "race suicide" was as much an issue in France as it was in Ireland (and the methods taken to combat it equally unsuccessful); the language of eugenics uneasily played around the fringes of pro- and anti-natalists alike across Europe; the re-imagining of sex within marriage as a form of domestic pleasure rather than duty was advocated in the United States and the UK by Sanger and Stopes and was brought into play by Shaw in the censorship debate; finally, censorship itself was not an Irish solution as many Anglophone, predominantly Protestant countries also felt the need to combat "degeneracy" by policing what was read. The issues raised by the censorship debate indicate the degree of concern and contradictory thinking within Ireland, in particular, and Europe, in general, concerning the relationship of sex, the family, religion, and the state. Anti- and pro-natalist campaigners often used similar arguments to very different ends and pockets of what we might now consider more progressive thought, such as in Austria and Weimar Germany, were to be found nestled alongside deeply conservative state policies, such as in Ireland and France (the two countries with the lowest rates of populations growth, it should be noted.)

In "Che Sciagura" and "Censorship in the Saorstat," however, Beckett was reacting to the particularities of an Irish context in sexual matters. Yet, as Diarmaid Ferriter suggests, "it is important to acknowledge that the sexual history of Ireland is just as complicated and multilayered as the sexual history of many other countries. Perhaps the real challenge is to identify the degree to which there are aspects of the Irish sexual experience that were unique. Does sexuality really have national characteristics?"[53] Ferriter cites an *Irish Times* editorial that claimed that "Ireland has enjoyed a high reputation for the cardinal virtues of social life. She was famous for her men's chivalry and for her women's modesty. Today, every honest Irishman must admit that this reputation is in danger." This call to defend modesty—to a mainly Protestant readership—might seem particular to Ireland, but such language of the rise of immorality and loss of chastity was common across Europe. The fear of "degeneracy" occasioned by changes in social, economic, and gender norms following the war were not confined to Ireland. However, in the process of creating an ideal self-image for the Free State, the reputation that the *Irish Times* felt to be in peril had to be secured to attain an idyllic Ireland, which de Valera glowingly characterized:

That Ireland which we dreamed of would be the home of a people who valued material wealth only as a basis of right living, of a people who were satisfied with frugal comfort and devoted their leisure to the things of the spirit; a land whose countryside would be bright with cosy homesteads, whose fields and villages would be joyous with the sounds of industry, the romping of sturdy children, the contests of athletic youths, the laughter of comely maidens; whose firesides would be the forums of the wisdom of serene old age.[54]

Again, such mythologizing is hardly unique to Ireland, but the degree to which sexual politics plays a part here should be noted. Children play a crucial role and they are to be "sturdy" and "athletic," which suggests, if not a trace of eugenics, then a desire for the improvement of the quality of the race. Where, one wonders, were these children to come from if the "leisure hours" were to be spent on the "things of the spirit"? A sexual politics can be inferred as underpinning much of de Valera's dream, but that must precisely be left unsaid.

This concern with, and yet unwillingness to publicly discuss, sexual matters in Ireland is epitomized by the *Report of the Committee on the Criminal Law Amendment Act (1880–85) and Juvenile Prostitution (1931)*, more commonly known as the Carrigan Committee Report. The report found that the sexual activities of the Irish were far from the ideal of chastity and chivalry the *Irish Times* had described as the past norm. As Ferriter summarizes:

> The Carrigan Committee report had revealed much about the reality and the perception of immoral conduct; one of its key phrases was that "we need to preserve the young from the contagion around them," as Monsignor Michael Brown of Maynooth College wrote in November 1932. [There was] an unrelenting pessimism about the Irish moral character, an obsession with what was visible as opposed to what was not, a belief that the Irish were different, and little mention of what went on in private, or the need for compassion or education.[55]

Ferriter's research into court records shows that a great deal was going on in private, as attested to by Francis Hackett: "Rape, infanticide, homosexuality, even incest, crop up all over the country."[56] The Carrigan Committee report was never published, on the advice of the Ministry of Justice. As Oliver St. John Gogarty commented: "If this country had produced great sinners there might be something to censor but even the Carrigon report [sic] was not made public so we didn't know what is the enormity of our crimes."[57] Nevertheless, the assessment was that the report demonstrated such a poor state of moral affairs that it was "clearly undesirable that such a view of the conditions in the Saor Stát be given wide circulation."[58] Instead, certain aspects of the Report were addressed through the 1935 Criminal Law Amendment Act: the amendments were drawn up behind closed doors. It was this act that finally saw the prohibition of contraception.

This unwillingness to discuss sexual matters publicly for fear that it would damage the image of a chaste Ireland makes Beckett's insistence on addressing sex throughout the 1930s an act of defiance. The awareness is repeatedly shown in *Murphy*, in which both Miss Counihan and Celia are (or were) prostitutes, rather than a chaste Irish "comely maiden" of de Valera's imaginings. After describing Miss Counihan's clinch with Wylie ("not in Wynn's hotel lest an action for libel should lie" (75)—a comment that speaks of Beckett's awareness of the possible Irish reception to the novel), the narrator briefly describes the cunning Miss Counihan:

> For an Irish girl Miss Counihan was quite exceptionally anthropoid. Wylie was not sure that he cared for her mouth, which was a large one. The kissing surface was greater than the rosebud's, but less highly toned. It is superfluous to describe her, she was just like any other beautiful Irish girl, except, as noted, more markedly anthropoid. How far this constitutes an advantage is what every man must decide for himself. (75)

Miss Counihan's Irishness is emphasized; indeed she is typically Irish, albeit rather more ape-like than most. This anthropoid tendency stresses a certain sexual bestiality within her that again contradicts any chaste paradigm of femininity. The desirability of such a bestial nature is left to the personal choice of the individual man rather than to some imposed, chaste (and yet fecund) ideal of Irish womanhood. That the passage is replete with sexual allusion is attested to by Wylie's preference for kissing a rosebud. This may appear as an innocent, romantic gesture of floral appreciation, but, of course, "rosebud" is slang for both the anus and the vagina. Embedded within the description of Miss Counihan is, then, a reference to a specifically nonreproductive form of sexual gratification that also plays across the gender norms. Miss Counihan's name itself suggests Beckett creating an uncomfortable relation between an ideal Irishness and a forthright sexuality. Chris Ackerley[59] and J. C. C. Mays[60] have both argued for Miss Counihan to be seen as a modern version of the Cathleen ni Houlihan, and Rina Kim has persuasively argued for a contrast between the chaste Cathleen ni Houlihan of Yeats's eponymous play and the decidedly sexual version provided by Beckett.[61] Ackerley rather coyly admits the other possibilities of her name as "cunnie" or "cunt" when he writes that "the name has teasing intimations of the cornice of desire."[62] Through the figure, name, and morals of Miss Counihan, Beckett is attacking the notion of the patriotically charged paradigm of a chaste Irish womanhood. He also does this with one eye fixed firmly on the censors. Of the "oyster kisses" section, the narrator tells us that the "above passage is carefully calculated to deprave the cultivated reader" (*Murphy* 75) as if to acknowledge and taunt a law in which the word " 'indecent' shall be construed as including suggestive of, or inciting to sexual immorality or unnatural vice or likely in any other similar way to corrupt or deprave."[63] This definition of indecent almost reads as a checklist of what Beckett has achieved in a few short paragraphs in *Murphy*. The methods that Beckett adopts in his "indecency" are those of allusion and association, for fear, as stated earlier in *Murphy*, "lest the filthy censors should lack an occasion to commit their filthy synecdoche" (50). By dubbing the censors themselves "filthy," it is almost as if Beckett is challenging them to find the filth in the allusive associations and therefore begging the question whether the "filth" found is the responsibility of the author or the reader. Sometimes a rosebud might just be a rosebud.

An awareness of the interconnection of the political and sexual persists in Beckett's subsequent novel, *Watt*, in two forms: the "Bando" tale of Arthur and the disastrously fecund Lynch family. "Bando" is suggested by Arthur to the gardener Mr. Graves as an effective aphrodisiac that will usher harmony into his marital relation. Unfortunately, it is banned in the country, which, in its topographical and social details, is undoubtedly the Irish Free State:

> It [Bando] cannot enter our ports, nor cross our northern borders, if not in the form of hasardous [sic] and surreptitious dribble, I mean piecemeal in ladies' underclothing, for example, or gentlemen's golfbags or the hollow missal of a broad minded priest, where on discovery it is immediately seized, and confiscated, by some gross customs official half-crazed with seminal intoxication and sold, at ten and even fifteen times its advertised value, to exhausted commercial travellers on their way home after an unprofitable circuit. (*W* 146)

The ban on Bando here closely, and rather paradoxically, resembles the ban on contraception within the Free State from 1935 onwards. In part, the reversal from a contraceptive to an aphrodisiac is a means of satirical disguise, yet the details of the transformative powers of Bando, of the dangers of "seminal intoxication," and the hazards of a "dribble" rather than a stream point to a trend within the interwar years of stressing the health and ultimately social concerns of free sexual expression. In " 'Civilized' Sexual Morality and Modern Nervous Illness," Freud was at the forefront of asserting the negative effects of an unhappy sex life. He argued that it "must above all be borne in mind that our cultural sexual morality restricts sexual intercourse even within marriage itself, since it imposes on married couples the necessity of contenting themselves, as a rule, with a very few procreative acts."[64] It therefore followed that sexual satisfaction was lost, and the "marriage becomes a failure in so far as it had promised the satisfaction of sexual needs." This result was partly due to the lack of effective contraception that would also allow for pleasure as "all devices hitherto invented for preventing contraception impair sexual enjoyment, hurt the fine sensibilities of both partners and even actually cause illness." His assessment—as Angus McLaren has suggested, Freud may have been thinking of his own unhappy marriage a little too much[65]—is unwaveringly depressing as married couples are "doomed" to "spiritual disillusionment and bodily deprivation." Sexual satisfaction is here placed at the very core of a successful marriage, and many "sexologists" and birth-control advocates in the interwar years increasingly argued that only a marriage based on mutual sexual satisfaction would be a happy one and one, ultimately, that would provide the proper conditions for healthy, happy offspring of a reasonable number. The goal of sex, for such campaigners as Theodore van de Velde (*Ideal Marriage: Its Physiology and Techniques* of 1926) and Ettie Rout (*Safe Marriage: A Return to Sanity* of 1922), was now not just procreation but mutual and, if possible, simultaneous orgasm. The vision of marital, and strictly heterosexual, relations was one of "married lovers" to whom Marie Stopes dedicated her book *Enduring Passion*. (The radical ambiguity of the title is one that Stopes did not intend, one assumes, but one that Beckett would have enjoyed, perhaps.) These campaigners for mutual sexual satisfaction also recognized the need for the removal, in Freud's words, of the "[f]ear of the consequences of sexual intercourse." A happy, healthy marriage was predicated on the use of contraception. This idea is certainly present in the list of benefits Arthur claimed accrued to him through the use of Bando:

> From being a moody listless, constipated man, covered with squames, shunned by my fellows, my breath fetid and my appetite depraved (for years I had eaten nothing but high fat rashers), I became, after four years of Bando, vivacious, restless, a popular nudist, regular in my daily health, *almost* a father and a lover of boiled potatoes. (*W* 145 [emphasis added])

The "almost" is a crucial qualification—a mishap, perhaps, that one might put down to the ban on contraception. The results of Bando are not only an increased potency but also a transformation from an introspective, isolated existence open to depravity to a social and healthy existence; a point further underlined by the "delinquencies of Louit, his fall and subsequent ascension, running Bando" (171). Such a fall and rise are at once sexual and social as depravity is avoided and heterosexual bonds are reinforced, not least as it is clear that Louit begins as a practicing homosexual in a relationship with the Bursar of an Irish university "whose association (for it was nothing less) [was] founded on a community of tastes, and even I fear practices, all too common in academic circles, and of which the most endearing was brandy on awakening, which they habitually did in each other's society" (146).

In order to illustrate the wonders of Bando, Arthur proposes to tell the story of this Mr. Louit. The story that is told seems to bear little or no relation to Bando at all. Indeed, at the end of a long digression, we are told that in "another place, [...] from another place, he might have told his tale to its end..." (171), yet Arthur is unable to do so within the Irish context of Mr. Knott's house and environs; again, another possible allusion to the banning of books concerning the promotion of contraception, or more general "indecencies." However, the apparent digression of Louit defrauding an academic committee by producing the savant, Mr. Nackybal, in defense of his dissertation on *The Mathematical Intuitions of the Visicelts*, only gets its fullest significance from the sexualized Bando framework provided. In brief, Louit is pandering to a desire to ground an Irish identity on a racial and rural paradigm. Mr. Nackybal, an illiterate "native of Burren" (149) with no formal education, has the apparent ability to calculate the cube-root of six-figured numbers. His rural innocence is stressed, as if intelligence as such were suspect. Of course, Nackybal is no such innocent mathematical genius but rather an urban Irishman—a Mr. Tisler who lives by the canal—who is perpetrating a fraud at the request of Louit. The very length of this apparent digression indicates a crucial point: while happiness is elsewhere being pursued through a new emphasis on mutual sexual satisfaction (aided by Bando and contraception), the Free State is spending considerable time and effort uncovering and celebrating an utterly fraudulent vision of the Celt as innocent, native sage, far removed from the temptations of the modern world.

Finally, the 28 souls of the Lynch family, from the 85-year-old patriarch to the four-year-old twins, Pat and Larry, are a catalogue of suffering and a Swiftian satire on Beckett's part of the ban on contraception and the de Valera vision of the fecund, rural Catholic family. The family is determined to reach their collective 1,000 years, and they breed regardless of the inevitable consequences: pain and death. Rather than de Valera's dream of "the romping of sturdy children, the contests of athletic youths, the laughter of comely maidens; [the] wisdom of serene old age,"[66] the Lynches of all ages, from the patriarch Tom, "confined to his bed with constant undiagnosed pains in the caecum" (84), to the young twins Pat and Larry, who suffer from rickets and malnutrition, are bound to a suffering in large part created by the sheer size of the family. Furthermore, the moral sanctity of the family is shown to be in danger from the family itself. When Ann (who has a "painful congenital disorder of an unmentionable kind" [85]) gives birth to twins, it is widely assumed that the father must be a member of the family, be it her cousin Sam (paralyzed from "no higher than the knees down and from no lower than the waist up..." [85]), or her cousin Tom (prone to paralyzing fits of depression and exaltation), who also has an eye on the young niece Bridie, or again her Uncle Jack who was "weak in the head" (91). The list is seemingly endless: "Other names mentioned in this connexion were those of Ann's uncles Joe, Bill and Jim, and of her nephews, Blind Bill and Maim Mat, Sean and Simon" (92). The family, due to its size and poor, cramped living conditions, is here seen to be a danger to morality rather than a guardian of morality. Incest is not viewed with horror but has become a natural assumption, and the reproductive success of the family has proved to be its own undoing, both physically and morally. In *Malone Dies* Beckett again emphasizes the questionable morality of the rural family. Mr. Lambert habitually uses violence against his wife to ensure sex (26), and the son, Edmund, "would have gladly slept with his sister, the father too, I mean the father would have gladly slept with his daughter [...] Incest then was in the air. Mrs. Lambert, the only member of the household who had no desire to sleep with anyone, saw it coming with indifference" (42). Sentencing a father to three years imprisonment for incest in 1936, Judge O'Donnell of the Cork circuit commented that such cases were "due to the conditions under which the poor lived, bad housing and poverty."[67] Beckett's Lynch and Lambert families may be exaggerated satirical figures, but, like all such figures, they are firmly rooted in the unfortunate social realities of the day.

CHAPTER 3

The Horrors of Reproduction

The previous chapters have argued for a distinction to be made between reproductive and nonreproductive forms of sexual expression in Beckett's works. The former is renounced, and the latter indulged, albeit with a string of caveats attached. Moreover, the debate over nonreproductive and reproductive forms of sexual expression has been seen to go beyond the merely personal to encompass political, religious, familial, and ethical concerns during the 1930s within Ireland in particular and Europe more generally. Yet the question remains: what is wrong with reproduction? In order to approach this question, Beckett's "First Love" offers something of a test-case; first because it demonstrates the extent to which issues of sexuality and psychology permeate Beckett's work as he begins the most intense period of creativity in his career, but also, the story is replete with misogynistic comments and ends with the protagonist-narrator rejecting his newly born child. These related issues of misogyny and misopedia (hatred of the child) are then further developed by tracing their import within Beckett's oeuvre, and, finally, the chapter concludes with the manner in which geriatric, impotent sex furthers a sense of the horrors of reproduction—a horror which permeates much of Beckett's prose.

"First Love"

The protagonist-narrator of "First Love" is horrified when his lover, Lulu/Anna, reveals that she is pregnant: "Abort! Abort!" he cries. Rather than taking on parental responsibility, he simply leaves while labor is in progress, followed by the cries as he walks away: "As long as I kept walking I didn't hear them, because of the footsteps. But as soon as I halted I heard them again, a little fainter each time, admittedly, but what does it matter, faint or loud, cry is cry, all that matters is that it should cease. For years I thought they would cease. Now I don't think so any more."[1] It may well be that the child is not his ("If it's lepping [in the womb] it's not mine" he comments [79]), especially as Lulu/Anna is a prostitute who receives clients in her room and the giggles and gasps of whom the protagonist can faintly hear. If the child is the protagonist's, it was conceived on his one "night of love," a night, importantly, which is not detailed:

> I woke next morning quite worn out, my clothes in disorder, the blanket likewise, and Anna beside me, naked naturally. One shudders to think of her exertions. I still had the stewpan in my grasp. It had not served. I looked at my member. If only it could have spoken. Enough about that. It was my night of love. (76)

That Beckett chose not to describe the actual sex scene should not be taken as a sign of some form of delicacy as this is a text, after all, in which the protagonist considers "kicking her [Anna] in the cunt" (66). Rather, the reticence here accentuates the passivity of the protagonist as if, harking back to Belacqua, Anna had raped him and then everything went kaputt. Indeed, the text is marked by gaps of reticence and forgetting. As Phil Baker has claimed, forgetting for Beckett was a synonym for repressing.[2] If this is the case, the protagonist is repressing his "night of love," his one instant of full coitus. That this ultimately led to a child might be the very reason for that repression.

However, the text plays with the reader's need or desire to ascribe psychological significance to many of the facets of the story, as the protagonist begs the question or questions: "I see no connexion between these remarks. But that one exists, and even more than one, I have little doubt, for my part. But what? Which?" (69) The remark all but demands a form of associative analysis, akin to Freudian practice in which, for example, the proximity of apparently unrelated material within a dream might hold some significance by dint of that proximity, or connections ("and even more than one") may collect about certain nodal points. These connections can themselves be apparently contradictory or counterintuitive. As Freud remarked in the so-called "Wolf-man" case history, there "was only a logical contradiction—which is not saying much."[3] The text would, therefore, seem to sanction a psychoanalytic reading, and such a reading has been attempted, for example, by J. D. O'Hara, who finds the story an unsuccessful application of the Wolf-man case, and Phil Baker, who sees a dominant thematic of birth trauma and the application of Otto Rank throughout the text. The problem, though, is the very foregrounding by the text of such a method. (A very similar moment occurs in *Molloy* when the narrator thinks that looking into his relation with his mother will bring light to bear on his plight.) Can one be sure that the text is endorsing a psychoanalytic approach or ridiculing a psychoanalytic drive to explain and explain away? Nevertheless, the text opens with an invitation to inquire into just such an associative connection: "I associate, rightly or wrongly, my marriage with the death of my father, in time" (61). The unstated nature of this association between the death of the father and the relationship with Lula/Anna provides a teasing framework in which to set the various details of the story, which, as O'Hara has suggested, amount to "sexuality, the father, evasions of the outer world, constipation, doubt, and childbirth."[4]

In keeping with the invitation to associate, one point of entry into the story is the one occasion when the protagonist himself makes a seemingly unconscious association. The protagonist is stripping his room in Anna's apartment of all its furniture and finally taking down some shelves when, "strange memory, I heard the word fibrome, or brone, I don't know which, never knew, never knew what it meant, and never had the curiosity to find out" (75). The word that slips into his head is most probably "fibroma," which, as Baker points out, is a "fibrous tumour, related to 'fibroid': a benign tumour of the wall of the uterus."[5] As he is clearing Anna's room of furniture so he can take possession of it, the benign tumor, rather than a foreshadowing of the impending pregnancy, may well be the protagonist himself who attaches himself to the wall of the room (and so, here, womb) when he turns the sofa to the wall and nestles in. The protagonist is then a form of benign growth in the womb in contrast to the malign growth that will be the baby born at the end of the story. If one were to follow this associative train, then the protagonist leaving the room would amount to some form of rebirth, and the terms of the story certainly lend themselves to such a reading: "What finished me was the birth of the child. It woke me up" (79). However, it seems that little benefit comes of this rebirth, as the protagonist wanders out of the story in a very similar fashion to which he wandered in, as he is expelled from shelter at the beginning and end of the story.

Indeed, images of expulsion dominate much of "First Love," in terms of expulsion from shelter and (or, rather, lack of expulsion) of fecal matter. Broadly speaking, a concern for the former might lead one to a reading of the story along the lines of Otto Rank's *The Trauma of Birth* (as Baker has indicated), and the latter would offer a more Freudian perspective (O'Hara). Yet it seems that the two need not be mutually exclusive. That Beckett was alive to the scatological possibilities of sexuality has been argued in Chapter 1, and here again there is a close connection between shit and sex. After all, the protagonist writes Lulu's "name in old cowshit [with his] devil's finger, into the bargain" (70). Although he claims that this action proves his love to be "pure and disinterested," the image leaves this somewhat open to doubt. That defecation and coitus are linked is again demonstrated by the narrator checking whether he has used the stewpan, which serves him as a bed-pan, as soon as he awakes from his "night of love"; tellingly, it is empty. His constipation is a further constant in the story, and ironically his difficulty in expelling allows him to be expelled from his family home:

> One day, on my return from stool, I found my room locked and my belongings in a heap before the door. This will give you some idea how constipated I was, at that juncture. It was, I am now convinced, anxiety constipation. But was I genuinely constipated? Somehow I think not. Softly, softly. And yet I must have been, for how otherwise account for those long, cruel sessions in the necessary house? (64)

In Freudian terms, defecation—in the pleasure of excreting and the withholding of excreta—forms a complex of associative possibilities:

> Since the column of faeces stimulates the erotogenic mucous membrane of the bowel, it plays the part of an active organ in regard to it; it behaves just as the penis does to the vaginal mucous membrane, and acts as it were as its forerunner during the cloacal period. The handing over of the faeces for the sake of (out of love for) some one else becomes a prototype of castration; it is the first occasion upon which an individual parts with a piece of his own body in order to gain the favour of some other person he loves. So that a person's love of his own penis, which is in other respects narcissistic, is not without an element of anal erotism. "Faeces", "baby" and "penis" thus form a unity, an unconscious concept (*sit venia verbo*)—the concept, namely, of "a little one" that can be separated from one's body.[6]

Constipation, therefore, also similarly suggests a plethora of possibilities. That the protagonist associates sex with Anna with defecation and yet remains constipated simultaneously suggests a fear of possible castration and the fear of the production of a real "little one," a child. (That the child itself will be the castrator will be considered later.) In the context of the death of the father, O'Hara may well be correct to draw a direct comparison to the "Wolf-man" of "From the History of an Infantile Neurosis" in which the analysand's constipation is indicative of his unconscious desire for his father and his wish to present him with a child, just as his mother had done.

The association between the death of the father and the "marriage" of "First Love" could then be that of the symbolic wish fulfillment of the protagonist's desire to take the mother's place in the father's affections, were it not for the fact that the protagonist remains constipated throughout. Freud's patient repeatedly complained that he felt that the world was obscured for him by a veil that was only torn apart when he was administered with an enema. Only when the patient remembered that he was born with a caul is Freud in a position to offer a full analysis: "Thus the caul was the veil which hid him from the world and hid the world from him. The complaint that he made was in reality a fulfilled wishful phantasy: it exhibited him as back once more in the womb, and was, in fact, a wishful phantasy of flight from the world."[7] At this point Rank's birth-trauma and Freud's analysis are allied, demonstrating that a merging of both readings is possible in "First Love." For Freud's patient, this "wishful phantasy" to be back in the womb is only surmounted through a form of passive (and so, for Freud, homosexual) sexuality:

> The necessary condition of his rebirth was that he should have an enema administered to him by a man. [...] This can only have meant that he had identified himself with his mother, and that the man was acting as his father, and that the enema was repeating the act of copulation, as the fruit of which the excrement-baby (which was once again himself) would be born. The phantasy of rebirth was therefore bound up closely with the necessary condition of sexual satisfaction from a man.[8]

That this opens up "First Love" and sexuality in Beckett more generally to a distinctly "queer" reading will be considered later. For the moment, it is important to note that the protagonist goes through no such process. He is indeed passive in his sexual relations with Anna, but this does not have a purgative effect, and the stewpan is empty come the morning. This would suggest that the protagonist does not wish to relinquish the womb-like state and that "rebirth" does not occur, which would account for the lack of change in the protagonist as he leaves; certainly, he has not been socialized by his experience of love nor has he assumed a masculine, productive identity.

Beckett's reading of Otto Rank's *The Trauma of Birth* in early 1935 might here suggest that the protagonist of "First Love" is unable to overcome the initial disaster of having been born. Rank suggested that:

> the essential factor in the development of neuroses seems to be that man, in the biological as in the cultural overcoming of the birth trauma, which

we call adjustment, comes to grief at the cross road of sexual gratification, which most nearly approaches the primal situation, yet does not completely re-establish it in the infantile meaning.[9]

For most people, the trauma of birth can be assuaged through successful heterosexual intercourse with "the gratification of partially returning to the mother" encompassed in the act.[10] The desire to return to the womb may be seen in Beckett's work prior to his reading of Rank (Belacqua's "womb-tomb" fantasy), and certainly after it in *Murphy* and *Watt* (featuring intrauterine memories), *Eleutheria* (Victor Krap taking to his room and bed), Molloy's intrauterine recall, Malone in his bed, Dan Rooney's blindness and his preference for the entombing office in *All That Fall*, Joe in *Eh Joe*, again careful to make sure that he is safely alone in his room, and through to the figures in fetal positions in the dark of the late prose texts.[11] In "First Love" the protagonist makes himself a second womb in Lulu/Anna's apartment, and while ensconced in this apparent safety, he hears the noises of sex as Lulu/Anna receives her clients, which may be suggestive of "both the primal scene and intrauterine disturbances caused by the mother's sexual activity."[12] This haven, however, is only temporary and is destroyed by the arrival of the child, as if a real expulsion from the womb necessitates a figural expulsion for the protagonist. In Rank, the symptoms of a neurotic inability to compensate for the trauma of birth cohere about a difficulty in heterosexual sexual relations; again the protagonist offers ample evidence of his difficulties in this area. First, of course, this is his only night of sex—at the age, we are told, of 25. Second, he displays a profound misogyny focused on the female genitals "because of its close relation to the shock of birth,"[13] as Rank argues. (He places this comment within the context of homosexuality, in particular.) When the actual business of sex is at issue, the protagonist also displays a marked detachment:

> She began to undress. When at their wit's end they undress, no doubt the wisest course. She took off everything, with a slowness fit to enflame an elephant, except her stockings, calculated presumably to bring my concupiscence to the boil. It was then I noticed the squint. Fortunately she was not the first naked woman to have crossed my path, so I could stay, I knew she would not explode. I asked to see the other room which I had not yet seen. (74)

Rather than taking up the invitation, the protagonist immediately wants to see the room, as if turning away from the womb-substitute of sex for the more satisfactory substitute of the room-as-womb. Moreover, as Christopher Ricks has pointed out, he cannot look at the body and prefers to focus on the face, at which point the squint is noticed. The female body is here offered as a foreign or bizarre site ("I knew she would not explode") from which the protagonist recoils. The precision of the prose—especially the "presumably"—also demonstrates a lack of engagement, as if the protagonist were watching an experiment, rather than taking part in a seduction. Indeed, he does not take part in the seduction: Lulu's striptease might have "enflamed an elephant," but it leaves the protagonist cold. For Rank, "The neurotic [...] fails in sexuality; which in this connection is as good as saying that he is not content with the gratification of partially returning to the mother, afforded in the sexual act and in the child, but has remained fixedly 'infantile' and even still desires to go *completely* or as a whole back into the mother"[14] (Rank's emphasis). Here, sex and the child are both rejected as insufficient compensation for the birth trauma. By denying the child, the protagonist would then be reasserting the need to entirely return to the womb. For Rank, procreation offers the male one mechanism with which to overcome the shock of birth, whereby the child that is born can become a figure with whom the male identifies inasmuch as it has recently been in the uterine state and at one with the mother. Alternatively, the child can be seen as a rival, as in the case of an older sibling's jealousy of a younger brother or sister as "the later coming child materializes the deepest wish tendency of the already present child to be again with the mother, and, as it were, spoils once and for all the chances of ever returning there."[15] In "First Love" this can be seen in the protagonist's identification with the new child and his need to leave Anna's house. "What that infant must have been going through!" (79). This is at once indicative of a genital horror—the "going through" is physically precise—and a moment of shared pain as the child is expelled once and for all from the "paradise" of the womb, to use Rank's term. However, the protagonist does not pursue this line of sympathy but is expelled into the world once again at the end of the story as if the hope of a return to the womb had been shattered by the emergence of a new life into the light. Tellingly, the cries that follow him down the road might be as much the cries of the newborn as of the mother, and the phrasing of "cry is cry" suggests a universal suffering occasioned by birth itself.

Beckett came to Rank as part of his own therapy with Wilfred Bion, which lasted for almost two years in 1934 and 1935, and was part of his extensive reading in psychology during this time. This reading encompassed secondary synoptic works such as Woodworth's *Contemporary Schools of Psychology* as well as works by Ernest Jones, Freud, Wilhelm Stekel, Alfred Adler, and others. The purpose of these readings, it has been argued, moved from a concern on Beckett's part to understand his own mental state to a more literary concern for appropriating concepts and phrases, in keeping with his note-taking prior to therapy. Whatever the actual purpose, it is important that figures such as Rank were in a sense already preaching to the converted inasmuch as Rank consciously placed himself within a tradition with which Beckett was very much aware—that of Schopenhauer. Rank repeatedly cites Schopenhauer in *The Trauma of Birth*. At one point, Rank commends Schopenhauer's "world as idea" as having "good psychological grounds"[16] and later places the philosopher within a pessimistic tradition stemming from Anaximander of Miletus, a further figure of whom Beckett was demonstrably aware, especially his (very Schopenhauerean) notion of "individual existence as atonement,"[17] which Rank also emphasizes. Indeed, the section on "Philosophic Speculation" in Rank's book draws upon many philosophers—many of the them pre-Socratic—of whom Beckett was aware, including Heraclitus and Anaxagoras. The point of coalescence for many of these figures, and one suspects for Beckett, is given by Rank via Nietzsche's approving comments of Schopenhauer: "The right standard by which to judge every human being is that he really is a being who ought not to exist at all, but who is expiating his existence by manifold forms of suffering and death..."[18] Perhaps, then, the protagonist's advice to "Abort! Abort!" is not as callous as it might first seem, for sexual reproduction is doubly damned: it banishes one from the true home of the womb, and it creates a further life condemned to suffering and death. It is this "birth to into death" (*MD* 114) that may account for Beckett's misogyny and his misopedia.

Beckett's Misogyny

Beckett has often, and rightly, been accused of misogyny. Susan Brienza writes that "insistent derogatory remarks about female characters take on the cumulative force of dogma"[19] in the early works, and Mary Bryden identifies "an essentialist and deeply misogynistic construction of Woman" in Beckett's predramatic prose.[20] However, dealing with the misogyny apparent in the works remains a delicate matter. After surveying the stereotypic and stereoscopic methods of characterization in Beckett's fiction, Rubin Rabinovitz admits that the question of "how to judge Beckett's most caustic descriptions of women" has been left unanswered. While ideas "about characterization can explain some of the disturbing factors in these works," Rabinovitz is still left troubled by Beckett's misogyny: "I admire Beckett's work [and it] is probably for this reason that I find myself wishing Beckett had never written these passages. For all the mitigating circumstances, their rancor still jars. [...] I would like to think that he now also regrets having written those caustic passages."[21] I have quoted Rabinovitz at some length because the comments exemplify some of the difficulties of dealing with misogyny in Beckett. The predominate tone here is one of regret, as if the image one has of Beckett is undermined by the misogyny of his fictions; as if such a hatred had no place in Beckett's thought, let alone a place in his works. Second, Rabinovitz clearly hopes that a proper scholarly approach (here the focus on methods of characterization) will in some way lessen the regrettable impact of misogyny in Beckett. "Mitigating circumstances" are offered, and yet they cannot expunge the stain of misogyny—it is, perhaps, just too frequently and too vehemently expressed in the works to be done away with so easily. Rabinovitz is honest, balanced, and troubled and recognizes that any attempt to deal with Beckett's misogyny runs the risk of seeming to excuse that misogyny or, at the least, lessen its damaging impact. For example, by placing Beckett within a tradition of misogyny, stretching from the pre-Socratics through the Church Fathers to the notoriously misogynistic Schopenhauer, might be enlightening but might also be accused of seeking to diminish Beckett's culpability. C. J. Ackerley, considering the techniques of the poem "Hell Crane to Starling" as used in *Dream*, argues that they "form set pieces in a tradition of misogynistic satire running from Juvenal to Chaucer and Burton."[22] The phrase "set pieces" creates a certain distance between the figure of Beckett and the words on the page, as if the author knowingly adopts a tradition that is questionable in its treatment of women to make a further satirical point. This might then leave Beckett somewhat free of the accusation of a personal misogyny. Similarly, the fact that Beckett made copious notes from Burton in the composition of *Dream* might point to either a desire to *use* a tradition of misogyny or a desire to be *of* a tradition of misogyny. To be as candid as Rabinovitz, I cannot say I regret the misogyny in Beckett's fiction as it opens up another avenue of inquiry into the themes of sex, reproduction, and death, which were highlighted in the previous reading of "First Love." Here, the question is not whether or not Beckett (however that word might be defined) may have been a misogynist. The question is rather: does misogyny play a significant role in the works? And, if so, what is the nature of that significance?

"First Love" amply demonstrates the misogyny that is so often to be found in Beckett's predramatic prose. His recoil from Lulu/Anna is on one level a physical reaction; he cannot bring himself to look at her body for too long and only focuses on her face in order for it to be disparaged. Their conversations are marked by his exasperation at her apparent stupidity. Her mere presence is repeatedly said to be "disturbing," and, of course, he contemplates a form of sexual violence against her: "I considered kicking her in the cunt" (66). Finally, the story (in-line with the "rape" of Belacqua in *Dream*) insists upon Lulu as the active agent of intercourse. However, one should not too easily rush to the conclusion that there is a rigid sexual binary in operation, along the lines of Lula/Him as active/passive, body/ mind. Certainly, Lulu takes the sexual lead in their first encounters, yet she elicits and then responds to the narrator's own physical response to her as she strokes his ankles: "But man is still today, at the age of twenty-five, at the mercy of an erection, physically too, from time to time, it's the common lot, even I was not immune, if that may be called an erection. It did not escape her, naturally, women smell a rigid phallus ten miles away and wonder, How on earth did he spot me from there?" (66). The narrator certainly suggests that Lulu is the one with carnality in mind, but this should not detract from the fact that an erection, of sorts, does occur. The comments that follow may indicate that the explanation of misogyny in Beckett's works most often given—that the female body distracts the mind of the male in his search for "self"—may be correct: "One is no longer oneself, on such occasions, and it is painful to be no longer oneself..." If only the sentence ended here, then all would be clear, but it continues: "...even more painful if possible than when one is. For when one is one knows what to do to be less so, whereas when one is not one is any old one irredeemably" (66–67). There is, then, little to choose between the pain of being oneself and the pain of not being oneself when lost in a physical state of arousal. It is not the case here that losing oneself in arousal is a barrier or distraction from finding one's true self, whatever that might be.

"First Love" is far from being an atypical example of the misogyny within the earlier prose and poetry, from the disgust at the female form in *Dream* to the offhand comment in *Malone Dies* that Moll is of no concern because she is "after all [...] only a female" (92). This disgust of the female form and dismissal of the female mind appears to fall into the oppositional binary that "First Love" can be seen to question. Those critics who have dealt with misogyny in the works have tended to assume that just such a binary is in operation. For example, James Acheson makes the general comment that "Beckett's men devote themselves to private religions of art or self [...], while his women act as either destructive temptresses or as exponents of what might be termed the heresy of love."[23] This clearly places the cerebral within the sphere of the male and the carnal within the sphere of the female. In comparison with the women in George Bernard Shaw, Kristin Morrison writes that "woman is the enslaving seductress who deflects man from his proper work, his proper self."[24] In a more theoretical vein, but adhering to the same binary assumption, Susan Brienza has described how the "male's impatience with the corporeal is displaced onto the woman as Other and expressed as aversion to or disgust with Woman as body, as clod."[25] As the title of Carol Helmstetter Cantrell's essay "Cartesian Man and the Woman Reader: A Feminist Approach to Beckett's *Molloy*" suggests, a degree of assumed Cartesian thought underpins many of the critical encounters with the undoubted misogyny of Beckett's works. It is important to note, however, that Mary Bryden does not adopt such an unquestioned Cartesian binary, and indeed warns against it. She points out that Cartesian dualism is "only by secondary, extra-curricular activity imprinted with gender segregation." Yet Bryden, quoting Carol Helmstetter Cantrell, concedes that "the effect of his [Descartes] thought was to rigidify and intensify the split between the two sides of the traditional system of polarities."[26] Bryden's work, drawing on the work of Deleuze, Guattari, and Cixous, argues that "the evolution of Beckett's artistic practices is [...] from an essentialist and deeply misogynistic construction of Woman towards more erratic, often contingent or indeterminate gender configurations."[27] However, in order to demonstrate such an evolution, Bryden begins Beckett's trajectory firmly within an oppositional, albeit not specifically Cartesian, structure "where the males of the early fiction ponder and agonise over the mind and the body as two separate and impermeable compartments, Woman is undoubtedly placed on the side of physical matter."[28]

These critical attempts at placing Beckett within a pseudo-Cartesian binary to deal with the misogyny of the works may adequately explain the Beckettian man's revulsion at the female form and his flight from it, yet they cannot account for the Beckettian man's frequent attraction to the female. If the female is so corporeal, what are Beckett's supposedly "Cartesian" men doing in a relation with something so regrettable? To say that Beckett's male characters in the predramatic prose simply flee from woman—rather like Gulliver fleeing from a lascivious Yahoo[29]—is to look only at one side of the story. The protagonist of "First Love" does not take to his heels at the first signs of an approach from Anna, after all; she may "disturb" him, but he does set up some kind of temporary home with her. Any attempt to think of the attraction toward the female need not diminish or excuse the misogyny of the works as such, but might rather reveal further grounds for the pervasive hatred of women that permeates the works.

Two early accounts of the male/female relation, John Fletcher's "Samuel Beckett and Jonathan Swift: Toward a Comparative Study" and Vivian Mercier's "Samuel Beckett and the Sheela-na-gig," provide just such further grounds. Fletcher's suggestive essay of comparisons between Beckett and Swift inevitably broaches the issue of the misogyny within both writers and claims that they "are both, in fact, convinced misogynists, attacking, it need hardly be said, woman's physical aspect."[30] Fletcher notes that both Beckett and Swift are "entirely devoid of idealism where physical love is concerned" and that this allows both to explore the "ridiculous" nature of sex and sexuality.[31] This is in line with many of the binary accounts of misogyny that we have already encountered. However, and most importantly, Fletcher argues that sex within Swift and Beckett must be viewed through the prism of a shared hatred of life, and goes on to argue that Beckett's misogyny is "no less deep-rooted than Swift's, and [shows] a similar recoil from female sexuality. For if existence is absurd, if death alone is desirable, it is not surprising that the human creature responsible for the transmission of life should inspire such dread."[32] The "not surprising" of the final sentence might seek to excuse misogyny (it seems to imply that all right-thinking *men* would be of the same opinion), yet the connection between misogyny and the "transmission of life" as being regrettable is a crucial link to be made. In turn, Mercier suggests that Beckett might be viewed (alongside Swift) from the perspective of a Gaelic tradition of the macabre and the grotesque, which can be typified in the female Sheela-na-gig figures that "have grossly exaggerated genitalia or a posture which directs attention to the genitalia".[33] Mercier admits that Beckett "might be described as *in* the Gaelic tradition but not *of* it," yet his place within the tradition hinges on the use of grotesque humor—which is often overtly sexual—that "serves as a defense mechanism against the holy dread with which we face the mysteries of reproduction."[34] Importantly, these mysteries of reproduction are, within the figure of the Sheela-na-gig, firmly allied to death, thus the "Sheela-na-gig symbolically reveals to us a universal truth [...] Sex implies death, for if there were no death there would be no need for reproduction. Besides, man has always found woman terrifying as well as alluring."[35] Both Fletcher and Mercier make the crucial connection between sex and death, but Mercier takes the argument further by suggesting that the relation between sex and death accounts for both the dread of, and attraction to, woman. He goes on: "The psychoanalysts say that this is because the female sex organ always suggests castration to him, as well as the first cruel expulsion from a nine-month paradise."[36] Mercier's terms take us back to the work of Otto Rank for whom the "importance of the castration fear is based [...] on the primal castration at birth, that is, on the separation of the child from the mother."[37] As noted earlier, Rank also connects misogyny with an "abhorrence of the female genitals, and this because of its close relation to the shock of birth."[38] Yet, the sexual attraction to the female remains, because the "only real possibility of an approximate reinstatement of the primal pleasure is given in sexual union, in the partial and purely physical return into the womb."[39] The "abhorrence" of the female form is, therefore, parallel with a desire to return to that very form.

The shape of this attraction to and then repulsion from the female can be seen on a larger scale in *The Unnamable* when the protagonist, as the avatar

Mahood, circles about the rotunda in which his family are housed. After years of wandering, Mahood is "returning to the fold" and telling himself that "yonder is the nest you should never have left." (29) Although the return to this rotunda, which has no windows but loopholes let in the walls (and may function as a precursor of the rotundas of the later short fictions), is styled as a return to home, Mahood remains ambivalent: "I had no wish to arrive, but I had to do my utmost, in order to arrive. A desirable goal, no, I never had time to dwell on that" (32). Mahood first claims that his journey to the family nest is stopped by the stench of the corpses of the family that has succumbed to food-poisoning. This ending is revised, and the second version sees Mahood entering into the rotunda and stepping through the "muck" of his decomposing relatives: "I like to fancy, even if it is not true, that it was in mother's entrails I spent the last days of my long voyage, and set out on the next" (36). The journey to the rotunda (itself perhaps symbolic of the womb) ends in a grotesque version of a return to the mother as he fancies he treads amongst her entrails. The rather disgusting imagery is itself suggestive of the attraction and repulsion that is at play in the story and underlines the unsuccessful nature of this return that sends him out again on a further journey. Furthermore, the story connects the figures of the mother and wife through an all-embracing, genitally inspired, misogyny. While circling the rotunda and under a belief in the first version of the story, the Unnamable comments that "the bouquet was this story of Mahood's in which I appear as upset at having been delivered so economically of a pack of blood relations, not to mention the two cunts into the bargain, the one for ever accursed that ejected me into this world, and the other, infundibuliform, in which pumping my likes, I tried to take my revenge." (35) The misogynistic reduction of the mother and the wife to their genitalia effectively collapses the relation between the trauma of birth and the attempts at overcoming that trauma through sex. That this attempt is unsuccessful is attested to by the sadistic "revenge" that Mahood is said to pursue in coitus. For Rank, such a failure in coitus points to a neurotic inability to overcome the initial horror at having been born. In the playful (and at times exasperating) manner of *The Unnamable,* the reader is encouraged to pay attention to this failed return to the "nest": "I must really lend myself to this story a little longer, there may possibly be a grain of truth in it" (33). That possible truth may be in the expulsion, return, and repulsion pattern occasioned by the birth trauma. It should be noticed, for example, that in the cases of Molloy and Lousse, and Malone and the woman who brings him the dish and pot, women are frequently depicted as offering womb-like shelter to the Beckettian man, yet such shelter is only temporary and unsatisfactory. The same pattern can also be seen in Molloy's need to return to his mother; a return that always ends in a flight from her. Just as Mahood's mother and wife are reduced to "two cunts," so Molloy's mother and his sexual partners are merged: "And God forbid me, to tell you the truth, my mother's image sometimes mingles with theirs, which is literally unendurable, like being crucified, I don't know why and I don't want to." (*M* 58) "Could a woman have stopped me as I swept towards mother?" Molloy wonders, and the answer is frequently "Yes," as, through sex, the lover offers a means of trying to deal with the initial expulsion into life. Of course, sex used to these ends does not find success, and Molloy and others are once more expelled into wandering. Misogyny, the trauma of birth, and the desire for death are all combined by Malone when he speaks of death as when "the world [...] parts at last its labia and lets me go" (14) and later as being expelled from the "great cunt of existence" (114). To echo the words of "First Love," one wonders what Malone "must have been going through."

The misogyny of the works is not only an attack on the threatening physicality of the female, although the terms of misogyny in *Dream* certainly suggest that this forms part of the complex. Yet, as the fear of, and need to return to, the female in the prose works has demonstrated, Beckett's misogyny also attests to the wish never to have been born and views birth as a form of banishment from home. That sexual intercourse is, in Beckett's world, nearly always a less than satisfactory affair goes on to attest that there can be no recompense for existence, as Rank suggested might be the case in the partial return to the mother through coitus. Beckett's male "lovers" appear to wish for full dissolution and not sex as some partial substitute. To be sure, this entails never forgiving the female for birth's expulsion from the paradise of nonexistence. However, it also means a constant pattern of expulsion, return, flight, and return as Beckett's male characters flee from, and yet are drawn back to, the site of the womb.

Beckett's Misopedia

If Beckett's misogyny, as argued above, is related to birth and the need to return to a prebirth state, it would seem reasonable to assume that Beckett would show a degree of fellow-feeling for those who have been banished from this haven more recently: those children scattered throughout his texts. Yet, as will be shown, the child is a figure of hate in Beckett's work. This hate should not be mitigated and as Beckett's misogyny has become increasingly recognized, the related hatred of the child, misopedia, needs also to be brought into the limelight, not in spite of but because of its objectionable nature.

As Daniela Caselli has noted, "Beckett and the child are a rather disconcerting couple."[40] No doubt this is in part due to the hatred attached to, or aimed at, the figure of the child, but also due to the critical neglect that the child in Beckett has suffered. Caselli rightly wonders why, in "an oeuvre which has allegedly been dissected to the point of exhaustion," the child has "remained almost completely invisible"; a sense reinforced by Terence Brown's assertion that the "Beckett universe is a curiously childless one."[41] Stephen Thompson argues that it is "as if the child were not the work of the oeuvre at all, nor indeed of the critic, but rather something to be seized upon as a natural resource, something ready to hand."[42] Far from questioning the child, the assumption is either that the child does not exist (and many, myself included, would habitually consider *Godot* to be a play with four characters, not five, for example), or, if the existence is noted, it is not worth pausing over. One possible reason for this occluded vision is, according to Thompson, that "the figure of the child, just because it stands for simplicity, transparency, self-evidence, is often read as being itself transparent and self-evident."[43] The child would then seem not only to resist interpretation, but also to form its own interpretative tautology. The child is natural and innocent and therefore self-affirming, obvious. They are open to be read precisely as they are and do not offer anything further. Such self-evidencing is dependent on an assumption of innocence, as if the child were a morally and ethically clean state, offering no interesting angles of view; as if, unlike the children one encounters every day, the literary child is beyond, or has not reached the sophistication of, telling a lie. Such innocence underlies Brown's appreciation of the figure of the boy (or boys) in *Godot*, in which an "innocent simplicity" and a "childish acceptance of the world" ultimately "challenges tonally the interrogative energy of the play's dialogue."[44] One assumes that a fall from such innocence and simplicity might be needed in order for the child to constitute a "character" worthy of more comment. However, the adult characters of Beckett's fiction and drama would not seem to share this view, for whenever a child impinges upon their world, they are bound to comment, albeit, most commonly, in the form of a curt rebuttal, a "cutting retort,"[45] or, most plainly, a "fuck off" (*ECEFL* 39). In Beckett's work, the child is seen and reacted to, or, more precisely, reacted against.

A further reason for the critical neglect of the child in Beckett's work might also be seen in relation to the rise of misogyny as a critical theme. While misogyny indicates the possibility of considering the morally dubious in Beckett, it may have obscured the related theme of misopedia, due mainly to the prism of Cartesianism through which Beckett's dread of woman has been figured. The parceling of attributes along gendered, Cartesian lines does not allow for the problem of the child. If one accepts that Beckett's male characters are unerringly allied to the mind, and the female to the body, then sexual reproduction becomes either a failure in the male's commitment to the mind or a victory of the female's corporeality. Such oppositional distinctions would place the child firmly within the realm of the female in such a case and would not address the child as child, but as a by-product of the male/female, mind/body dichotomy. Also, a gendered Cartesianism chooses the sexual act itself as the site of conflict, with the male unwilling and the female rapacious or devious, and thus neglects the phenomenon of the child and its relation to reproductive sexuality. This neglect of the remains of the sexuality in favor of clear, Cartesian dualities, similarly neglects what might be a further stimulus for Beckett's misogyny, that is, his misopedia. Rather than the problem with sex being the sullying of the pure mind by the impure body, of the male intellect by female emotion, the problem could be that sex might mean children. Thus, a consideration of misopedia must entail a dual shift in emphasis: away from the sexual act itself to focus rather on its supposed goal of reproduction and away from Cartesian paradigms of the mind/body, male/female dichotomy.

*   *   *

John Calder has tried to defend Beckett from the charge of misopedia. In *The Philosophy of Samuel Beckett,* Calder admits that Beckett's "attitude towards children in general was always ambiguous" before seeking to distance Beckett from the hatred of children to be found in the works: "the anger that he might more logically have directed towards their parents is occasionally transferred, not seriously of course, to children themselves, because the kindest of men in life could be quite wicked in literature."[46] Calder initially attempts to mitigate the misopedia of the works with reference to Beckett's own essential goodness. When Beckett is nasty—and he can be certainly nasty when it comes to children—it is only "from the jaundiced lips of one of his fictional outcasts," as Calder puts it. It would be tempting to agree with Calder if misopedia were present in just one or two of the "jaundiced" characters of the works, but it is simply too widespread to be passed-off as local color of character. The murderous desire of Dan Rooney to "nip some young doom in the blood" in *All That Fall* (*CDW* 191) is merely one of the most forthright expressions of misopedia in the works. Terence Brown suggests that Rooney's misopedia is related to his Protestantism, which explains his "misanthropic fear of consanguinity, reproduction, fertility" as a threat to "self-hood's imagined integrity of being."[47] This may hold true for Rooney, yet the list of child-haters is a long one: Clov in *Endgame* is ready to deal swift death with a gaff to the boy outside the room; the messenger boy in *Waiting for Godot* is harassed, interrogated, and threatened; Mercier, in *Mercier and Camier,* tells his own children to "fuck off out of here" (23), and Mr. Madden in the same novel says of children that they are the "offscourings of fornication" (31); in *Molloy*, Moran habitually mistreats Jacques Jr., and Molloy himself declares that it would have been impossible ever to have helped his son; the protagonist of "First Love" prefers abortion to fatherhood and flees as soon as his child is born; Dr. Piouk in *Eleutheria* recommends drowning babies; Henry in *Embers* describes his child, Addie, as a "horrid little creature" (*CDW* 256); the protagonist of "The End" describes his own, now adult, son as "an insufferable son of a bitch" (*ECEFL* 45); and the protagonist of "The Expelled" (of whom more later) confesses that he loathes children. It may well be that all these characters share a jaundiced view of the world, but it is impossible to deny that Beckett repeatedly returns to misopedia and that hatred toward the child is part of his artistic palette.

Apparently in contradiction to the misopedia he admits is present in the works, John Calder also claims that whenever there is a child in the fiction, "the boy is nearly always the young Samuel Beckett himself, either as he remembered himself, or symbolically." This boy, Calder assures us, is "fresh-faced and eager for the life ahead."[48] This is an instance of the transparent, self-evident child that Thompson described. The adult Beckett can be glimpsed through the clear film of the child, who stands as a mere proxy, not a definable entity in its own right. The reader is then encouraged to pass through this uninteresting skein of the child in order to approach the much more interesting "character" of Beckett (although which "Beckett" is not specified). The figure of the child is, therefore, a guarantor of an uncomplicated, unmediated identity: Beckett *is* the young boy of the fictions. Moreover, Calder assumes that the figure of the child is innocent, "eager" for experience to etch on the *tabula rasa* of childhood. It is the supposed innocence of the child that makes the hatred aimed toward that figure unwarranted. Both of these assumptions are flawed when considering the child in Beckett, but it is the assumption that the child is innocent that makes misopedia seem so unjust and so, according to Calder, unworthy of Beckett's serious adhesion. The question is therefore begged: what makes children worthy of hatred?

An answer might be found by tracing a "lynch-pin" of misopedia in Beckett's works, which runs from the murderous misopedia of "The Expelled" back to *Watt* and on to the equally murderous *All That Fall*.

The narrator of the "The Expelled" is impeded in his route by a child in a baby-harness. It occasions the following diatribe:

> I would have crushed him gladly, I loathe children, and it would have been doing him a service, but I was afraid of reprisals. Everyone is a parent, that is what keeps you from hoping. One should reserve, on busy

streets, special tracks for these nasty little creatures, their prams, hoops, sweets, scooters, skates, grandpas, grandmas, nannies, balloons and balls, all their foul little happiness in a word. [...] They never lynch children, babies, no matter what they do they are whitewashed in advance. I personally would lynch them with the utmost pleasure, I don't say I'd lend a hand, no, I am not a violent man, but I'd encourage the others and stand them drinks when it was done. (*ECEFL* 8)

No doubt the narrator does have a jaundiced view of the world, but the terms of his loathing deserve some scrutiny. The narrator takes issue with the concept that children are born in or are in a state of innocence. Babies are "whitewashed in advance" by those who wish to see them as innocent and who wish to preserve such assumed innocence, and the narrator's desire to lynch them firmly suggests that he is not of the same opinion. What then could the child be guilty of? The answer, by way of Augustine and Schopenhauer, Leopardi, Calderón, and all the other ages' sages, is the sin of having been born.

Augustine is, of course, largely, but perhaps erroneously, credited with the rigorous conceptualization of original sin. In his debates with the Pelagians and, more specifically, in "On the Merits and Forgiveness of Sins, and on the Baptism of Infants," Augustine takes issues with the heretical view that children must have been born innocent, and, in so doing, formulates the logical necessity for original sin:

[...] as nothing else is effected when infants are baptized except that they are incorporated into the church, in other words, that they are united with the body and members of Christ, unless this benefit has been bestowed upon them, they are manifestly in danger of damnation. Damned, however, they could not be if they really had no sin. Now, since their tender age could not possibly have contracted sin in its own life, it remains for us, even if we are as yet unable to understand, at least to believe that infants inherit original sin.[49]

Given the premise that God is good, and therefore cannot be unjust, the necessity for baptism to prevent damnation must surely mean that sin exists that needs to be expunged through the grace of God, and that it can only be expunged precisely through the action of that grace. Augustine frequently reiterates the burden that the first sin placed on all mankind, as here expressed in Book 13 of *The City of God*:

...the whole human race was in the first man, and it was to pass from him through the woman into his progeny, when the married pair had received the divine sentence of condemnation. And it was not man as first made, but what man became after his sin and punishment, that was thus begotten, as far as concerned the origin of sin and death.[50]

As death and suffering are passed down through the generations, so death and suffering are themselves generated by the generation of offspring, and so "death is perpetuated by propagation from the first man, and is without doubt the penalty of all who are born..."[51] What is a crucial theme in Beckett's misopedia, and misogyny for that matter, is precisely the child's role as guarantor of future suffering and, ultimately, death, as if the child, however unwittingly, is both the sign and principle of regrettable generation.

Far removed from Augustine in purpose and intent, but in agreement with him when it comes to the fundamental, original problem of humanity, lies Schopenhauer. In both *The World as Will and Representation* and the later compiled *Essays and Aphorisms,* Schopenhauer returns to the same point: "That our existence itself implies guilt is proved by the fact of death."[52] Death is not here, as with Augustine, the punishment for and consequence of sin, but the necessary corollary of life in the first place; a logical conclusion once one has removed God as an agent of punishment and yet one still faces the twin evils of suffering and death. With "the production of a new body," he writes, "suffering and death, as belonging to the phenomenon of life, are also affirmed anew."[53] Suffering and death are therefore continued by new forms of life. Beckett adopted Schopenhauer on this point in his *Proust* essay when he paraphrased Schopenhauer stating that the "true sense of the tragedy is the deeper insight that what the hero atones for is not his particular sins, but original sin, in other words, the guilt of existence itself."[54] The child is then far from being innocent. Rather he or she is the guarantor of the continuing curse of consciousness and pain "disturbing the blessed calm of nothingness."[55] In a valuable meditation on the child as a theatrical presence within *Waiting for Godot,* Stephen Thompson, taking issue with Colin Duckworth, writes that "[t]he child is thus read as an emissary from, and so guarantee of, another scene." Thompson goes on to argue: "This, it seems to me, is what makes the Boy a problem: his physical presence on the scene."[56] The child's very presence does indeed act as an emissary of something removed from this present stage: it is an emissary of the future. The futurity of the child is precisely what has been attacked more recently by Lee Edelman, who writes that "the Child has come to embody for us the telos of the social order."[57] Denial of the child would then be a political denial by those marginalized by a ubiquitous pro-procreative order, for if "there is *no baby* and, in consequence, *no future,* then the blame must fall on the fatal lure of sterile, narcissistic enjoyments understood as inherently destructive of meaning and therefore as responsible for the undoing of social organization, collective reality, and, inevitably, life itself."[58] From Augustine to Schopenhauer to Edelman, the child is seen to be the guarantor of futurity. The nature of the continuance into the future might alter from the perpetuation of sin and death to a maintaining of a repressive social order, yet, in all these cases, the child can be viewed as far from welcome precisely because it heralds an entirely regrettable future. As Edelman suggests, and as Dr. Piouk concurs, the remedy might be to bring "life itself" to an end.

Schopenhauer is rather more resigned to the fact of children than the protagonist of "The Expelled." He writes that noticing that all life is essentially suffering and that there is little choice but to live is "in fact calculated to instil in us indulgence towards one another: for what can be expected of beings placed in such a situation as we are?"[59] The narrator of the story seems singularly lacking in such indulgence toward the figure of the child, but there is a murderously logical form of pity at work here that again finds a correlative in Schopenhauer. The narrator claims that falling upon and killing the child would in effect be an act of mercy; it would be "doing him a service" to cut his life of inevitable suffering short. This is not indulgence but intervention. However, Schopenhauer advocates something rather similar, albeit at the prefetal stage:

> If the act of procreation were neither the outcome of a desire nor accompanied by feelings of pleasure, but a matter to be decided on the basis of purely rational considerations, is it likely the human race would still exist? Would each of us not rather have felt so much pity for the coming generation as to prefer to spare it the burden of existence, or at least not wish to take upon himself to impose that burden upon it in cold blood?[60]

Rather than dispensing with the child once it has been born, we are enjoined not to let them into the world in the first place. If one accepts that existence is not to be borne and so one should not be born into it, the strict logic of Dr. Piouk in *Eleutheria* comes into play. As the solution to the problem of humanity, he advocates the following: "I would establish teams of abortionists, controlled by the State. I would apply the death penalty to any woman guilty of giving birth. I would drown all newborn babies" (*E* 44). Dr. Piouk's extreme position neatly brings together the dual themes of misopedia and misogyny. Women are to be condemned and killed only because they bring forth children, not, according to him, on account of their own natures or actions. Importantly, Piouk's strictures do not exclude all expressions of sexuality (homosexuality is to be encouraged and condoms distributed), and only focus on reproduction. His continuing interest in sex per se is evidenced by his pursuit of Victor Krap's fiancée, Mlle Skunk. Despite his pursuing personal sexual satisfaction, Dr. Piouk nevertheless proposes mass infanticide as a solution to the "problem of humanity," and this "cold-blooded" solution needs to be weighed against the "cold-blooded" decision to have children, as Schopenhauer put it.

To return to the "lynch-pin" of misopedia running through works, Beckett chose to stress that children needed "lynching" rather than hanging, or a more generic killing, in "The Expelled." The word refers us back to where Beckett offers the consequences of not lynching children in the grotesquely extended Lynch family of *Watt*. The 28 souls of the family from the 85-year-old patriarch to the four-year-old twins, Pat and Larry, are a catalogue of suffering. Determined to reach their collective 1,000 years, they breed regardless of the inevitable consequences: pain and death. The Lynches well know that the hemophiliac line of the family, for example, will only perpetuate the condition, and yet they do not stop:

> [I]t was very wrong of Sean, knowing what he was and knowing what Kate was, to do what he did to Kate, so that she conceived and brought forth Rose, and indeed it was very wrong of her to let him, and indeed it was very wrong of Sean again, knowing what he was and what Kate was and now what Rose was, to do again what he did again to Kate, so that Kate conceived again and brought forth Cerise, and indeed it was very wrong of her again to let him again... (*W* 100–101)

The rigid repetition not only reinforces the banality of this ongoing carnality but also suggests the mechanistic quality of such unthinking procreation, or, as Schopenhauer puts it "the will's objectification as a mere μηχανή, a means for preserving the individual and the species, just like any organ of the body."[61] Slaves to the will-to-live, the Lynches produce slaves of the will-to-live, imprisoned within inevitable suffering and, unfortunately for the Lynches' dreams, inevitable death as a phenomenon of life.

It is just after being pelted by the Lynch twins that the most famous of Beckett's misopediasts, Dan Rooney, fantasizes about killing a child. He may have already done so and pushed a child from the train on which he was travelling. His initial outburst against children is reminiscent of certain aspects to be found in "The Expelled": "And the brats, the happy little healthy little howling neighbours brats [...] what must it be like on a working-day? A Wednesday? A Friday? What must it be like on a Friday!" (*CDW* 193). Rather like the narrator of the story, Dan's exasperated anger runs away with him and forms almost a panic-stricken indictment of the lively, happy presence of children. One recalls that the narrator of "The Expelled" is forced from the pavement by the little creature for whom there is not enough room, and this crowding is made all the worse by the accoutrements of childhood. The words of the Unnamable are apposite here, when he says that "[w]here there are people, it is said, there are things" (*U* 2), for the child brings in its wake a list of yet further things in a world already crowded with them. It is just such a sense of the encroaching presence of the child that informs Dan's first diatribe against them. Sean Kennedy has suggested that this sense of encroachment may also bear witness to the precarious position of the Irish Protestants represented in the play and that the Catholic Lynch twins "embody the perceived threat of absorption that the seemingly inexorable rise of the Catholic community posed to the Protestant community in the early years of the Free State."[62]

Dan Rooney's wish to kill a child, while in-line with the desire expressed in "The Expelled," does however have a rather different tone:

> Did you ever wish to kill a child? [...] Nip some young doom in the bud. [...] Many a time at night, in winter on the black road home, I nearly attacked the boy. [...] Poor Jerry! [...] What restrained me then? [...] Not fear of man. (*CDW* 191)

The question he asks of himself, "what restrained me then?" can no longer be answered in the terms of "The Expelled," where restraint was only a social constraint, for Dan no longer fears man. It would be tempting to posit a recognition of a divine displeasure at murdering children. Alternatively, in keeping with the Schopenhauerean framework I have laid down, a note of regretful indulgence has entered into the misopedia, an ability, perhaps, "to view the so-called imperfections of the majority of men [...] without surprise and without indignation."[63] Nevertheless, the misopedia of Dan Rooney is still informed by the wish to bring the continuation of suffering to an end. In the phrase to "nip some young doom in the bud," the replacement of "bloom" by "doom" strongly suggests that it is in blooming that one is doomed, that life itself is the disaster that one should wish to avoid. Nipping doom in the bud would, then, be to short-circuit the mechanical progress of life into death, to cheat death of its necessary precursor, life.

Thus far, the focus has been on the desire within misopedia to bring suffering and death to an end through the death of the child. This would, of course, be consonant with many of Beckett's characters' wishes to have done with it all. Nevertheless, continuance of the individual, the "I can't go, I'll go on" paradox, also has a role within Beckett's misopedia. Even that most virulent of misopediasts, Dr. Piouk, still retains the desire to secure a longevity by proxy in the form of the child, someone that can "receive the torch from my hands, when they are no longer strong enough to carry it" (*E* 45). Similarly, Hamm, who is so concerned that humanity might spring from a crab-louse, shows a curious equanimity when Clov announces the presence of the boy outside the shelter. Rather than wishing to kill the child, he envisages the boy as a replacement of Clov, and, through the figure of adoption through which Clov himself was brought into service, as a means of going on. However, continuance through one's offspring comes with its own inherent dangers, symbolically captured in an instance of apparently gratuitous misopedia in "The End":

> There was a strange light which follows a day of persistent rain, when the sun comes out and the sky clears too late to be of any use. The earth makes a sound as of sighs and the last drops fall from the emptied cloudless sky. A small boy, stretching out his hands and looking up at the blue sky, asked his mother how such a thing was possible. Fuck off, she said. (*ECEFL* 39)

This rebuke, tempered in different versions of this scene in *Malone Dies* and *Company,* is consistent with Mercier's reaction to the appearance of his own offspring, yet it is in *Malone Dies* that a disturbing mythological context to such expressions of misopedia can be discerned. Having recently hit upon the idea that what is needed is to be born, Malone ends the passage in cannibalistic mode:

> Yes, a little creature, I shall try and make a little creature, to hold in my arms, a little creature in my image, no matter what I say. And seeing what a poor thing I have made, or how like myself, I shall eat it. Then be alone for a long time, unhappy, not knowing what my prayer should be nor to whom. (*MD* 53)

A number of facets of the story of Cronus can be seen to be at play within this anthropophagite desire. First, Cronus was responsible for the usurpation and castration of his father, Uranus (sky) at the urgings of his mother, Earth. The blood (and in some accounts semen) from the wound dropped to Earth and impregnated her. As ruler, Cronus feared that he would be usurped by his own children, and so ate them annually, until Rhea hid their son Zeus and duped Cronus with a stone wrapped in swaddling. Cronus was indeed deposed by Zeus and through the auspices of an emetic, the children consumed were vomited back out into the world. The brief description from *Malone Dies* bears strong resemblances to this story. Malone figures himself in god-like role, making things in his own image, only then to consume them. For Malone there seems to be two contradictory desires. First, he wishes to perpetuate himself, to create a means of continuance via the "little creature" (an echo of "The Expelled" and of *Embers*). Second, he wishes to obliterate the child precisely because it is "like myself." Such a contradiction is embodied in the Cronus myth, where Cronus fears that he will suffer the same fate as Uranus because his own children will bear too strong a resemblance to their father. The childhood section previously quoted from "The End" benefits from this context in that it symbolically revisits Cronus's castration of Uranus as the sky-god. By suppressing the word "rain," the "last drops" that fall from the sky are open to be interpreted as Uranus's semen and blood which then impregnate a sexualized sighing earth. The boy's outstretched arms, not, I take it, toward the mother but toward Uranus, may be a figuration of Cronus's reaching to and castration of his father. The child is then to be feared and negated through the violence of the "fuck off" retort.

Although Mary A. Doll, in *Beckett and Myth*, has identified Cronus as a vital archetype within Beckett, oddly she has not identified Malone's eating of his own children with Cronus, and has instead chosen to interpret the consumed offspring as a positive that needs to be vomited forth: "The old man, for example, Beckett's favourite character type, is egoism rigidified by excessive rationalism. This type is characterized by the myth of Cronus, which we Westerners must confront if we are ever to go beyond a repressive need to swallow imagination, as Cronus did metaphorically when he swallowed his children."[64] Certainly, birth and aesthetic creation are important within Beckett, although it is arguably more a case of aesthetic creation replacing sexual reproduction than Doll's account would allow. What the Cronus myth, in conjunction with misopedia, reveals is a desire to both go on—by proxy through the form of the child—and yet to be the end by eating one's own children, as if time consumed continuance.

This same complex of desire for, and fear of, continuance through offspring is played out in the only fully depicted father and son relation in Beckett's oeuvre; Moran's relations with Jacques Jr. in *Molloy*. Of course, the act of naming his son after himself already signs a desire for continuance, yet Moran assures the reader that the identical name "cannot lead to confusion" (*M* 95) for he is quick to assert the differences between himself and his inheritor and possible usurper:

> If I had been my son I would have left me long ago. He was not worthy of me, not in the same class at all. I could not escape this conclusion. Cold

comfort that is, to feel superior to one's son, and hardly sufficient to calm the remorse of having begotten him. (*M* 108)

Despite such self-reassurance that his son cannot resemble him, the possibility that Moran Senior and Junior are alike, and so the latter might replace the former, continues to worry Moran. He is enraged by Dr. Py's claim that Jacques Jr. "has naturally very bad teeth." The wounding word is "naturally," for Jacques Jr. has inherited his poor dental health from his father, who is now "down to [his] incisors, the nippers" (107). In an apparent contradiction, Moran's pedagogy is largely devoted to making Jacques precisely like his father. For example, he is keen that Jacques should inherit his walk: "I wanted him to walk like his father, with little rapid steps, his head up, his breathing even and economical, his arms swinging, looking neither to left nor right, apparently oblivious to everything and in reality missing nothing" (134).

The vexed question of how Moran and his son are to set out to simply walk together demonstrates the contradictions inherent within their relations. Moran is adamant that Jacques walks behind him, leaving Moran in his rightful place "in the van," as he later puts, but Moran cannot trust that his son will be capable of following him and that Moran "waking from [his] reverie, would turn and find him gone" (134). The reverse is considered, with Moran following Jacques, the better for Moran to monitor and correct his errant son: "I could keep my eye on him and intervene, at the least false movement he might make" (135). But the sight of his son *before* him is too much for Moran to bear. Between these two options, lies a third: a pseudo-umbilical linkage: "I toyed briefly with the idea of attaching him to me by means of a long rope, its two ends tied about our waists." This cord, which is later imagined as a chain, binds the two Jacques together but is also a symbol of fettered separation; they may be physically linked, but the rope is a long one, which is expressive of the desire both to escape the son and keep a watchful eye over him. Despite Moran's hope for the rope, it should be pointed out that it would not solve the problem of who is to go "in the van." Importantly, the rope as umbilical solution (which is no solution at all) is also figured by Beckett as shadowed by the death of Moran:

> . . . he might have undone his knots in silence and escaped, leaving me to go on my way alone, followed by a long rope trailing in the dust, like a burgess of Calais. Until such time as the rope, catching on some fixed or heavy object, should stop me dead in my stride. (134)

As depicted in Rodin's statue "The Burghers of Calais" (and as pointed out by Ackerley and Gontarski in *The Grove Companion to Samuel Beckett*[65]), the reference is to an incident in the Hundred Years' War in which the elders of Calais surrendered themselves to the English in return for the lifting of the siege of the town. Almost naked and with nooses around their necks, these elders would almost certainly have been executed had it not been for the intervention of Edward III's wife, Philippa of Hainault. The image is one of the patriarchs sacrificing themselves for the good of the community they have led, and this image is apposite by itself but becomes more so for Beckett's nuanced rendering. Here, Moran doesn't imagine sacrificing himself for the good of his son, but the son forcing him to become a sacrifice by deceitfully abandoning him, the better to go on living elsewhere, one assumes.

Given such considerations, it is to be expected that Moran's greatest fear, as he steps out with his son on his mission, is that the habitual violence that Moran visits on Jacques will be turned upon himself. Although Moran does not dwell on this violence, it is clear that it is severe. In addition to the "little clouts" that he feels free to administer, Moran also sets upon his son wielding the "heavy massive-handled winter umbrella" (129) he has chosen for the journey, even "holding it by the end with both hands"—thus bringing the massive handle to bear—the better to beat his child (131). When Moran confiscates Jacques's Scout knife, he suspects that "[h]e would doubtless at that moment have cut my throat, with that selfsame knife I was putting so placidly in my pocket. But he was still a little on the young side, my son, a little on the soft side, for the great deeds of vengeance. But time was on his side..." (136).

In terms of the Cronus myth, the symbolic castration of Jacques Jr. as Moran pockets his knife might be seen to forestall the castration and usurpation of the father. Moran may have defeated Jacques in this instance, but it is feared that the day will come when his son, who is almost the same size as Moran, will finally take his place.

The child, as figured in the mythology of Malone's dream of cannibal infanticide and Moran's relations with his son, is seen as a cursed blessing of possible continuance. The father needs and yet fears the avatar who will usurp him. The misopedia of the works is, therefore, not only directed at the child's guarantee of future life and therefore future suffering, but also, in contradiction to and inherent within that misopedia, is the need to keep going through the child-as-proxy, as the father fears to be replaced by the child in whom he will go on. Malone eating his own offspring might then be seen as part of Beckett's ongoing search for a means of continuation removed from sexual reproduction, of the will to go on while not submitting to the will-to-live.

Impotent Sex

Reproduction—that doubly damned process in Beckett's work—may be wholly regrettable as the expression and continuance of the will-to-live, yet this does not necessarily entail turning aside from intercourse altogether. Once the possibility of making new life has been removed from the sexual liaison, many of Beckett's characters persevere with heterosexual penetrative sex. Logically, one might suspect that once issue is not at issue, then sex should at least offer some pleasure, if little else. In *Malone Dies,* Macmann's affair with his keeper, Moll, is predicated on the impotence of both parties. Both are long past their primes ("Oh would we had but met sixty years ago!" (89)), and their bodies are in quite an advanced state of decay, and yet they pursue what little sexual pleasure remains with a form of grim determination.

> The first phase, that of the bed, was characterized by the evolution of the relationship between Macmann and his keeper. There sprang up gradually between them a kind of intimacy which, at a given moment, led them to lie together and copulate as best they could. For given their age and scant experience of carnal love, it was only natural they should not succeed, at the first shot, in giving each other the impression they were made for each other. The spectacle was then offered of Macmann trying to bundle his sex into his partner's like a pillow into a pillow-slip, folding it in two and stuffing it in with his fingers. But far from losing heart they warmed to their work. And though both were completely impotent they finally succeeded, summoning to their aid all the resources of the skin, the mucus and the imagination, in striking from their feeble clips a kind of sombre gratification. (89)

This passage has been quoted at length for two reasons: the emphasis on the impotence of Macmann and Moll, and the disjunction between the pleasure of the lovers and the disgust of the reader (albeit, a disgust tinged, I would argue, with amusement). Given their advanced years, it is not surprising that Macmann and Moll are indeed impotent. We are now a world away from the business of sex as conducted by Murphy and Celia, or Belacqua and his fair and middling women. Thus the dangers inherent within youthful coitus—among them, of course, pregnancy—are now long behind the elderly Macmann and Moll who can therefore indulge in sex for pleasure alone. Once the hazards of sex are put aside, Beckett can use Macmann and Moll as a set-piece study in the grotesquery of heterosexual relations. In the Macmann and Moll affair, carnal love is shorn of the romantic associations of youth and physical beauty and the business and the emotional results of sex can be examined and parodied. As a love object, Moll is characterized as being far from promising as she is "immoderately ill-favoured of both face and body" (86). While this repeated focus on her ugliness, and especially her thick lips, may betray a certain misogyny, it should be remembered that Macmann is also described as being a derelict who even Moll doubts was ever a good-looking man: "even when you were of an age to quicken the pulse of beauty, did you exhibit the other requisites? I doubt it." (91) Age has leveled the beautiful and the ugly so that now they have become "scarcely less hideous than even [their] best favoured contemporaries." What remains are two failing bodies and a certain innocence in their sexual relations as both have had "scant experience of carnal love." Despite this sexual naiveté, their sexual experiments are not confined to vaginally penetrative sex. In an example of one of her letters to Macmann, Moll wishes to persevere with "tetty-beshy," despite "all these bones that mak[e] it awkward" (91). "Tetty-beshy" is a corruption of a term from philately, *tête-bêche*, which are two stamps joined together and upside-down in relation to each other, or "head to tail," and therefore the term is a euphemism for mutual simultaneous oral sex: a 69, in contemporary terms. Even for figures so aged and so inexperienced, the varieties of sexual expression are broad, and it is noticeable that nonreproductive forms of sexual expression are highlighted as Moll offers Macmann "oyster kisses just where you want" and so earns the sobriquet "Sucky Moll."

These particulars of geriatric sex no doubt leave the reader uncomfortable. This points to a general prejudice that equates sex with youth and hence with procreation. Geriatric sex is pointless, in that reproduction is not a possibility, and so the *telos* of sex is removed and sex is denied a significance beyond its own actions. The result is a focus on those actions in terms of the body, but also in terms of the emotional actions that stem from, and may be seen to justify, sexual activity. So, in their geriatric affair, Macmann and Moll indulge in the clichés of youthful romance: Moll presents Macmann with letters "tied together by a favour" (90) containing the *carpe diem* advice that "at last it is the season of love, let us make the most of it, there are pears that only ripen in December"; Macmann is her "Sweetheart!" and their "hearts labour as one" (91). On his part, Macmann, "towards the close of this idyll," is moved to love poetry and is allowed to enjoy the cliché of "two is company" (89). In this elderly affair, the gestures of romantic love are made to appear ridiculous as they bear little relation to the details of two bodies working upon each other. The same disjunction between the reality of the physical and the language of love placed upon it can be seen in two of Watt's affairs. The first, with Mrs. Watson, is couched in the language of respectable wooing. The love interest is "an old lady of delicate upbringing, and advantageous person [...] whom he had pursued with his assiduities on no fewer than three occasions" (60). The physical disjunction is that the lady in question "was amputated above the knee" who, when she finally gives in to Watt's advances, "unstrapped her wooden leg and laid aside her crutch" as if in a pastiche of a striptease. The second affair, with the fishwoman, Mrs. Gorman, is characterized as impotent from the outset: "That a trifling and in all probability tractable obstruction of some endocrinal Bandusia, that a mere matter of forty-five minutes by the clock, should effectively as death itself, or as the Hellespont, separate lovers" (*W* 121–22). As with Macmann and Moll, there is a degree of communion between the two lovers as they exchange places in each other's lap. However, the relationship is, by necessity, unconsummated and so the discourse applied to it is that of a chaste, yet unique love that urges them to demur: "Why was this? Was it the echo murmuring in their hearts [...] of past passion, of ancient error, warning them not to sully, not to trail, in the cloaca of clonic gratification, a flower so fair, so rare, so sweet so frail?" (121). The clichéd language of almost courtly love is deployed, but what attracted the two to each other? The answer to which Watt inclined finally was that "were they not perhaps drawn, Mrs. Gorman to Watt, Watt to Mrs. Gorman, she by the bottle of stout, he by the smell of fish?"(122) The clichéd language and rituals of love are thoroughly undermined by the reality of the two bodies, their needs and preferences.

Beckett's use of the clichés of love in this depiction of Macmann's and Watt's affairs not only undermines that romanticism but also allies the sexual acts with death through the dead-yet-living language of the cliché. "A cliché," writes Christopher Ricks, "is a dead piece of language, of which one cliché might be that it is dead but won't lie down."[66] Elizabeth Barry has gone on to argue that the "death instinct proves itself to be very much alive in Beckett's work, restoring a kind of deathly energy to a moribund language."[67] To use the clichés of romantic love in the description of geriatric sex is, then, to embed within the language itself an uncomfortable, but apt, amalgam of death and life. Macmann's and Moll's affair—which is continued virtually up to the point of her death—is imbued with a language that is redundant ("Sweetheart!" "hearts labour as one"[91]) yet new within the context of their experiences. The moribund language of love speaks through these geriatrics who are themselves becoming moribund. Indeed, Macmann's sexual desire for Moll is not abated by her rapid demise, as he still desires to "take her, all stinking, yellow, bald and vomiting, in his arms" (94). The entire liaison is conducted within the shadow of death, as Macmann's love poetry demonstrates:

Hairy Mac and Sucky Molly
In the ending days and nights

Of unending melancholy
Love it is at last unites.

And:

To the lifelong promised land
Of the nearest cemetery
With his Sucky hand in hand
Love it is at last leads Hairy. (92)

As death is the "promised land" so a deathliness stalks the language of Macmann's poetry through its repetition, in particular the play between "ending" life and an "unending" unhappiness, and in the phrase "love it is at last," which is used at the close of each poem. Love, then, is viewed in combination with ending, although it is left open to doubt whether this last love will last beyond the last. This is neatly expressed as the "exaltation of love regarded as a kind of lethal glue" (92): the unification of two people is shadowed by and, one could argue, predicated on mortality. Vivien Mercier has argued of Macmann and Moll's affair that "it is calculated to under-mine the reverence for life and awe before the reproductive processes of all but the most wholesome personalities."[68] By removing reproduction as a possibility for Macmann and Moll, the focus is then on the absurdity of the physical acts themselves, as if once the end of sex has been taken away the business of sex therefore lacks its proper significance. Mercier has rightly argued that sex "implies death, for if there was no death there would be no need for reproduction,"[69] but in Beckett's text reproduction has already been excised thus leaving death alone as the end-point of sex. If, in *Godot*, Beckett can collapse birth and death as to "give birth astride of a grave" (*CDW* 83), so in the Macmann relations, sex and death are similarly col-lapsed into each other: "we have sex beside the grave," one might suggest. This might account for Macmann's fetish for Moll's tooth carved into a crucifix "to represent the famous sacrifice" of Christ. The tooth is already dead and rotting yet it acts as an enlivening element in their intercourse and "in the pleasure he was later to enjoy, when he put his tongue in her mouth and let it wander over her gums, this rotten crucifix had assuredly its part" (93). The crucifixion—a death that will ensure life—is literally embodied as an already dead tooth that is a fetish object in a nonreproduc-tive sexual relationship. The fact that the tooth falls out as Moll further deteriorates toward death suggests the hope expressed in the crucifixion is entirely illusory: there will be death and no resurrection. This point is further underlined by the association of birth and death as Moll begins her final illness in which "she was subject to fits of vomiting" (94). We are told: "Half a century younger she might have been taken for pregnant." The sex between Macmann and Moll will not result in further life, and the vomiting only presages death.

Macmann and Moll, Watt and Mrs. Gorman, in their particulars and the pattern of their relations may seem merely an exercise in the grotesque, yet Beckett's impotent lovers follow closely Schopenhauer's description of the delusions and realities of love as set out in the second volume of *The World as Will and Representation*. Schopenhauer argues that individual sex is actually geared toward the end-point of the procreation of the species in the service of the will-to-live. All individual considerations—such as why one is attracted to a particular partner, who, for the lover, seems to be without parallel—are in fact merely a form of disguise for the purposes of the will-to-live, which wants to ensure the survival of the "type" proper to the species. The seriousness with which the lover takes his or her "unique" love is justified as, unbeknownst to the lovers, what "is decided by it is nothing less than the *composition of the next generation*" and so the "high importance of the matter is not a question of the *individual* weal and woe, as in all other matters, but of the existence and special constitution of the human race in times to come..."[70] In order for the will-to-live to continue in the proper type of human species, individuals are sexually attracted to those who can counteract or complement the defects or qualities of the procreative partner:

> Accordingly, the neutralization [...] of the two individualities by each other requires that the particular degree of *his* manliness shall correspond to the particular degree of *her* womanliness, so that one-sidedness of each exactly cancels that of the other. Accordingly, the most manly man will look for the most womanly woman and *vice versa*; and in just the same way will every individual look for the one corresponding to him or her in degree of sexuality.[71]

So, Schopenhauer tells us, "women often love ugly men, but never an unmanly man, because they cannot neutralize his defects." In the passage that introduces the Watt and Mrs. Gorman affair, the question of the degree of manliness and womanliness that either possess is rigorously, and ridiculously, detailed until we are told that Watt was "neither a man's man nor a woman's man" and that Mrs. Gorman was "neither a woman's man nor a woman's woman" (*W* 120). It is then admitted that neither manliness nor womanliness was really at issue, as Watt was attracted by the smell of fish and Mrs. Gorman by the bottle of stout. Also, the idea of complementing

each other the better to serve the will-to-live is parodied by the permutations of sitting on each others lap. Certainly, the fact that when one tires
the other takes over would seem to suggest a degree of togetherness, yet the
business of "introverting" (*W* 121) leaves them only enough time to achieve
one complete double-kiss, so their complementary nature actually prevents
consummation rather than encourages it.

Schopenhauer also details the attributes that attract men to women and
women to men who believe they are acting on their own sexual impulse but
who are, nevertheless, acting under the larger demands of the will-to-live.
The first among the criteria is age:

> [A]n old woman, that is to say a woman who no longer menstruates,
> excites our aversion. Youth without beauty always has attraction; beauty
> without youth has none. Here the purpose that unconsciously guides us
> is clearly the possibility of procreation in general. Therefore every indi-
> vidual loses attraction for the opposite sex to the extent that he or she is
> removed from the fittest period for procreation or conception.[72]

The primacy of age and therefore health in Schopenhauer's thinking sharply
contrasts with the detailed and very physical nature of Beckett's geriatric sex.
Point for point, it can be argued that Beckett very much has Schopenhauer
in mind in this connection. For example, a "deformed figure" is an unat-
tractive proposition with a view to procreation, and all figures involved in
Beckett's impotent sex are in many ways less than perfectly formed. Further,
a "full female bosom exerts an exceptional charm on the male, being directly
connected with the woman's functions of propagation..."[73] and yet we note
that Mrs. Gorman has had her left breast removed "in the heat of a surgical operation" (120) and one also recalls the flat chests of Ruth/Edith and
Lousse in *Molloy*. Schopenhauer also claims that a "mouth small because
of small maxillae is very essential as a specific characteristic of the human
countenance,"[74] and, of course, Moll's mouth is repeatedly described as
large and too full-lipped. Finally, Moll's remaining, rotting tooth would
have not passed muster for Schopenhauer, for the "teeth are also important
to us, because they are essential to nourishment, and are above all heredi-
tary."[75] On each count, Beckett's lovers are the least likely candidates to
prove useful as procreators and therefore to continue the will-to-live. By
refusing health, beauty, and potency to his characters, Beckett mitigates
against the continuation of, as Schopenhauer puts it, the "true type [that]
is always re-established. This takes place under the guidance of that sense
of beauty which generally directs the sexual impulse, and without which
this impulse sinks to the level of a disgusting need."[76] Beckett refuses to

allow his characters to be co-opted into serving both the will-to-live and the future, which, as we have seen, is shadowed by what might be called the "tyranny of the child." For Schopenhauer (who is not dissimilar to Edelman in this respect), the child who is not yet born "is already kindled in the meeting of [the lovers'] longing glances, and it announces itself as *future* individuality…"[77] However, once this *telos* has been removed, we are left with that mix of grotesque comedy and the clichés of love that, according to Schopenhauer, "give to his very physical desires such a hyperphysical clothing that love becomes a poetical episode even in the life of the most prosaic person; in this latter case, the matter sometimes assumes a comic aspect." Macmann and Watt are, it would seem, prosaic men.

The impotent sex in which Beckett's geriatrics indulge necessarily severs the connection between sex and the regrettable possibility of future children. In similar vein, Malone is happy to relate that Macmann is childless and that the cycle of birth and death will be broken:

> …he was no more than human, than the son and grandson and great-grandson of humans. But between him and those grave sober men, first bearded, then moustached, there was this difference, that his semen had never done any harm to anyone. So his link with his species was through his ascendants only, who were all dead, in the fond hope that they had perpetuated themselves. (68)

In accordance with Schopenhauer's thinking, Macmann's semen is ethically issueless. As far as Schopenhauer is concerned, procreation means the continuance of life endlessly, for "…the satisfaction of the sexual impulse goes beyond the affirmation of one's own existence that fills so short a time; it affirms life for an indefinite time beyond the death of the individual."[78] If life persists, then the necessary concomitants of life, suffering and death, persist endlessly too. Better, then, to put a halt to the wheel of procreation. One way of achieving this, in addition to aged impotence, might be Molloy's wish for castration:

> I would have been happier, livelier, amputated at the groin. And if they had removed a few testicles into the bargain I wouldn't have objected. For from such testicles as mine, dangling at mid-thigh at the end of a meagre cord, there was nothing more to be squeezed, not a drop. So that non che la speme il desiderio, and I longed to see them gone… (33)

The quotation from Leopardi's *A Se Stesso* is apt not just for its death of desire, but, within the context of Beckett's work, it once again returns us to the Schopenhauer inspired *Proust* where the same lines from Leopardi were quoted. Of course, Schopenhauer never fails to emphasize that the genitals are the root of all lively evil:

> Far more than any other external member of the body, the genitals are subject merely to the will, and not at all to knowledge. [...] the genitals are the real *focus* of the will, and are therefore the opposite pole to the brain, the representative of knowledge [...] The genitals are the life-preserving principle assuring to time endless life.[79]

If the desire is to see the ablation of desire and the overcoming of the will, then the genitals are a proper focus for rancor and a castration fantasy becomes more of a rational mode of negating the will-to-live. That the will is objectified in the unruly genitals is reason enough for one to wish to see them "long gone," but the crime is compounded by the fact that the action of the genitals sees life perpetuated in time, and therefore suffering and death similarly perpetuated. In the Lynch family of *Watt* this is most clearly demonstrated by Sam, who is the most sexually driven among them. He amply demonstrates Schopenhauer's point that the will-to-live is focussed on the genitals, for Sam's genitals are about all that functions as he is "paralysed by a merciful providence from no higher than the knees down and from no lower than the waist up..." (*W* 98–99). This disabling nevertheless enables him to sire 20 children in wedlock (four of whom survived) and possible countless others due to his "having committed adultery locally on a large scale" (104). The more Lynches are born, however, the more they inevitably feed death, and their millennial hopes, so nearly gained, recede further and further away. Moreover, the catalogue of illness, disease, and disability with which the Lynch family are inflicted clearly shows the curse that the siring of each child entails as suffering is passed from generation to generation, culminating in the rickety legs and balloon bellies and heads of little Pat and little Larry. If sexual reproduction is left to run wild, the result is scions of suffering. While there is a satiric edge to Beckett's Lynch family, traceable to the discourses of procreation which surrounded the creation of the Free State and the fear of losing out in the reproduction stakes to the Protestant minority, as Sean Kennedy has set out in relation to *First Love*,[80] the satirizing of rampant reproduction can also clearly be felt within a discourse of the undesirability of the continuance of suffering through the continuance of the human, for, as Schopenhauer approvingly quotes Clement of Alexandria: "Those who have castrated themselves from all sin for the sake of the kingdom of heaven, are blessed; *they abstain from the world*."[81]

This ethical renunciation of reproductive sexuality in favor of impotent forms is clearly seen in the sexual affairs of Molloy. He does recall one sexual encounter with a woman named Ruth or Edith, but there is considerable doubt as to whether actual vaginal intercourse occurred at all. First, Molloy is unsure whether Ruth/Edith was not, in reality, a man, as she "was an eminently flat woman [...] Perhaps she too was a man, yet another of them. But in that case surely our testicles would have collided, while we writhed. Perhaps she held hers tight in her hand, on purpose to avoid it" (56). Second, the method of their congress, with Ruth/Edith bent over the couch because of her rheumatism, combined with the doubt over gender, leads Molloy to question which orifice he actually penetrated, as he wonders: "is it true love, in the rectum?" (56). The incident is also presaged by a Schopenhauerean moment of turning away from the will. Edith accosted Molloy while he was rummaging in a rubbish dump in the hope, he says, of "finding something to disgust me for ever with eating" (57). This desire never again to eat might not need a Schopenhauerean gloss, but the philosopher made an explicit relation between eating and sexual reproduction: "The process of nourishment is a constant generation; the process of generation is a higher power of nourishment. The pleasure that accompanies procreation is a higher power of the agreeableness of life."[82] In a rather fanciful manner, perhaps, eating is seen as the same expression of the will as is found in sexual generation, albeit in diluted form. To turn away from nourishment is then to turn away from the higher power of that manifestation of the will in the form of sexual reproduction. (It should be noted that in the matter of nourishment and excrement, Schopenhauer stands in direct contradiction to Freud. In the former, excrement, as a constant throwing away of matter, is the same as death, albeit at a lower power. For Freud, via the theory of anal birth, excrement is associated with birth.) Molloy's hope to stop nourishing himself is then also a hope against generation in its higher power manifestation as sexual reproduction. It is crucial, then, that the sexual play between Molloy and Edith should be free from any possibility of issue, and the only issue arising from their sexual encounter is financial as Ruth pays Molloy after every session.

This turning away from sexual reproduction is perhaps even more marked in the somewhat submerged figure of the chambermaid, whose story Molloy fails to relate. She is mentioned in the first paragraph in the novel, but when it seems as if her story might suitably be told as a continuation of the Ruth/Edith encounter, Molloy angrily refuses:

Don't talk to me about the chambermaid. I should never have mentioned her, she was long before, I was sick, perhaps there was no chambermaid, ever, in my life. Molloy, or life without a chambermaid. (58)

The renunciation of the chambermaid is also a renunciation of the only positive act of sexual reproduction in Molloy's narrative. Not only does Molloy appear to actually have had intercourse with her but she also bore him a son, for we are told in the opening paragraph that the son that Molloy might have somewhere is a result of his congress with "a little chambermaid" (3). By denying the role, and even the existence, of the little chambermaid, Molloy is attempting to cancel out his regrettable indulgence in sexual reproduction and his debatable role in perpetuating the will-to-live and the continuance of the species.

CHAPTER 4

Alternating and Alternative Sexualities

"...but all men are homo-sexy, I wish to Christ I had been born a Lesbian" (*Dream* 154). As the Alba's wearied plea demonstrates, the possibility of sexualities other than the heterosexual is a feature of Beckett's work from its very beginnings. There is no surprise here at the very concept of homosexuality, rather a recognition of alternative sexualities as not only an option but perhaps even as a preferable option. The terms of the Alba's plea also identify a dichotomy of thought concerning orientation toward a sexual object. If, as she asserts, all men are "homo-sexy" then this category would include those whom society at large might regard as heterosexual. Alternatively, the "homo-ness" of which she speaks might indicate that, no matter what the actual sexual object involved, the lover only ever loves the same in the other in a form of narcissism; a possibility that Leo Bersani has captured when he writes that "we love [...] inaccurate replications of ourselves. [...] All love is, in a sense, homoerotic. Even in the love between a man and a woman, each partner rejoices in finding himself, or herself, in the other."[1] This also suggests a certain fluidity in the choice of sexual object for, as long as the need to see one's self in another is satisfied, then male or female becomes an irrelevance. In contrast, the Alba's wish to have been born as a Lesbian points to an innate disposition toward a certain sexual object. According to the Alba, rather than a fluid choice, one is either born a Lesbian, or not, and one can sense the Alba's disgust at having been born into a heterosexual orientation that gives her so little room to maneuver.

The Alba's brief comment hinges upon two contrasting conceptions of sex and identity. Either one has identity within a fixed definition based on sexual preference (one *is*, or *is not*, a Lesbian), or sexual preference does not constitute an identity as such but might be a means toward, or a reflection of, one's identity. The difference may be characterized as that between *essence* and *acts*. We are accustomed to approach this difference, especially in regard to "transgressive" sexualities, through the prism of Foucault. With the proliferation of discourses around, and therefore surveillance of, "aberrant" forms of sexual practice, a shift occurred in which what were once "acts" now became indicators of an essential sexual identity. "Homosexuality," he writes, "appeared as one of the forms of sexuality when it was transposed from the practice of sodomy onto a kind of anterior androgyny, a hermaphrodism of the soul. The sodomite had been a temporary aberration; the homosexual was now a species."[2] Foucault dates this shift as occurring in 1870 with the publication of Carl Westphal's *Archiv für Neurologie* and in Vol. 2 of the *History of Sexuality* Foucault uses the example of Ancient Greece to examine the fluidity of sexual choice when the designation of a sexual "species" does not apply.

Prior to Foucault's cut-off point of 1870, the view of homosexuality as a question of *acts* rather than *essence* is well demonstrated by Beckett's loadstone, Schopenhauer. He does not write of homosexuality as such—indeed the term was not available to him—but only of the act of pederasty. The act, at first, "appears to be a monstrosity [and] contrary to nature,"[3] not least because the will-to-live perpetuates itself through the reproduction of children. Yet, somewhat ingenuously, Schopenhauer goes on to argue for the naturalness of the act precisely because the strength of will-to-live is preserved by the weak (in particular the aged and also immature males) being diverted into a safe, nonreproductive form of sex, leaving the "healthy" to reproduce and maintain the quality of the species. When the immature male gains maturity, he may then safely engage in procreative sex, just as the aged pederast had once had sexual relations with his wife and sired children. "Accordingly," Schopenhauer writes,

> there was here no question of moral admonition against this vice, but of a proper understanding of the essential nature of the matter. For the rest, the true, ultimate and profoundly metaphysical reason to the objectionable nature of pederasty is that, whereas in it the will-to-live affirms itself, the effect of that affirmation, which opens the path to salvation, and hence the resumption of life, is completely cut off.[4]

One might find the terms of Schopenhauer's argument absurd, offensive and occasionally just factually wrong (he claims, for instance, that pederasty is a more common choice for older men), yet it rather helpfully removes the sexual act from a question of sexual identity and proposes that the choice of sexual object changes when the end of the sex itself changes. He also hints that turning from heterosexual, procreative sex to nonreproductive forms will have the ultimately ethical benefit of curtailing the will-to-live through the death of the species itself. It is in this spirit that Dr. Piouk in *Eleutheria* offers the practice of homosexual sex as an answer to the problem of humanity. Perhaps most importantly, Schopenhauer's eccentric account of homosexual acts allows for the deployment of those acts as a position to be adopted without the individual thereby being categorized as a distinct social identity and so open to control, surveillance, and the admonition of power.

The somewhat elderly Mercier certainly turns away from sanctioned pro- creative sex, yet what he then turns to might be more difficult to ascertain:

> I said yes? Said Mercier. I? Impossible. The last time I abused that term was at my wedding. To Toffana. The mother of my children. Mine own. Toffana. You never met her. A tundish. Like fucking a quag. To think it was for this hectolitre of excrement I renegued my dearest dream. He paused coquettishly. But Camier was in no playful mood. So that Mercier resumed perforce, You ask me which. Then let me whisper it in your ear. That of leaving the species to get on as best it could without me. (*MC* 69)

The misogynistic abuse leveled at Mercier's wife, and the dismissive rejec- tion of his children, are familiar components of the desire to leave the spe- cies to "get on as best as it could without me," that is, refusing to engender offspring, as we have seen in Chapter 3. Yet, given the apparently violent rejection of heterosexual procreative sex ("Like fucking a quag"), what is one to make of the coquettish pause that follows? Is one to infer that Mercier's "dearest dream," consonant with leaving no offspring behind, entails homo- sexual relations? If Camier was in a more playful mood, would a homosexual relation between the two bloom? After all, it is Mercier and Camier, among the clearest of pseudo-couples in Beckett's prose, who claim that if there were no women they would "explore other channels" (59); a phrase that has a certain corporeal specificity.

When we first see Mercier and Camier together, they run into each other's arms (an embrace that Didi and Gogo repeat in *Godot*), and their coming together is shadowed by the (more literal) coming together of two dogs: "They had not finished in each other's arms and yet felt awkward about resuming. The dogs for their part were already copulating, with the utmost naturalness" (5). The awkwardness of the human couple is belied by the naturalness of the dogs, which implies that the human interac- tion might in some way be "abnormal," as if Mercier and Camier wish to remain in each other's arms until they have "finished" but fear to do so, even though they are sheltering in a pagoda that is "a friend to lovers" (4). Mercier and Camier might also here remind us of the heteronormative approach assumed for that other pseudo-couple, Vladimir and Estragon, for, as Peter Boxall has put it: "In what could be thought of as an extraordinary demonstration of mass denial, Beckett studies has worked under the assumption that Vladimir and Estragon are just good friends. Like Holmes and Watson, they may have breakfast together, but in the critical imagination they have remained absolutely straight."[5] It may be tempting to merely reverse this critical assumption by effectively "outing" key Beckett characters, be it Mercier and Camier, Didi and Gogo, Hamm and Clov, or Molloy. The kisses and embraces that pass between these characters would offer an opportunity for just such a reversal, as would Molloy's question of whether or not "it is true love in the rectum" in his sexual relations with Ruth/Edith, who may also be a man. Yet, as this final example suggests, the boundaries between homosexual and heterosexual, male and female, may not be sufficiently well-defined to allow a simple crossing of borders and reallocation of established sexual identities, and, indeed, may call into question just such allocations.

Sexual Preference and Identity

Mercier and Camier may *suggest* exploring same sex desire, but the sexual practices of the two protagonists indicate that heterosexual sex is still also desirable and available. When they ask a policeman directions to a brothel, they are more than willing to defend their right to "venery" and that to renounce it "because of a simple falling off in erotogenesis would be puerile" (75). Yet it is with Helen that sexual activity is most regular. She may have "terminated" the "nice little suck-offs" (20) that were once on offer (it is unclear whether or not Helen is a prostitute, but it can certainly be inferred), yet heterosexual sex is still on the agenda, as when Camier takes advantage to do "what one can" (59). The one time these activities are described, mutual masturbation between all three of them is the preferred act:

> They passed a peaceful night, for them, without any debauch of any kind. All next day was spent within doors. Time tending to drag, they manstuprated mildly, without fatigue. Before the blazing fire, in the two-fold light of lamp and leaden day, they squirmed gently on the carpet, their naked bodies mingled, fingering and fondling with the languorous tact of hands arranging flowers, while the rain beat on the panes. How delicious that must have been! (57)

This is arguably the most positive description of sex in the whole of Beckett's oeuvre and, while it is clear *what* is being done, it is not so clear who is doing it to whom. As the bodies mingle, so the boundaries between individual homosexual and heterosexual sex acts also mingle. Of course, the sex acts indulged in preclude any worries about procreation, and therefore, arguably, they can be enjoyed for the momentary respite they can offer, or at least offer some way of passing the time. However, one instance in the novel demonstrates an awareness of the possible boundaries between homosexual and heterosexual acts. Camier goes to embrace Mercier "who promptly recoiled. I was only going to embrace you, said Camier. I'll do it some other time, when you're less yourself, if I think of it" (22). If Mercier's recoil here is a recognition and rejection of a sexual element in Camier's advance, then such advances are only welcome when Mercier is less himself, when he is not policing the boundaries of a heterosexually conditioned selfhood.

As Mercier recoils from Camier, so Murphy attempts to recoil from the attentions of Austin Ticklepenny, but "Murphy had such an enormous contempt for rape that he found it no trouble to go quite limp at the first sign of its application" (55) as Ticklepenny traps Murphy's legs beneath a café table. "Limp" here strains to make it clear that Murphy is not aroused by Ticklepenny's fondlings and thus maintains Murphy within a strict heterosexuality. Indeed, Ticklepenny, who is perhaps the most clear example of a gay man in Beckett's work, is shown from the outset to be an invasion of Murphy's person as he thrusts his visiting card beneath Murphy's nose. The physicality is here perhaps reminiscent of the corporeal insistence of women in Beckett's early prose and, as those women are often treated with misogyny, it is hard not to see a certain homophobia in Beckett's treatment of Ticklepenny. Despite his crucial role in the plot of the novel, Ticklepenny is asserted to be of no importance and therefore "does not merit any particular description" (55). His effeminacy is accentuated not only by his physical approaches to Murphy beneath the table but also by his breaking into tears and "snivelling" on two occasions during their first meeting (56,59). He is also described as a "creature" (55) and an "animal" (119) for whom Murphy demonstrates a marked degree of contempt. Yet, as Jennifer Jeffers has argued, this contempt is not solely generated by Ticklepenny's sexuality: "Ticklepenny, a caricature of Austin Clarke, the Irish Catholic poet and Dublin acquaintance of Beckett, is interesting, not because he is homosexual, per se, but because Beckett singles out a Gaelic poet to feminize."[6] Beckett, as an Anglo-Irish Protestant writer, thereby takes revenge on the poetry favored by the Free State in its desire for an indisputable Irishness by making one of its favored poets homosexual, because, in "a heterosexual patriarchy, the surest way to put down a man is to render him homosexual."[7]

Jeffers does not pursue this point beyond the "masculine protest" that she sees Beckett engaging in as a way of compensating for a loss of privilege and identity after the creation of the Irish Free State, yet her insight is valuable not only for the light it throws on Beckett's psychological reactions to Ireland. Jeffers's point also identifies a moment in which Beckett makes a structural and political *use* of homosexuality. In *Murphy* the terms of that use err on the side of the homophobic, but it should be noticed that Ticklepenny's homosexuality is being used to undermine an imposition of identity on the political level. One can glimpse here a first indication of what will become an important facet of Beckett's politics of sexual orientation in which the possibilities of homosexual acts are seen to be inimical to the creation of an all-encompassing, rigid identity. In *Watt*, Louit bears the burden of undermining this identitarianism through his running of Bando. As Chapter 2 noted, Louit's smuggling of this banned aphrodisiac is a satire on the Free State's banning of contraceptives in the service of creating a new vision of a Catholic Ireland. Louit's homosexuality, as evidenced by his relationship with the College Bursar with whom he wakes in the morning "habitually" (*W* 146), already places him outside of the practice and rhetoric of the state's desired Irish male who is enjoined to reproduce and thus secure Ireland's future. Louit's transgression is, then, not only sexual but also social as his smuggling activities and sexual preferences cross the borders, as it were, of a state-sanctioned identity. In this sense, both Ticklepenny's and Louit's sexuality is disruptive of order and subverts a vision of a heterosexual, patriarchal identity politics.

The degree to which transgressive sexuality can be disruptive in this way can be gauged by what occurs when clear heterosexual relations form the core of Beckett's work. For a play about an extramarital affair, *Play* offers little for the present book's concern with sexuality and its depictions. This might seem surprising, but the very *banality* of the affair in *Play* is precisely the point. The title itself might suggest this. Of course, one might wish to emphasize the witticism of *Play* as mere "play" or a game and that the man and two women of the affair are merely engaging in "game-play" in their betrayals. Alternatively, the title might also play with its own redundancy, as if flaunting the clichéd nature of the "eternal triangle" that lies at its core and that Beckett makes literal in the purgatorial extension of the man caught between two women. Harold Pinter's play of betrayal, itself redundantly entitled *Betrayal*, has both *Play* and Joyce's *Exiles* in its hinterland and captures the lack of significance of the basic premise of the extramarital affair. When the wronged husband, Robert, reveals to Jerry, his supposed best friend, that he has known for quite a while about Jerry's long-standing affair with his wife, he comments: "Well, it's not very important, is it?" And later: "You don't seem to understand that I don't give a shit about any of this."[8] The bourgeois nature of Pinter's play (Robert is a publisher and Jerry an author's agent) is also present in Beckett's *Play*: all the characters are comfortably off (Woman 2 even has a butler), both women like green tea, and moments of crisis are often played out against the gentle noise of someone mowing the lawn. The text is replete with situational and verbal clichés that underline the triteness of the whole affair: Man swears to both women that he "could not live without her" (*CDW* 309 and 311); Woman 1 has her husband followed by a private detective (308); Woman 1 threatens to "settle the hash" of Woman 2 (309); Man returns to Woman 1 "at home all heart to heart, new leaf and bygones bygones" (311). The clichéd nature of the text brings together the two possible resonances of the title. The characters were "playing" their roles in a preestablished, traditional drama and indulging in a game, the rules of which were laid down long before. As Man comments, "I know now, all that was just...play" (313).

Heterosexual sex is at the center of the relations between the characters of *Play*. Man is said to have a "horror of the merely Platonic thing" (308) and keeps having sex with both partners throughout the affair. The wife even commends her husband on this point: "I confess my first feeling was one of wonderment. What a male!" (309). But the heteronormative sex engaged in appears to be without significance; it is merely part of the tired tale of the eternal triangle. This lack of significance is precisely what is at issue in the purgatorial torture of the light that interrogates the characters as they are trapped in their urns. Woman 1 wonders if the light is meant to elicit "penitence, yes, at a pinch, atonement, one was resigned, but no, that doesn't seem to be the point either" (316). Man wonders if the light is "looking for something. In my face. Some truth. In my eyes," but then admits: "Not even" (317). This admission is supported by Woman 1 who comes to see the light as "mere eye. Just looking." Significance is not forthcoming, despite the apparent wishes of the protagonists who suggest that if significance can finally be found, the torture will stop. Instead, the protagonists are bound into a meaningless regurgitation of their affair as the text of the play is then (all but identically) repeated. This repetition also indicates the repetitious nature of *Play* itself as it once more plays out the eternal triangle paradigm. "No doubt," says Woman 2. "I make the same mistake as when it was the sun that shone, of looking for sense where possibly there is none" (314). In the words of *Murphy*: "The sun shone, having no alternative, on the nothing new" (3). The punishment is then fitting as the characters endlessly repeat their real-life affair that was itself a repetition of a cliché of sexual mores. The man and two women of the play are trapped within a narrow heterosexual identity and are therefore doomed to play out this identity in perpetuity.

The fixed dimensions of the urns in which they are caught are indicative of the restrictions placed upon them and also indicative of the fact that any crossing of borders would be impossible. There is no scope within their sexual identities for flux and, therefore, disruption; the three heterosexuals will continue under the torture of the interrogating light.

The disruptive possibilities within the heterosexual scenario of *Play* are severely curtailed, but the reverse—that homosexual identities allow for disruption—may not necessarily hold true if the term "homosexual" itself becomes a rigid form of identity in opposition to, but conditioned by, the heteronormal. It may be that a fluidity in sexual orientation, or an indifference to sexual difference, might prove to be more subversive than a form of counteridentity. This possibility is raised in Beckett's oeuvre by the lack of identifiably homosexual characters beyond those of Louit and Ticklepenny, or, more accurately, the lack of certainty one feels about applying the term homosexual without making the application conditional. In "Beckett and Homoeroticism"—an essay that functions as an erudite rallying call to investigate the queerness of Beckett—Peter Boxall chooses the main point of contention as Molloy's relations with Lousse and Ruth/Edith. Boxall quotes the following passage: "Perhaps after all she put me in her rectum. A matter of complete indifference to me, I needn't tell you. But is it true love, in the rectum? That's what bothers me sometimes. Have I known true love, after all" (56). Boxall then rightly states: "The extent to which we accept Molloy's claim that the difference between the anus and the vagina is a matter of complete indifference is perhaps here key."[9] He goes on to criticize AnJanette Brush for effectively closing down the transgressive possibilities within the Lousse and Ruth/Edith sexual relations with Molloy. Of particular concern is the male/female confusion within the descriptions of their congress, in which "perhaps she too was a man" who held "her" testicles "tight in her hand" on purpose to avoid their colliding. Brush argues that "these multiple confusions/blurrings take place only within the figure of *her*..."[10] For Brush, the third-person pronoun curtails the gender confusions that the passage creates, as if the gender-specific language obliterates the *physical* confusion of the passage. One wonders if the same thing would occur if the personal pronoun was "he" rather than "she." Thankfully, Beckett maintains a tension (to use Boxall's word) between possible sexual identities, when the identification of just one would effectively close down the transgressive possibilities. Molloy's sexual relations with Ruth/Edith will not allow for a simple containment as either homosexual or heterosexual but rather allow for a play between these two (supposed) poles.

So, although Molloy is bothered on occasion by the question of whether true love can be found in the rectum or not, it might be that his "indifference" to whether it makes a difference might be genuine. He admits, for example, that "he would have made love to a goat, to know what love was" (57). Further, he is again apparently indifferent about the nature of the intercourse with Edith:

> I would have preferred it seems to me an orifice less arid and roomy, that would have given me a higher opinion of love it seems to me. However. Twixt finger and thumb 'tis heaven in comparison. But love is no doubt above such base contingencies. And not when you are comfortable, but when your frantic member casts about for a rubbing-place, and the unction of a little mucus membrane, and meeting with none does not beat a retreat, but retains its tumefaction, it is then no doubt that true love comes to pass, and wings away, high above the tight fit and the loose. (57)

The choice here is between masturbation and some form of intercourse, yet, even here, the orifice in question is not specified. All that is specified is the need of a mucous membrane; mouth, anus, vagina, all seem to be acceptable when Molloy is prey to tumefaction. It is noteworthy, perhaps, that the tumefaction occurs *before* an orifice is sought. It is not the case that an erection occurs in response to the "right" sexual object, whatever gender or whichever sexual preference is thereby involved. Edith's gender and, therefore, the nature of Molloy's sexual relations with her, remain undecided even after Edith's death, to which Molloy is also indifferent. He reasons that as Edith died in the bath her sex would have been discovered, so she "must have been a woman after all, if she hadn't it would have got around, in the neighbourhood" (58). His reasoning is faulty because the people in the neighborhood were "extraordinarily reserved [...] about everything connected with sexual matters. And it is quite possible that the fact of having found a man when they should have found a woman was immediately repressed and forgotten..." Beckett seems to be suggesting here that the gender identifications with which the society at large are comfortable are so sacrosanct that the transgression of gender norms—Edith was a man—cannot be tolerated and must be returned to the strict male/female dyad; a dyad that Molloy's indifference effectively undermines, for, having had some form of sex with Ruth and Lousse, Molloy is still not clear whether they were women or men and is merely "willing to go on thinking of her as an old woman" (58) as a matter of a hypothetical preference rather than an expression of sexual orientation.

Queer Indifference: Beckett, Bersani, and Edelman

Molloy's indifference to the nature of his sexual acts—and one should note he is also indifferent to any moral consideration of those acts—suggests a similar indifference to the supposed relation between sexual preference and identity. Leo Bersani (for whom Beckett is an important and often used resource) has raised the question of the desirability of such a sexuality and identity relation. He wonders

> ...why should sexual preference be the key to identity in the first place? And, more fundamentally, why should preference itself be understood only as a function of the homo-heterosexual dyad? That dyad imprisons the eroticized body within a rigidly gendered sexuality, in which pleasure is at once recognized and legitimized as a function of general differences between the sexes.[11]

For Bersani, the homo-heterosexual dyad limits both the access to, and sites of, erotic pleasure and imprisons the individual within a policed form of identity politics. He is acutely aware of the difficulties of escaping the implications of a homo-heterosexual binary. On one hand an "intentionally oppositional gay identity, by its very coherence, only repeats the restrictive and immobilizing analyses it set out to resist," and yet "de-gaying gayness can only fortify homophobic oppression; it accomplishes in its own way the principal aim of homophobia: the elimination of gays."[12] As has been seen, I have resisted the option of "outing" Molloy as such an act would reify him within an identity based on sexual preference. It would also render him "safely" marginalized. To return to Mercier, who only welcomes Camier's embraces when he is "less himself," one can see the restrictive nature of the relation between identity and heterosexuality, and Bersani suggests that a switching from one side of the sexual dyad to the other would not call into question the nature and effects of that dyad as such.

The either/or nature of allocating sexual identity based on sexual preference is often questionable in Beckett's work. Malone claims that "there is so little difference between a man and a woman, between mine I mean" (5), and if one takes this lack of difference seriously, then the homo-heterosexual dyad becomes unsettled, as can be seen in the short story "Enough" of 1965. The story entails two people, the narrator and an older male, who seem to walk perpetually, spending their days and nights in mathematical calculation or picking out constellations among the stars. The hand in hand tread, the mathematics, and the stars are all very much Beckettian motifs and so, one could argue, are the explicit sexual acts used to characterize the relationship:

> I only had the desires he manifested. But he must have desired them all. All his desires and needs. When he was silent he must have been like me.

When he told me to lick his penis I hastened to do so. I drew satisfaction from it. We must have had the same satisfactions. The same needs and the same satisfactions.[13]

This passage is taken from only the second paragraph of the story, and the narrator has only spoken in the first person. The sex of the narrator is not known at this stage and so the heterosexuality or homosexuality of the act cannot be ascertained. However, given that this is a Beckett short story with a first-person narrator and given the nature of the vast majority of Beckett's prose, the *assumption* one makes is that this is an instance of homosexual sex. It may be, though, that a social predilection for the heteronormative will encourage the reader to quickly substitute male for female solely on the basis of the oral sex. Yet, the sex of the narrator continues as indeterminate, and the references to other sexual acts are similarly nonspecific. For example, the old man "did not like to feel against his skin the skin of another. Mucous membrane is a different matter" (187). As in *Molloy*, mucous membrane is not enough to indicate which orifice is intended, allowing now for fellatio, anal sex, and, contrary to the prior assumption, vaginal penetration. It is only in the final sentence of the text that the sex of the narrator is given an apparently undeniable indicator: "Enough my old breasts feel his old hand" (192). This anatomical specificity is left to the last possible moment and, to one troubled by the possibility of the homosexual nature of the sex described, perhaps this is met with a sigh of heteronormative relief. Yet, when the story is read for the first time, the sex of the narrator and therefore the nature of the sex acts performed are formulated, challenged, and reformulated a number of times as the reader attempts to bring the sexual relation into one or the other of the designations in the dyad: is this homosexual sex or heterosexual sex? Less obvious factors within the story might make one adopt further assumptions. Given that the narrator only desires what the man desires, and that the fellatio is not reciprocated, then the dynamics of the relation are those of the powerful and the submissive. If the narrator is a woman, this lays Beckett once again open to the charge of misogyny (or, more kindly, the contention that Beckett reveals the unequal power relations between male and female), yet, as the reading of Rank demonstrated earlier, one could read the passivity of the narrator as indicative of homosexual compliance. All these options are predicated upon a rigid identity of the individual based on the relations between biology and sexual preference, and run dangerously close to forms of caricature that women and gay men would find offensive. Instead of this, the story's suspension of certainty causes the reader to question the nature of the identifications that are made on the basis of sexual acts and whether male or female protagonists might be most "appropriate" for those acts.

Throughout this discussion, I have been resisting "rigidly gendered sexuality" (to use Bersani's terms) connected to sexual preference as a basis for identity in order to retain a range of subversive possibilities precisely in terms of identity. In one sense, this is to keep Molloy and others as marginalized individuals who refuse to accept established marginal identities, such as "the homosexual." Molloy himself is again instructive in his refusal to accept a form of homosexual community offered to him by the charcoal burner in the forest. Molloy admits that "I might have loved him, I think, if I had been seventy years younger" (84) before asserting a difference between the love reserved for old men and the "true love" with the woman he now mistakenly names Rose. This assertion of difference is already compromised by the confusion of difference in the actual description of the Ruth/Edith affair. Rather like Ruth/Edith and Lousse, the charcoal burner offers Molloy both shelter and company: "He was all over me, begging me to share his hut, believe it or not" (85). Molloy does not see this offer as one of compassion (for which he has a dread) or of two lonely men finding company together; instead he sees within it the threat of containment: "...he wanted to keep me near him [...] for when I made to go, he held me back by the sleeve. So I smartly freed a crutch and dealt him a good dint on the skull. That calmed him. The dirty old brute" (85). The charcoal burner may be placed alongside Lousse and Ruth/Edith and, for that matter, Lulu/Anna in "First Love" inasmuch as all offer shelter and some form of homo- or heterosexual community (or, as is often the case, a confusion of the two) that is then rejected by the Beckettian male who seems determined to remain marginal.

Peter Boxall rightly identifies the homoerotic encounter in "The Calmative" as being of prime importance for any queer reading of Beckett. He argues that it "is through the erotics of this encounter with the other that the narrator seeks to find a new home, to find a new relationality in which the conflicting needs and pathologies which produce the story might be worked through, and might open onto a new form of community or placedness."[14] Relationality and community are, then, precisely at issue, and while it is clear that the masculinity of the stranger whom the protagonist meets cannot "be feminized," as Boxall puts it, and therefore brought simply into some form of displaced heterosexual relation, it is yet unclear whether a homosexual relation is any more viable. The homosexual-heterosexual dyad is again blurred in this encounter with the man with the shining teeth who is in a heterosexual relation with Pauline but, who is "going to leave her and set up with another, younger and plumper" (*ECEFL* 29). This heterosexuality is initially carried forward into the stranger's seduction:

Are thighs much in your thoughts, he said, arses, cunts and environs? I didn't follow. No more erections naturally, he said. Erections? I said. The penis, he said, you know what the penis is, there, between the legs. Ah that! I said. It thickens, lengthens, stiffens and rises, he said, does it not? I assented, though they were not the terms I would have used. (*ECEFL* 30)

While this seduction begins in a clear anatomical heterosexuality it quickly becomes a homoerotic paean to the potency of the penis. It is this potency that is questioned by the narrator who distances himself with the dry caveat of "they were not the terms I would have used." Indeed, the narrator's lack of comprehension—"I didn't follow," "Erections?"—indicates a degree of separation between him and the stranger on such sexual specifics. This lack of shared feeling continues when the stranger suggests that the narrator exchanges something for the phial, which, one notices, he doesn't actually want: "Want it? he said. No, but I said yes, so as not to vex him." So the narrator refuses to exchange his hat or a lace for the promised phial. He will however, exchange a kiss, for "a kiss is not a bootlace, he must have seen from my face that all passion was not quite spent" (31). That the narrator is willing to exchange a kiss when he is unwilling to exchange his hat or a bootlace suggests either that a new mode of relationality based on homo-erotic exchange might be possible or indicates an indifference to the value placed upon the kiss itself.[15] Bootlaces and hats are of greater importance, one might say, than a moment of homoerotic contact. That moment is also delicately poised; the narrator prepares to kiss the stranger on the mouth, but his advance is deflected:

He took off his hat, a bowler, and tapped the middle of his forehead. There, he said, and there only. He had a noble brow, white and high. He leaned forward, closing his eyes. Quick, he said. I pursed my lips as mother had taught me and brought them down where he had said. Enough, he said. (31)

The more overt sexual possibilities of the kiss are redirected toward a desex-ualized, yet still homoerotic, peck on the forehead. The mention of the mother underlines the childlike nature of the kiss bestowed and thereby the stranger takes on the role of parent, and more specifically father, rather than of lover. This might come as no surprise, given that the figure of the father haunts the three novellas and "First Love" and, in the latter case, the death of the father is explicitly connected to the expulsion into wandering of the narrator that leads to his "marriage" with Lulu/Anna. Just as the narrator of "First Love" fails to find a "placedness," to use Boxall's term, so the narrator of "The Calmative" similarly fails to find a place, despite the intervention of the eroticized father figure in the form of the stranger. After the encounter the narrator moves through a mix of hallucination, dream, and memory in which images of community and placedness are recognized but rejected. So, he thinks of "ringing at the door [of a house] and asking for shelter and protection till morning. But suddenly I was on my way again" (33). And when he falls to the pavement he is "in a throng" yet the crowd "pay no heed" to him, and then "the throng fell away, the light came back and I had no need to raise my head from the ground to know I was back in the same blinding void as before." The final few sentences relate this wandering and the void back to the figure of the father, who taught him to read the stars and who read him the heroic stories of Joe Breem at bedtime. However, neither of these father-connected attributes will help him place himself:

> But up with me again [...] A blessing he was not waiting for me, poor old Breem, or Breen. I said, The sea is east, it's west I must go, to the left of north. But in vain I raised without hope my eyes to the sky to look for the Bears. For the light I stepped in put out the stars, assuming they were there, which I doubted, remembering the clouds. (33)

Breem or Breen here applies to the childhood stories and also to the figure of the stranger with the shining teeth, and both are *fortunately* absent, leaving the narrator alone and unable to find his way. Finally, if anything might promise access to community through the homoerotic exchange with the stranger, it would arguably be the phial that is purchased by the kiss. Yet, when this phial reappears in "The End," it contains a calmative that the narrator takes (in a "real" or imagined scenario) as he scuttles his coffin-like boat and commits suicide as the "sea, the sky, the mountains and the islands closed in and crushed me in a mighty systole, then scattered to the uttermost confines of space" (*ECEFL* 56–7). Rather than leading to relation, the calmative bought at the price of a kiss leads to an Oceanic dispersion in an image, both in the ocean itself and the womb-like boat in which he effectively entombs himself, of a return to nonbeing. As the phial in "The Calmative" is drawn from a "big black bag, like a *midwife's*" (30), we have once again an instance of birth into death, of a desire to return to a state prior to any relation at all.

Yet it is this very failure to relate that might indicate the valuable queerness of Beckett's writing. As we have seen, Bersani is keenly aware of the dangers of established communal identities based on sexual preference. The concept of "homo-ness" that Bersani adumbrates in *Homos* and elsewhere speaks to a new form of relation not necessarily grounded in specific sexual acts:

> If homosexuality is a privileged vehicle for homo-ness, the latter designates a mode of connectedness to the world that it would be absurd

to reduce to sexual preference. An anticommunal mode of connected-ness we might all share, or a new way of coming together: that, and not assimilation into already constituted communities, should be the goal of any adventure in bringing out, and celebrating, the "homo" in all of us.[16]

Here is not the place to question whether the bringing out of "homo-ness" in all, regardless of sexual preference, might mean the disappearance of "the homosexual," which Bersani feared would occur through a process of "de-gaying" the gay. Here is the place to note the paradox of an "anticommunal mode of connectedness" and how apposite this description might be for the dispersal of the narrator at the end of "The End." If one assumes that the narrator is the same figure as the narrator of "The Calmative," then we have a rejection of established modes of community (in that case, it *happens* to be one that might be designated as homosexual) followed by a dissipation and merging into unexpected forms of connectedness, with the sky, the sea, the islands in a "mighty systole" in which individual identity is no longer discernible, nor relevant.[17] This new mode of connectedness presupposes an indifference to those modes of relation that are currently sanctioned—an indifference that so many of Beckett's character's exemplify. Yet, as the comments quoted above indicate, homosexuality is given a privileged position by Bersani as a preferred route toward such new modes of relation. "Perhaps," he writes,

inherent in gay desire is a revolutionary inaptitude for heteroized social-ity. This of course means sociality as we know it, and the most politically disruptive aspect of the homo-ness [. . .] in gay desire is a redefinition of sociality so radical that it may appear to require a provisional withdrawal from relationality itself.[18]

Certainly, one would recognize the "withdrawal from relationality" in Beckett's figures, but, as has been shown, whether or not those figures are, or should be taken to be, engaging in "gay desire" is very much open to ques-tion. Nevertheless, after considering the works of Gide, Proust, and Genet as "gay outlaws," Bersani closes *Homos* by adding Beckett to the list: "The cult of failure and the cult of waste: Beckett and Genet belong to a radical modernity anxious to save art from the preemptive operations of institution-alized culture. [. . .] And so they compel us, perhaps in spite of themselves, to re-think what we mean and what we expect from communication, and from community."[19] As Calvin Thomas has asked: "How should one account for the relatively unexpected appearance of Samuel Beckett on the final page of

Leo Bersani's *Homos*?"[20] His answer is that, for Bersani, Beckett's aesthetic of failure is predicated on the lack of relation between the subject and object in art or in the terms of *The Three Dialogues* between the artist and the occasion. In *Acts of Impoverishment*, Bersani states that Beckett's work "performs the inestimable service of representing the unrelated subject..." and that this might be "the precondition for any viable reconstruction of [new] social relations. For such a reconstruction will have to take into account the persistence of unrelatedness, the priority of unrelatedness in the social itself, a priority that perhaps only an art removed from culturally inspired goals of relationality can remind us."[21] Bersani's focus is on the aesthetic level as laid down in *The Three Dialogues*, not on the sexual practices of Beckett's characters. This is in direct contrast to Bersani's interest in the relation of the individual to homosexual community and in the practice of certain sexual acts that privilege a form of indifference in the works of Gide, Proust, and, especially, Genet. It may be that Genet and Beckett are approaching the same goal that Bersani prizes albeit through different means, but this begs the question of why Bersani might miss (or wish to miss) the implications of homosexual acts within Beckett. Calvin Thomas has identified an important divergence between Beckett and Bersani precisely as regards the benefits of sex itself. For Bersani, as Thomas puts it, "Nothing is more crucial for Bersani's project than his emphasis on the self-shattering capacities of both sexual and aesthetic experience." Following Leplanche, Bersani argues that the jouissance of the sexual moment amounts to a disintegration and dispersal of the self, as he relates through his reading of Freud in *The Freudian Body* and in *Homos* itself: "I call jouissance "self-shattering" in that it disrupts the ego's coherence and dissolves its boundaries. [...] self-shattering is intrinsic to the homo-ness in homosexuality. Homo-ness is an anti-identitarian identity."[22] That Mercier recoiled away from homosexual contact, and therefore possible *jouissance*, when he was most "himself" would seem to support this notion in Beckett were it not for the lack of any form of *jouissance* in the sex Beckett's characters indulge in. Of the Ruth/ Edith affair, Thomas is right to wonder "how this feeble encounter qualifies as *jouissance*. It certainly seems demeaning enough, but it falls noticeably short of any exuberantly sexual self-discard. Indeed, Molloy seems to have been divested of self well before having arrived at Ruth's rectum." Beckett's characters are already self-shattered, leaving little room for the benefits of sexual *jouissance*. Paradoxically for Bersani's theory in which indifference plays such a crucial role, it may be that Beckett's characters are not only indifferent to the different sexes of sexual partners but are indifferent to sex itself. To return to Molloy's tumefactions, penetrative sex may be "heaven" in comparison to masturbation but the desire expressed is more that of the desire to scratch an itch than it is to divest the self in sexual excess. For Molloy, any orifice will do the job of scratching the itch of the sexual.

For the characters of Beckett's fiction, homo- or heterosexual sex acts seem to promise little in terms of community or of self-divestiture as a prelude to a new form relationality. Yet, their indifference to sexual difference and their refusal to be contained within the homo-heterosexual dyad suggest a fluidity that will not be dammed by established social identities, no matter how transgressive or marginalized these identities might appear to be. However, this does not necessarily exhaust the queer possibilities, for, as Thomas has suggested, "…failure to reproduce the person might be regarded […] at least as one of the queerest elements of Beckett's impoverishing art." We have seen in Chapter 3 how misopedia is inflected in Beckett by a dread of the future and the unchecked progression of the will-to-live through birth, suffering, and death. For Lee Edelman, in *No Future: Queer Theory and the Death Drive*, an antagonism to the child and therefore to the future and social order as such is a mark of an aggressive form of the queer. For him, "the Child […] marks the fetishistic fixation of heteronormativity: an erotically charged investment in the rigid sameness of identity that is central to the compulsory narrative of reproductive futurism."[23] In order to combat this futurism that subordinates the individual, the figure of the *sinthom*osexual [sic] is one who would "fuck the social order of the Child in whose name we're collectively terrorized; fuck Annie; fuck the waif from *Les Mis*; fuck the poor, innocent kid on the Net; fuck both Laws both with capital *l*s and small; fuck the whole network of Symbolic relations and the future that serves as its prop."[24] The aggressiveness of Edelman's prose— intentionally not for the ears of children—is as one with the aggressively antisocial stance of the *sinthom*osexual. The term derives from Lacan's *sinthome*, which "designates a signifying formulation beyond analysis, a kernel of enjoyment immune to the efficacy of the symbolic." The *sinthome* knots together the real, symbolic, and the imaginary, yet "since meaning (*sens*) is already figured within the knot, at the intersection of the symbolic and the imaginary, it follows that the function of the *sinthome* […] is inevitably beyond meaning."[25] For Edelman, the figure of the *sinthom*osexual is therefore a challenge to order as "order is […] ultimately grounded in something [the *sinthome*] that is not of the order itself" and one who insists "on access to jouissance in place of access to sense, on identification with one's sinthome instead of belief in its meaning."[26] The *sinthom*osexual is therefore meaningless in the sense that it calls into question those structures that establish meaning and value; indeed, it is contrary to, or a negation of, value and meaning that are fantastically guaranteed by futurity. The figure is therefore seen by the social order as negative, utterly transgressive, and antagonistic for if "there is *no baby* and, in consequence, *no future*, then the blame must fall on the fatal lure of sterile, narcissistic enjoyments understood as inherently destructive of meaning and therefore as responsible for the undoing of social organization, collective reality, and, inevitably, life itself."[27] To bring Edelman and Beckett together, we might recall Watt's two outbursts in *Mercier and Camier:* "Bugger life!" and, a little later, "Fuck life!" (94, 96). From the perspective of the heteronormal social order, this is precisely what the *sinthom*osexual threatens and what Beckett's misopedia reveals.

Edelman's *sinthom*osexual is a radically subversive figure, but one that designates a *position* rather than a set of sexual preferences and practices. For him, "queerness can never define an identity; it can only disturb one," and we have seen how Beckett's men do not easily fit into a definite sexual identity. The correlative of this is that logically anyone can *assume* the position of the *sinthom*osexual, a possibility that Edelman exemplifies in the figure of the birds from Hitchcock's film of the same name—a force beyond the social that, unaccountably, attacks the future on which that social is based; the birds are also representative of the inhumanity that lies at the heart of *sinthom*osexuality—an inhumanity that the social order lays as a charge against the *sinthom*osexual, but that should also therefore be embraced. The rejection of compassion (or, rather, false compassion) that this inhumanity entails is exemplified by the "evil henchman" Leonard of Hitchcock's *North by Northwest* who revels in crushing the fingers of the hero as he hangs from a precipice on Mount Rushmore and begs for help. The *sinthom*osexual therefore acts *against* the "human" and refuses any form of redemptive possibility:

> In breaking our hold on the future, the *sinthom*osexual [...] forsakes all causes, all social action, all responsibility for a better tomorrow or for the perfection of social forms. Against the promise of such activism, he performs, instead, an act: the act of repudiating the social, of stepping, or trying to step, with Leonard, beyond compulsory compassion, beyond the future and the snare of images keeping us always in its thrall.[28]

There is much in this queer, antisocial, uncompassionate, and inhuman figure that may remind us of Beckett's characters, especially in terms of the hatred of the child and dread of reproduction. Further, we have already seen the violence with which Molloy treats the charcoal burner, who is, after all (although perhaps with ulterior motives) only offering him compassionate shelter and companionship. Molloy similarly reacts against the "compulsory compassion" visited upon him by the social workers at the police station ("Against the charitable gesture there is no defence" [21]). Mercier and Camier, for their part, beat a policeman to death with a certain glee, and Moran clubs to death a fellow wanderer who resembles him in many ways—which may be taken as a further repudiation of sameness and, therefore, of community. All the characters of *Godot* take their opportunities to abuse or beat Lucky, who is himself aggressive at a demonstration of compassionate care. In *Endgame*, Hamm is the epitome of inhumanity: having failed to help Mother Pegg in her darkness, and, in the past, shown utter disregard for the plight of his starving tenants, so he now abuses Clov, Nagg, and Nell and is unconcerned at the latter's death. Rather than being moved to compassionate regret in reaction to the voice that reminds him of the suicide of a one-time lover, Joe of *Eh Joe* mentally strangles both the voice and memory in order to remain alone and inviolable. There is, indeed, a great deal of callousness in Beckett's men that is activated by the threat of society—in the form of loving communion, social values, or indeed social law as embodied by figures of authority—and that callousness ensures their remaining beyond the reach of the social.

Yet still there is the nagging doubt as to whether or not one can relate such *sinthom*osexual traits of Molloy and others to an access to *jouissance* that Edelman, following Lacan, describes as being "sometimes translated as 'enjoyment': a movement beyond the pleasure principle, beyond the distinctions of pleasure and pain, a violent passage beyond the bounds of identity, meaning and law."[29] Pleasure, pain, violence, and nonidentity are all implicit within sadomasochism, and it is to Beckett's deployment of this sexual possibility to which one can turn in order to discern, or abandon, the *jouissance* that Edelman and Bersani, in very different ways, see as the center of a queer sexuality and sociality.

Sadism and Relation in How It Is

I apologize for having to revert to this lewd orifice, 'tis my muse would have it so. Perhaps it is less to be thought of as the eyesore here called by its name than as a symbol of those passed over in silence, a distinction due perhaps to is centrality and its air of being a link between me and the other excrement. We underestimate this little hole, it seems to me, we it call it the arsehole and affect to despise it. But is it not rather the true portal of our being... (*M* 80–81)

Molloy's apostrophe to the anus prompts Peter Boxall to ask, "could the rectum, as a site of transgressive sexuality and a site of homoerotic desire, be the portal to [...] a new relationality?"[30] The question of relationality and the anus is most usefully focused on *How It Is*, not only because the text explicitly focuses on the anus as a possible site for some form of communication and (possibly) identity but also because Bersani and, in very different ways, Alain Badiou have both chosen the text as one in which the conditions for a limited happiness based on forms of relation occur. For Badiou, this happiness is one of hope and love in an encounter with the other, and for Bersani, it is the emergence of new forms of sociability.

Certainly, the anus has a degree of centrality within *How It Is* that confers upon it some of the distinction that Molloy suggests. It is through Pim's "right buttock [that] first contact" is made (45) and as the unnamed narrator trains Pim to sing, speak, cry, and so forth, it is through the buttocks and anus that these commands are often relayed. So, in order to get Pim to speak, the narrator employs a can opener:

> Take the opener in my right hand move it down along the spine and drive it into the arse not the hole not such a fool the cheek a cheek he cries I withdraw it thump on skull the cries cease it's mechanical end of first lesson second series and here parenthesis. (57)

An index finger in the anus is the command for Pim to soften his speech or song, and, in a bold extension to the divine, the narrator relishes the thought that "had I only the little finger to raise to be wafted straight to Abraham's bosom I'd tell him to stick it up" (31). Even before the training of Pim, in the (possible) memories of a heterosexual relation in his teens with a girl, the narrator comments "the arse I have" (23) and "the rump I have" (24). The arse also takes on a central position, via the name, within identity itself. Just as the protagonist foisted the name of Pim onto that unfortunate figure, so in turn the protagonist imagines that he will have a name scored upon him: "BOM scored by the finger-nail athwart the arse the vowel in the hole..." (52).

The centrality of the anus is no doubt accentuated also by the fact that both Pim and the narrator are male. At first, the sex of the figure in the mud the protagonist encounters is uncertain, before a "testicle or two" are grasped (46). The same-sex relation of the two figures, "we're two little old men," is emphasized through the comment that there is "something wrong there" (46). While this phrase is a constant refrain, especially in part one of the novel, the "something wrong" in this specific instant might be the shared sex of the two figures. In an important passage that creates the necessary sexualized context, a possible memory of "life in the light" demonstrates a progressive turning away from heteronormative, procreative sex:

> Pam Prim we made love every day then every third day then the Saturday then just the odd time to get rid of it tried to revive it through the arse too late she fell from the window or jumped broken column (52)

Rather like Mercier despairing of "fucking a quag," it appears that the figure in the life in the light has wearied of "straight" sex, leaving the way open for alternative possibilities.

Yet, the focus on the anus in *How It Is* may not be separable from the violence within the relation of the protagonist and Pim—a violence that strongly suggests a sadomasochistic element. The nature of this sadomasochism, and whether it may allow for a new form of relation beyond that which is sanctioned in the heteronormal, is complicated by the debatable nature of sadomasochism itself, that might be seen as 1) a pathology, 2) an acceptable sexual expression that confers a sense of identity and even insight on behalf of the consensual practitioners, 3) an unacceptable repetition of the violence inherent in patriarchal control, 4) a parody and therefore undermining of the violence inherent in patriarchal control, or 5) something that does not exist at all—an unfortunate confusion of two quite distinct phenomena: sadism and masochism.

The sadomasochism of the book is integral to the training that Pim receives at the hands of the narrator. Once singing and speech are gained by clawing at the armpits and thrusting the can opener in the anus, a second stage is entered into in which the protagonist uses his long fingernails to scratch questions into the back of the unfortunate Pim. This again is a long, drawn-out process in which "bloody him all over with Roman capitals gorge on his fables" (53). Throughout all this, the physical nature of this form of torture into speech is crucial. Pim's back is bloodied into sensitivity, as is the armpit into which the figure nails are continually jabbed. Imagining what Pim must be thinking of this regimen of pain, the protagonist offers: "sadism pure and simple no since I may not cry" (54). Giving the name of sadism to what is occurring is perhaps inevitable, yet it raises as many questions as it answers. First, if what Pim imagines the protagonist's aims to be is correct, then pain is not the only desired outcome. If this is the case, then pain is not the end of the brutality but the means through which a further objective is achieved. The aims of sadism will be returned to later. Secondly, the phrasing allows for at least two levels of sadism: that which is "pure and simple" and a further level with less pure and more complicated aims. Sadism is therefore offered as anything other than a simple desire to inflict pain and a pleasure in doing so.

In what the novel describes as "justice," the protagonist who inflicts such pain on Pim will in turn become the victim of such torture:

happy time in its way part two we're talking of part two with Pim how it was good moments for me we're talking of me for him too we're talking

of him too happy too in his way I'll know it later his way of happiness I'll
have it later I have not yet had all (43)

Now a third figure, Bom, will be the sadist to the protagonist's masochist,
and an identical, albeit reversed, process of training through torture will
be undergone. The arrival of Bom to torture the protagonist is not related
within the novel, given that it would so closely resemble the torturing of
Pim that nothing new would be gained. It seems as if it matters little who
is the torturer and who the victim in this "mechanical" sadomasochistic
economy.

It would appear from this brief, sadomasochistic description that forms of
happiness or a new sociability would not be thinkable within such a world;
that, in particular, the torture inflicted and endured would preclude any
notion of happiness at all. And yet, the protagonist speaks of happiness and
pleasure within the site of reciprocal torture. It would be tempting to take
this happiness as ironic, yet it is precisely in this realm of torture that both
Badiou and Bersani mount their claims for the hope, love, and sociability
of the text.

The love of which Badiou speaks, and for which he sees the necessary
conditions within *How It Is*, might need to be differentiated from romantic conceptions of the word. For Badiou, "Beckett never reduces love to
the amalgam of sentimentality and sexuality endorsed by common opinion. Love as a matter of *truth* (and not of opinion) depends upon a pure
event: an encounter whose strength radically exceeds both sentimentality
and sexuality."[31] Such an event in *How It Is* is that between the protagonist
and the figure he names Pim and the procedures of the event as truth will
be detailed shortly. Yet this turn in Beckett's writing—the emergence of
the possibility of the encounter at all, and, proceeding from that, the possibility of love as truth—comes after the dead end of solipsism, best seen in
The Unnamable. It is within such a text that Badiou situates the notion of
torture. This torture occurs within the psyche of the individual subject and
is, indeed, an interrogation of the subject itself: "...an inner violence is necessary, a superegoic perseverance capable of literally submitting the subject
of the *cogito* to the question, to torture."[32] This torturing of the cogito in an
impossible attempt to produce "the pure and silent point of enunciation as
such"[33] inevitably leads to a hopeless impasse. An encounter with an Other,
beyond the solipsism of the cogito, is necessary if hope is to be a possibility.
This point cannot be overstated: love (and the happiness contingent upon it)
cannot occur within the One. For Badiou, *How It Is* forms a pivotal moment
within Beckett's work in that suddenly the One becomes the Two. Badiou
then elaborates on this arithmetic of love, in which One + Two = infinity.

The two in question are not to be thought as part of the numerical conventions of love in which two become one, for "love is neither fusion or effusion. Rather it is the often painstaking condition required for the Two to exist as Two."[34] The two must remain as two distinct Ones, as it were, with the "+" functioning as both a condition of the separation and connection of those distinct Ones. In other words, the other must remain as other in the process of becoming, and continuing as, the Two. This initial opening up to alterity allows for the infinity of such openings as "there is the infinity of the sensible world that the Two traverses and unfolds, where, little by little, it deciphers a truth about the Two itself."[35] The complex abstract numericality that Badiou adopts does not obscure the fact that the process in which "what Beckett quite rightly calls happiness" emerges, that of One + Two = Infinity, clearly depends on their being a second figure onto which the first can be added. For Badiou, the "two coherent ontological theses" of the world of *How It Is* are "the thesis of the One and the thesis of the Infinite," thus privileging the Two as the site of mediation between these two poles. Without Two, there is just the nothing of a dead end solitary cogito.

The figure of the two, or, to put it another way, the encounter with the Other, is also crucial to Bersani's claims for the sociability of *How It Is*. The torture, which Badiou associates with *The Unnamable*, is recognized by Bersani within the processes of *How It Is* through which the Other is encountered. He focuses on the torturing-into-speech that the protagonist inflicts on Pim. Through this process of brutal demands for words, Beckett, according to Bersani, is reflecting upon the method by which all human subjects are defined as subjects and then brought into social relations:

> The Beckettian fable of *How It Is* reenacts this entry into relations as a coercion, a coercion that is, however, psychologically unmotivated. To be tortured is the precondition for being humanized, but this has nothing to do with any sadism on the part of the torturer or any masochism on the part of the victim. Rather, the torture consists in the fact that as soon as we begin to listen to voices we can't help hearing an injunction to speak.[36]

The sadomasochism of the relations is here set aside—an issue that I would argue cannot be set aside quite so easily—and the focus is on the socialization of the subject through coercive violence. Bersani argues that Beckett identifies the violence of this socialization, but also inflects the process with the possibility of pleasure within sociability. So, the reciprocity of the torture is a "moral imperative" that obeys and reenacts the "deep structure" of the process of socialization itself and thus "we enter and maintain linguistic intersubjectivity in a reign of terror, and it is, Beckett proposes, the reciprocity of the terroristic process that we name justice."[37] Bersani proposes, then, that Beckett not only recognizes the terror of both becoming a subject and then taking one's place amidst other subjects but also allows for the result of such a reciprocal terror to be a degree of pleasure:

> Thus the grim regimen of justice is just slightly inflected in *How It Is* by the pleasure of the victim's company. Society, then, would not only reproduce the structure of coercion which made it possible, but might even be a pleasant result of that structure. Most unexpectedly, sociality might—from within the operations of torture but perhaps also in excess of them—generate sociability.[38]

As we have seen for both Bersani and Badiou, although in very different ways, the encounter with an Other is of crucial importance. It allows for the emergence of a degree of pleasurable socialization for the former, and, for the latter, the truth process of love, whereby one encounters alterity and opens up to the infinite possibility of encounters.

My question on returning to the text of *How It Is* is simple, but the answer might not be so: are there two in *How It Is*? If two, then all is feasible within Bersani's and Badiou's interpretations; if less than two, or more than two, then a problem might arise. To support his calculations of the truth process within *How It Is*, Badiou quotes the following passage:

> in other words in simple words I quote on either I am alone and no further problem or else we are innumerable and no further problem either (108)

While this would seem to support that only the one or the infinite are possible within this hellish world, as Badiou contends, there is a difficulty in that the protagonist is not here portrayed as being one at all. Even as he states that he is "alone" he claims that he is quoting some other source, that the word "alone" is not therefore his, but another's. The one that Badiou sees here is already compromised by the act of quotation. The protagonist, even if we wish to see him as quoting from an inner voice, is not a singularity, but already a plurality of possible subjects. To use a phrase of Bersani's, the protagonist is already "self-shattered" rather than a solitary ego coming into an encounter with the Other.

Neither Bersani nor Badiou account for the end of the novel. Apparently out of logical necessity the protagonist asserts the possibility of a million figures in the mud and the need for a deity to arrange the sacks. From one, we have indeed reached closer to infinity, but these millions are only necessities in what amounts to a fictional construct. In order for the justice of the system to work, either three or innumerable figures in the mud are needed. That this is an act of the imagination—a novelistic peopling of this barren world—is attested to by the protagonist himself: "and if on the contrary I alone then no further problem a solution which without a serious effort of the imagination it would seem difficult to avoid" (102). Indeed, the imagination does fail, and in the final pages of the novel the protagonist cancels out all his imaginative hypotheses—from Krim and Kram to the innumerable others, and even the sacks—as "all balls." He is left then alone: "never any Pim no nor any Bom no never anyone no only me no answer only me yes so that was true yes it was true about me yes" (128) In what will later inform the work *Company*, a figure in the dark imagines it all to fend off being alone, to at least taste a moment of company. It would seem, therefore, that the protagonist never encounters an Other at all.

In order to think through this renunciation, it is necessary to return to the notion of sadism that Bersani sees within *How It Is* but that he minimizes. Thus far the terms sadism, masochism, and sadomasochism have been used somewhat loosely, and intentionally so for the problem of definition (as Pim's comment makes clear) is precisely at issue. This definitional difficulty has been felt since the creation of the composite term sadomasochism by Krafft-Ebing in his *Psychopathia Sexualis*. This composite begged the question of the relation between the two elements. To a certain extent, common sense dictated that for masochism to function practically it would need sadism as stimulant and vice versa. This, however, oversimplified the relation, for what pleasure would accrue to the sadist if they knew that their victim was deriving pleasure from the pain being inflicted? The reversibility of sadism into masochism was initially integral to Freud's thinking on the matter. He posited that guilt was the necessary component that would transform sadism into masochism, as he stated in "A Child is Being Beaten":

> …a sense of guilt is invariably the factor that transforms sadism into masochism. But this is certainly not the whole content of masochism. The sense of guilt cannot have won the field alone; a share must also fall to the love-impulse.[…] This being beaten is now a convergence of the sense of guilt and sexual love. *It is not only the punishment for the forbidden genital relation, but also the regressive substitute for that relation,* and from this latter source derives the libidinal excitation which is from this time forward attached to it, and which finds its outlet in masturbatory acts. Here for the first time we have the essence of masochism.[39]

In this scheme, masochism has no originary status, but is seen as growing out of a primary sadistic drive. As such, sadomasochism as a term is valid, since the masochism cannot exist without a prior sadistic phase and the sadistic instinctual drive toward the outside and toward mastery (what Freud terms the "will to power") is, in masochism, "turned round upon the self—that is to say, by means of regression from an object to the ego."[40] Freud posits the source of the guilt within the necessary overcoming of the Oedipal complex. In what is an unusually female perspective for Freud, the guilty turn from sadism to masochism occurs from the repression of incestuous desire for the father. The derivative nature of masochism was somewhat questioned by Freud in later work, particularly "The Economic Problem of Masochism" in which he recognizes "original, erotogenic masochism";[41] however, the essentially inverted relation between sadism and masochism was maintained, allowing for a conflation of the two phenomena in a single composite term.[42]

In Freud's terms, sadomasochism does seem an apt description for what occurs in *How It Is*; there is an apparent reciprocal nature to the turn and turn about of torturer and victim, as if "justice" were to be found in the reversal of positions. The very proof of this justice is that the torturing of the protagonist does not need to be related, because it would be a mere exercise in repetition. Certainly, the sadistic half of the relation bears some comparison to Freud's description. The actions of the protagonist upon Pim are from the very beginning figured as one of "will to power." As soon as Pim is encountered, the protagonist speaks of "a touch of ownership already on the miraculous flesh" (43) and, perhaps with greater moral significance, it is clear that the actions of the protagonist are nonconsensual: "who but for me he would never Pim we're talking of Pim never be but for me anything but a dumb limp lump flat for ever in the mud but I'll quicken him you wait and see" (44). Dumb and limp, Pim has no choice but to suffer the blows that the protagonist visits upon him. This lack of consent is, of course, a further problem that in many ways lies at the heart of the controversy surrounding current S/M practice. For the moment, it is enough to note that the action of the protagonist is aimed outward toward a display of mastery. In this will to power, Pim is objectified, at one point even being reduced to a convenient holder for the can opener: "I put away the tool between his thighs" (59)

As the sadistic half of the equation seems to fit Freud's conception, so the reversal of the roles would seem to support a Freudian reading. Yet, the crucial element of guilt within a Freudian account of the change from sadism to masochism is nowhere to be found in *How It Is*. Rather than a psychic inversion from a projection outwards to a guilt-induced interiority, the mechanism of exchange is precisely that—a mechanism. There is no expression of guilt or a transitional phase in which guilt is seen to be at work. The protagonist was a sadist; he will be a masochist, and that is just how it is.

This lack of guilt points to a possibility, much described in contemporary pro-S/M thinking, which views sadomasochism not so much as an inversion of sadism into masochism, but as a single phenomenon that contains a continuum within it. In short, within S/M, there are no sadists and no masochists, but instead there are SM-ers, as some practitioners prefer to be known. In "Maid to Order: Commercial Fetishism and Gender Power," McClintock notes that S/M challenges norms of identity, power, and gender, by, among other things, pushing the "boundaries of sanctioned gender role behaviour by allowing either gender to assume dominant and submissive roles; [and by mocking] the concept of a unitary, fixed identity by allowing participants to move fluidly in an out of an S/M sexual identity and by facilitating participants' adoption of various fantasy and S/M roles," as Kathy Sisson has summarized.[43] The stress on the fluidity of S/M participants, with a ready exchange between "tops" and "bottoms," with one person now adopting a supposedly dominant role and then subsequently adopting a supposedly submissive one, does not adhere to the separation of sadism and masochism apparent in Freud. Moreover, this mechanism of exchange of positions also counters one key objection to S/M as a practice within gay and lesbian circles in particular. If, as Freud suggests, masochism is a form of guilt-driven sadism-on-the-self, then this seems to imply that the practicing gay or lesbian masochist needs punishment in order to assuage a sense of guilt over their sexuality. Rather than a celebration of queerness and an extension of transgressive behavior, masochism is, it is argued, a form of homophobia directed toward one's own person, an internalized homophobia. For example, Sheila Jeffreys has argued that "sadomasochism and other forms of self-harm should be seen as the result of oppressive forces such as sexual abuse, bullying, physical violence, hatred and contempt, rather than celebrated as 'transgressive' or even as signature gay practices."[44] This anti-S/M thinking has led to the denial of "choice" practiced by, in particular, lesbian SM-ers, as Lorena Leigh Saxe has argued. Saxe goes so far as to assert that S/M reveals that "our desires are socially constructed and thus our 'consent' to sexual activity is not really free: it is not free in the sense of being the autonomous choice of an atomic individual."[45] In contrast to this, Foucault stated that S/M is not "a reproduction, within the erotic relationship, of the structure of power. It is an acting out of power structures by a strategic game that is able to give sexual or bodily pleasure."[46] Therefore, through the fluidity of its protagonist's identities, through its play, S/M mocks and thereby undermines notions of stable power relations and identities. It is, in short, playfully transgressive. Putting to one side the "playful" aspect of this account, the conception of sadomasochism as a continuum rather than a reversal allows for the guilt of which Freud writes to be excised from the phenomena. Rather than a guilt to be assuaged, now there are roles that can be knowingly adopted.

However, it is precisely on this point of the "playfulness" (or *jouissance*) of contemporary S/M practice that *How It Is* again seems to be divergent. While guilt may have been removed from the sadomasochism of the novel, it has hardly been replaced by a sense of free-play and a joy in the possibilities of exploring alternative identities. Although the protagonist is currently a "top" and will become a "bottom," this is a mechanical, structural reversal rather than a witting adoption and parody of available identities. Indeed, identity as such is felt not so much as something to be played with, but as something that is entailed within the structure of power itself, for the apparent aim of the sadism inflicted on Pim, and subsequently on the protagonist himself, revolves around the obligation to have an identity and bear witness to it.

> I nothing only say this say that your life above YOUR LIFE pause my life ABOVE long pause above IN THE in the LIGHT pause light his life above in the light... (62)

And, a little later:

> soon unbearable thump on skull long silence vast stretch of time soon unbearable opener arse or capitals if he has lost the thread YOUR LIFE CUNT ABOVE CUNT HERE CUNT (65)

Pim is obliged (and the word is repeated) to have had some form of life prior to existence in the mud, and, moreover, he is obliged to recount that life to the torturing protagonist. He in turn will then recount the *same life* when he becomes the victim of Bom. The life in the light is then an obligation that is passed on from victim to torturer, supposedly ad infinitum, and the life that is recounted is not sole and unique, but shared by all victims: "dear Pim come back from the living he got it from another that dog's life to take and to leave I'll give it to another [...] that only one life above from age to age eternally" (63). Obliged to have an existence, the victim is obliged to pass on that existence and coerced into doing so. This "obligation to express" is not the playful accessing of alternative subjectivities, but the drudgery of becoming a subjectivity as such.

It should come as little surprise, perhaps, that the playfulness of which Foucault speaks in connection with S/M identities is absent from Beckett's forms of sadism. One need only remember the difficulties that Malone in *Malone Dies* has in his determined attempts to "play" with the surrogate identities he creates: "Such is the earnestness from which [...] I have never been able to depart. From now on it will be different. I shall never do anything any more from now on but play" (4). And yet Malone is unable to keep the earnestness at bay, for he "was already in the toils of earnestness" and relapses to "darkness, to nothingness, to earnestness, to home..." (20). Beckett acknowledges the possibility of playing, and yet playing is repeatedly seen as not overcoming the unfortunate consequences of having any subjectivity at all. Moreover, the obligation to have an existence and to express it is seen within *How It Is* to be the result of the application of power. The torturer exerts power in its crudest form to coerce an acquiescent existence from the victim. Rather than an endorsement of Foucault's playful optimism as regards S/M, *How It Is* would seem to be closer in spirit to Leo Bersani's opposition to such an optimism. Bersani writes that: "S/M lifts a social repression in laying bare the reality behind the subterfuges, but in its open embrace of the structures themselves and its undisguised appetite for the ecstasy they promise, it is fully complicit with a culture of death."[47] *How It Is* similarly lays bare the structures, yet subjectivity, itself regrettable in Beckettian thought, is seen as being tortured into speech by the imposition of power and play is not a palliative for that.

One reason, perhaps, for the absence of the possibility of *jouissance* of which Foucault writes within the knowing adoption of identities within S/M could be that there is no structural inversion between sadism and masochism within *How It Is*; rather than sadomasochism as the sexual and violent paradigm at work in the novel, it may be that *How It Is* remains firmly within sadism "pure and simple." As Gilles Deleuze has demonstrated, sadism and masochism, so often combined, can and should remain distinct. For Deleuze,

> the masochist is able to change into a sadist by expiating, the sadist into a masochist on condition that he does not expiate. If its existence is too hastily taken for granted the sadomasochistic entity is liable to become a crude syndrome that fails to satisfy the demands of genuine symptomatology.[48]

He argues that the term "sadomasochism" has long obscured the utterly different dynamics and causalities of two distinct phenomena. One key point is the access to pleasure the sadist has when she or he is the victim rather than the torturer. On the face of it, the self-proclaimed sadist taking pleasure in the submissive role would seem to attest to the reversibility of sadism and masochism, yet Deleuze argues that the "pain he suffers is an ultimate pleasure, not because it satisfies a need to expiate or a feeling of guilt, but because it confirms him in his inalienable power and gives him supreme certitude."[49] The pleasure then accrues not from a reversal of positions but from the ultimate success of the sadistic pleasure in crime, as La Borgèse in Sade's *Juliette* attests: "I would wish that my aberrations lead me like the lowest of creatures to the fate which befits their wantonness: for me the scaffold would be a throne of exquisite bliss."[50] The apparently masochistic pleasure derives from an overarching sadistic project, and the psychic processes of sadism and masochism, according to Deleuze, could not be more distinct. Interestingly, Deleuze (in contradistinction to Bataille) firmly allies the sadistic drive with that loftiest of Enlightenment qualities: reason. He claims that "[Sade] is interested in [...] demonstrating that reasoning itself is a form of violence, and that he is on the side of violence..." This insight would again seem to be supported by *How It Is*. In order for the system of perpetual pairings of torturer and victim to work, the protagonist occupies much of Book three with reasoned calculations of the necessary attributes that must be in place. He reasons out, for example, the permutations of a million figures in the mud and how the sacks would have to be distributed between them and, again at the coaxing of reason, even posits the necessity of a deity to organize the proper positioning of those sacks. This generation of a further 999,997 individuals out of apparently reasoned necessity bears witness to an underlying repetitiveness in sadistic reason, to which Deleuze also points:

> This is the clue to the meaning of repetitiveness in Sade's writing and of the monotony of sadism. [...] the libertine is confined to illustrate his total demonstration with partial inductive processes borrowed from secondary nature. He cannot do more than accelerate and condense the motions of partial violence. The condensation on the other hand implies that violence must not be dissipated under the sway of inspiration or impulse, or even governed by the pleasures it might afford, since those pleasures would still bind him to secondary nature, but it must be exercised in cold blood, and condensed by this very coldness, the coldness of demonstrative reason. Hence the well-known *apathy* of the libertine...[51]

Apathy is key here. The sadist, according to Deleuze, is not in the throes of passion but in the cold-blooded demonstration of "how it is." This same apathy marks the novel, for although sexual passion is hinted at and remains part of the supposed "light in the life" that forms the necessary context of the sadism described, sexual satisfaction is itself not the aim of the sadism and is not apparent within the sadistic acts performed. Indeed, the narrator claims that he "forgave nothing never could never disapproved anything really not even cruelty to animals never loved anything" (34). Within this overarching disinterest, the aim of the torture is to coerce existence from the lumpen, dumb Pim and for that existence to be witnessed by the protagonist and then in turn transferred to Bom. Bereft of a unique subjectivity (one might argue blessedly bereft) the protagonist violently claims that of his victim. As Deleuze argues: "The ultimate victims of the sadist are the mother and the ego. *His ego exists only in the external world*: this is fundamental significance of sadistic apathy. *The sadist has no other ego than that of his victims.*"[52] The sadism in *How It Is* is dependent on just this projection of the ego onto the external world, with the aim of it then to be reflected back onto, and appropriated by, the protagonist, as he himself makes clear: "cruelty suffering so paltry and brief/the paltry need of a life a voice of one who has neither" (106). The means to this end are those of the violence proper to sadism. Yet that is not quite the whole story, for the sadism here is not "pure and simple." Not only does the protagonist violently and with reason drag Pim into existence, he also insists that Pim loves him, most explicitly stated as "DO YOU LOVE ME CUNT" (105). The phrasing and the graphic use of capital letters throughout the phrase demonstrate the violently hostile demand to be loved, and thereby to be witnessed. It is love demanded, quite literally, with menaces from a Pim who has been tortured into speech and subjectivity for the purpose of giving the protagonist some form of identity. Love, existence, and witnessing are all seen as cold, apathetic exertions of violent power.

However, if there is a form of love expressed in *How It Is*, it is paradoxically through this very renunciation of an apparent "other." Badiou and Bersani may be correct in sensing the hope of happiness that the text occasionally expresses. However, they do not take into account an ethical question: at what cost is such limited happiness bought, and is the price of torture, coercion, and violence too high for such a reward? The return to the single figure, alone without company, is an ethical decision not to force subjectivity onto another. Alone again, the hope then arises that the mechanical economy of sadistic violence inherent within such a subjectivity can be brought to a close, possibly, although it is far from certain, through death of the narrating subject itself: "DIE screams I MAY DIE screams I SHALL DIE screams good" (129).

Yet, even as the narrator renounces company, a form of relation via the anus may still be traced in what amounts to a recognition of the universality of suffering.[53] The "other" can be laid to one side precisely because the suffering takes no cognisance of the individual:

> …what the fuck I quote does it matter who suffers faint waver here faint tremor
> the fuck who suffers who makes suffer who cries who to be left in the peace in the dark the mud […] always the same imagination looking for a hole that he may be seen no more in this faery who drinks that drop of piss of being and who with his last gasp pisses it to drink the moment it's someone each in his turn as our justice wills and never any end it wills that too all dead or none (115)

The equation of being with waste that is recycled from individual to individual effectively posits the individual as no more than a conduit and makes that which is "willed" of more importance than the figure that momentarily contains that "willing." The terms are evocative of Schopenhauer's conception of the will-to-live that takes on the figure of the individual *in time*, yet which of itself persists beyond the individual in perpetuity. The desire to "be seen no more in this faery" through an act of imaginative suspension is consonant with a recognition that while one may imagine one is an individual one is in fact little more than a passageway of the will. And, as Schopenhauer makes clear on many occasions, while we are prey to the will, we are prey to the suffering inherent within desire and life.

The being as waste equation is most clearly marked in *How It Is* as a relation between the figures in the mud and fecal elimination. They are likened to "shit in the guts" (108) within a world of mud that is "nothing more than all our shit […] billions of us crawling and shitting in their shit hugging like a treasure in their arms the wherewithal to crawl and shit a little more…" (44). William Hutchings's article "Shat into Grace" admirably insists on the universality of this fecal relation and that the scatology of the book's vision "is even more all-encompassing than Swift's, since no person, place, or thing is exempted from the universal characterization of dung."[54] This, Hutchings argues, applies to a previous life as much as to, what he calls, the postmortem world of the novel itself. However, Hutchings does see a way out of the shit. "Life," he argues, "is a sequence of rites of 'passage' through one meatus or another—urethral and vaginal ones first, then (life-long) the oral and anal. […] At death the soul is 'born upwards' in the ultimate oral expulsion, so that the postmortem effort to be "shat into grace" from the cosmic body begins."[55] Can one, though, be "shat into grace," to use Hutchings's adaptation of Beckett's words, and finally eliminated in death? Hutchings's phrase is derived from the following verselet:

> ...we are talking of a procession advancing in jerks or spasms like shit in the guts till one wonders days of great gaiety if we shall not end one after another or two by two being shat into the open air the light of day the regimen of grace (108)

The passage is part of the section in which the narrator posits a "him in charge of the sacks" as a God-like figure who oversees all, and the language is certainly redolent of Judeo-Christian salvation with the "lumfs," to use Little Hans's term, falling two-by-two like animals leaving the Ark. Of course, this omniscient figure is ultimately rejected by the novel, which leaves the religious language of the passage open to doubt, not least the concept of grace. It will be noticed, however, that the narrator does not say he will be "shat into grace" but rather shat into a *regimen of grace.* Rather than accessing grace directly, the waste expelled would be subject to a prescribed course of treatment, an atonement, under the auspices of grace. Beckett here has a very precise conception of the workings of grace, which is not gratuitous but functions precisely to overcome the original sin of having been born. However, once the figure of the deity is removed in the novel, then the concept of grace is also made redundant, leaving only the suffering inherent to birth and subsequent life intact.

Nevertheless, Hutchings is surely correct to note the relation between anal and vaginal expulsion, a relation that then posits life itself as "being" a shit, and this necessarily returns us to the anus of Molloy's mother, the orifice through which (as was seen in Chapter 1) Molloy imagines he was born and through which he had his "first taste of the shit." Molloy, as waste product within a world of waste, is a foreshadowing of the literal birth-into-shit of *How It Is.* Within the later novel, images repeatedly revolve around a fetal/fecal combination with the protagonist in the mud huddling his sack likened to a fetus: "the knees drawn up the back bent in a hoop the tiny head near the knees curled around the sack Belacqua fallen over on his side..." (18). The Belacqua allusion not only recalls a pre-life existence in the womb from which the protagonist will be expelled but also a postmortem existence as one of Dante's figures in purgatory. As such, the image of Belacqua as fetus and as excrement effectively collapses the supposed poles of birth and death. The narrator similarly sees himself in another image as "quite tiny the same as now more or less only tinier quite tiny no more objects no more food and I live the air sustains me the mud I live on" (12). As Hutchings has pointed out, this suggests the tiny narrator as a fetus "amid the placental sac's amniotic mud,"[56] yet, as the fetus is "the same as" the narrator, then the fetus is also being offered as a form of excrement that will soon be eliminated into life. Once eliminated, the child will in turn excrete his "gift" to the world: "I pissed and shat another image in my crib never so clean since" (5). The fetal/fecal and anal/vaginal conflation is epitomized by a "good old question" the narrator puts to himself: "if always like that since the world world for me from the murmurs of my mother shat into the incredible tohu-bohu" (35). Although "tohu-bohu" is idiomatic French for confusion, which is apposite enough, its Biblical resonances precisely address the scenario of *How It Is* in which the protagonist is dumped. It connotes a formlessness (the original Hebrew for the state of the cosmos prior to God's injunction for light at Genesis 1:2) and the "tohu" part alone a wilderness or, quite literally, a *waste*land. The world of *How It Is* is a tohu-bohu, a formlessness in which the narrator and the other excrement merge. In this sense, the narrator is fundamentally expelled into an excremental wasteland.

This fetal/fecal and anus/vagina conflation casts a somewhat different light on what Peter Boxall has described as Molloy's "paean to the arsehole" in which he wonders whether the anus may be the "true portal of our being" as now our being is nothing more, nor less, than fecal matter. Although that paean admits for the possibility of penetration ("Nothing goes in, or so little, that is not rejected on the spot, or very nearly"[81]), which Boxall correctly notes, the anus is still figured primarily as a site of elimination: "Almost everything revolts it that comes from without and what comes from within does not seem to receive a very warm welcome either" (*M* 81). Yet, the elimination itself forms a mode of relationality, which Molloy characterizes as a "link between me and the other excrement" (80). The anus/vagina as site of expulsion allows for the alliance of birth into suffering (the expulsion from the womb) with birth as shit into the shit. Although this may offer some form of relation—a sense, perhaps, that we are all in this together, that all must be expelled as waste into a world of waste—it is open to question whether the terms of this relation as such are acceptable. If this is the only relation that may be guaranteed, perhaps a denial of all relation might be preferable.

CHAPTER 5

Sex and Aesthetics

The turn toward alternative expressions of sexuality and away from heterosexual penetration has been shown to be predicated on the horror of physical reproduction. For Beckett, such reproduction entails the production of new life and, therefore, the continuation of suffering. The logical solution to this problem of humanity is precisely that offered by Dr. Piouk in *Eleutheria*—the cessation of the species. Yet such a renunciation of the world creates a particular set of problems for the artist whose business it is to create new, peopled worlds. The aesthetic, practical, and ultimately ethical difficulties in which this places Beckett, which have already been encountered in *How It Is* in the previous chapter, provide much of the impetus for his restless exploration of form and media in the postwar works.

Fighting the Will-to-Live: Sterility, Suffering, and Continuance

The opportunities for physical reproduction in Beckett's works are greatly reduced as a series of sterile scenarios—from the postapocalyptic landscape of *Endgame* to the infertile inhabitants of Foxrock and environs in *All That Fall*—denude the natural world of its procreative capacities. If one takes *Happy Days*, for instance, then the possibilities of sexuality and Schopenhauer's will-to-live playing a role would seem to be all but eliminated. The play's setting in a barren landscape, by which the once sexually active Winnie (accentuated by her still prominent décolletage in the first act) is slowly being consumed, transfers that sterility onto Winnie herself. Although one might wish to figure Winnie's return to earth as a form of returning to the womb (and hence, of course, death), one should not, therefore, neglect the less figural moments of sexual interest in the play. Sterility is a given in the world of Winnie and Willie. However, this sterility is predicated on a still remaining sexual interest. Willie's pornographic postcard is a case in point. With a mix of prudishness and shocked fascination, Winnie itemizes what she sees:

> Heavens what are they up to! [*She looks for spectacles, puts them on and examines card.*] No but this is just genuine pure filth! [*Examines card.*] Make any nice-minded person want to vomit! [*Impatience of Willie's fingers. She looks for glass, takes it up and examines card through glass. Long pause.*] What does that creature in the background think he's doing? [*Looks closer.*] Oh no really! [*Impatience of fingers. Last long look. She lays down glass, takes edge of card between right forefinger and thumb, averts head, takes nose between left forefinger and thumb.*] Pah! [*Drops card.*] Take it away! [*Willie's arm disappears. His hand reappears immediately, holding card. Winnie takes off spectacles, lays them down, gazes before her. During what follows Willie continues to relish card, varying angles and distances from his eyes.*] Hog's setae. [*Puzzled expression.*] What exactly is a hog? (CDW 144)

The comic interplay between the expression of disgust and Winnie's closer and closer examination of the card maintains both an almost puritanical disdain alongside a compelling prurience. Winnie is interested but will not let herself appear to be so. What the card depicts—a couple in a (perhaps unusual) sex act with a masturbating voyeur looking on—might be taken from a *More Pricks than Kicks* story and so is a recognizably Beckettian sexual scene, mixing scopophilia and masturbation with coitus. Just as Malone watched a couple from his bedroom window, Winnie cannot at first imagine what is actually occurring, but once she does realize she provides the supposedly necessary moral indignation of "just genuine pure filth." The phrasing perfectly captures her ambivalence toward the sex depicted, for the words of condemnation are themselves words of value. The sex act is "just" or fitting; it is "genuine" rather than copied, derived, or faked; it is "pure" or inimical and disinterested. The final "filth" has excremental overtones, which in a Freudian account would also be something to be valued rather than shunned as abhorrent. Indeed Winnie treats the card as excrement, not only in her holding her nose up at it and wanting it to be taken away but also in her fascination with the sex seen on the card. Winnie then proceeds as if the card had never been seen and turns to talk of the hair of her toothbrush. Yet this apparent non sequitur is in fact (in a rather Joycean way) indicative of a current of unacknowledged connection. Winnie turns to think of the hog—a castrated male pig, as Willie informs us—as soon as she has seen sexual acts. The castration could then be seen as an answer to the sexuality on display on the card. "The creatures" indulging in such sexual activity might be better off castrated as the hog has been. The "happy expression" on Winnie's face when Willie finally defines a hog for her "increases" when he continues that the "castrated male swine" are "reared for slaughter" (159). As the swine is castrated, it cannot be reared for rearing and so only death remains.

This might account for Winnie's disgust at the sexually explicit card, but it doesn't quite account for her interest in that same card. Given her condition, why does sexual interest persevere? Willie and Winnie laugh together only once in the play, and then at one of God's "little jokes" (150). She sees some ants carrying little white balls:

Willie: Eggs.
Winnie: [*Arresting gesture.*] What?
Willie: Eggs [*Pause. Gesture to lay down glasses.*] Formication.
Winnie: [*Arresting gesture.*] What?
[*Pause.*]
Willie: Formication.
[*Pause. She lays down spectacles, gazes before her. Finally.*]
Winnie. [*Murmur.*] God. [*Pause. Willie laughs quietly. After a moment she joins in. They laugh together.…*] (150)

The joke, one of God's "poorer ones," takes a while for it to be registered by the characters, based, as it is, upon the confusion between "formication" and "fornication." Winnie naturally first mistakes the word for "fornication" not only because it is much more common but also because she is watching the results of fornication in the shape of the ant's eggs being carried before her. She mentally, and quite rightly, connects eggs with sex. "Formication" though means something quite different: "a sensation like insects crawling over the skin."[1] The pun between fornication and formication suggests that the former is an itch that cannot be scratched, a perpetual irritant on the skin itself, which, according to some medical opinion, will only get worse if one gives in to the urge to scratch. God's joke is not just the near-homonymy of the words but that He has given us a drive that is beyond our control and however much we try to sate it, it will only return all the more forcefully. Sex is the itch that cannot be scratched, but, at least, one can try to ensure that the present generation is the last to suffer from it.

Such sterility as seen in *Happy Days* does not prevent the continued suffering existence of Winnie and Willie. Yet there is at least the hope that

Willie and Winnie may be the last of their kind; the very reason Malone praises the ethically issueless sperm of Macmann. The world of *Happy Days* and the physical condition of the protagonists suggest that Beckett is working to reduce the possibilities for the resurgence of the will-to-live and, in the shape of Winnie being sucked back into the earth, almost reversing the regrettable process of parturition. Beckett's sterile worlds may seek to prevent the continuation of the species, but can do little to assuage the suffering of those already condemned to live. In this respect, *All That Fall* captures both the imperative to bring procreation to a halt and the suffering inherent within the continuing life of the individual.

There has long been a critical consensus regarding the reading of the biblical allusion that gives *All That Fall* its title. Dan and Maddy Rooney's "wild laughter" at the thought that the "Lord upholdeth all that fall" is taken as a bitter and ironic reflection on the absence of the Lord and the inevitability of falling. The reading gains credence from two main themes: that decay and suffering dominate much of the play, and the assumption that the Beckettian world does not have a Lord to fall back on, hence making the suffering experienced essentially meaningless. However, this persuasive ironic reading of "the Lord upholdeth all that fall" has had the unfortunate effect of precluding a contrary reading wherein the play demonstrates that the words of the Bible are, unfortunately, far too accurate; the Lord *does* uphold all that fall, condemning them to go on, when to fall, to cease, would be the greatest benefit. Or, perhaps more accurately, one might say that, even in the absence of the Lord, falling is not gifted to the residents of Boghill.

It is beyond doubt that decay and concomitant suffering permeate *All That Fall*. Mrs. Rooney's journey to the station is a catalogue of illness and decline, be it her own or that of her neighbors. Clas Zilliacus sums up the view of many when he writes: "The incidents in the play serve as a stave for a threnody on the theme of decay and meaningless death."[2] I hope to qualify Zilliacus's statement by noting a contrary strain in the play, wherein, rather than decay leading to death, we are presented with the annoyingly stubborn survival of life. Dying is not being dead.

Mr. Slocum's car is a case in point. "All morning she went like a dream and now she is dead" (*CDW* 178). A meaningless death, perhaps, but, of course, the car is not fully certified dead. In a rather grim joke, once it is dead it is choked, and the choking brings the car roaring back to life. Further, Mr. Barrell asks: "Who's that crucifying his gearbox, Tommy?" (178). Death of the car through crucifixion inevitably leads to a resurrection. Similarly, Mr. Tyler's back tire may be deflated, yet he still insists on pedaling on. The mechanisms of life go on regardless of suffering and take no account of the wishes of the likes of Maddy Rooney. Rather like Clov in

Endgame, she dreams of "dissolution" and a time when the last dust will fall. Unfortunately, the dust will not fall for Maddy: "This dust will not settle in our time. And when it does some great roaring machine will come and whirl it all skyhigh again" (176).

The point is comically underlined by Beckett's use of the sound effects of animals:

All is still. No living soul in sight. There is no one to ask. The world is feeding. The wind—[*Brief wind.*]—scarcely stirs the leaves and the birds—[*Brief chirp.*]—are tired of singing. The cows—[*Brief moo.*]—and sheep—[*Brief baa.*]—ruminate in silence. The dogs—[*Brief bark.*]—are hushed and the hens—[*Brief cackle.*]—sprawl torpid in the dust. We are alone. There is no one to ask. (192)

Maddy's paean to stillness is undercut by the stubborn vivacity of the animals to which she refers. In a letter to Zilliacus, Beckett claimed that he "would have preferred true animal sounds to the BBC human imitators,"[3] which would have made the contrast between the human conscious wish and the intrusive will-to-live interjections of the animals all the more apparent. According to Schopenhauer, the "animal learns to know death only when he dies." The human figure, however, "*consciously* draws every hour nearer his death."[4] (My emphasis.) One might consciously draw near, which does not necessarily entail reaching, while the will-to-live refuses to acquiesce.

As the animals and machines refuse to lie down into death, so, contrary to their wishes, the majority of the human characters remain alive. Christy's wife and daughter are no better and no worse, respectively. Mr. Tyler's daughter, after a full hysterectomy, remains "Fair, fair." Mr. Slocum's mother manages to keep going and is kept "out of pain." The old lady remains to play "Death and the Maiden" in her ruined, but habitable, house. In a rather literal demonstration of my reading of the "Lord upholdeth all that fall," it is suggested that Hardy fell, but found an arm to sustain him, as Mr. Tyler relates: "We used to climb together. [Pause] I saved his life once. [Pause] I have not forgotten it" (174).

The wish to fall, never again to rise, is consistently expressed throughout the play. Maddy, for example, begs, of no one in particular: "Oh let me just flop down flat on the road like a big fat jelly out of a bowl and never move again" (174). She complains that the spell spent in her sick bed was "not long enough" (180) and certainly not long enough for her to drift "gently down into the higher life" (181). Similarly, Dan wishes to be "buried alive" within the mausoleum of his workplace, nor would he mind being entombed within the never moving train carriage, if only his prostate would allow, but short of fully certified death and hoped for ease, Dan knows full well that he will be drummed back into the restless row of the world:

> [T]he dusting, sweeping, airing, scrubbing, waxing, waning, washing, mangling, drying, mowing, clipping, raking, rolling, scuffling, shovelling, grinding, tearing, pounding, banging, and slamming.(193)

What begins as a catalogue of onerous daily chores becomes more a list of the manner in which Dan would vent his frustration upon the material world and, more importantly perhaps, how the material world would violently act upon him once he has been loosed from the stultified sanctuary of his office.

Dan suspects that he will not be allowed simply to fall into lethargy in preparation for, and imitation of, death, and the play amply suggests that his suspicion is correct. In an important exchange, Dan asks of Maddy:

> *Mr. Rooney* [. . .] But why do we not sit down somewhere? Are we afraid we shall never rise again?
> *Mrs. Rooney*: Sit down on what?
> *Mr. Rooney*: On a bench, for example.
> *Mrs. Rooney*: There is no bench.
> *Mr. Rooney*: Then on a bank. Let us sit down upon a bank.
> *Mrs. Rooney*: There is no bank.
> *Mr. Rooney*: Then we cannot. [Pause] I dream of other roads, in other lands. Of another home, another—[he hesitates]—another home. (192)

Maddy and Dan do not sit because they fear never to rise, they do not sit for fear that the Lord will not upholdeth all that so fall. Rather they do not sit because there is no opportunity to sit. Maddy and Dan's world is so arranged that the final fall is not an option. The Lord, if one must be posited, insists on holding them up. Yet Dan's dream is of a land, a true home, where one can sit and truly never rise again. That land is not Boghill. One might wish to qualify Zilliacus, and say that "meaningless death" is present in the play, but also there is the annoyingly stubborn presence of the continuation of meaningless life, of precisely *not* falling.

Yet, despite this pattern of continuance in the play, there is undeniably death. However, the three fully certified deaths of the play—of Minnie, of a hen, and of the child on the train—are closely allied not just with the death of the individual but with the death of procreative possibilities and, hence, with the death of the species. While *this* generation pants on, the hope might remain that the suffering can end through an end of regeneration.

The death of little Minnie, and the subsequent childlessness of Maddy, "may have been the outcome of a miscarriage which rendered Maddy sterile,"[5] as Zilliacus has perceptively suggested. The "may" is well-advised, but certainly the play associates Minnie with the end of procreation, for she too, had she lived, would have been entering menopause, a sense reinforced by Mr. Tyler's forever grandchildless state. As noted earlier, the sterility of the play is again in evidence by the figure of the Christy's hinny, which as the offspring of a donkey and a male horse, is unable to procreate. When the hinny finally falls, no little hinnies will take up the burden of dung.

The death of the hen, a seemingly inconsequential moment in the play, overtly focuses on death as the cessation not only of the individual but also of the continuation of the species through procreation:

Mind the hen [*Scream of brakes. Squawk of hen.*] Oh, mother, you have squashed her, drive on, drive on, [...] What a death! One minute picking happy in the dung, on the road, in the sun, with now and then a dust bath, and then—bang!—all her troubles over. [*Pause.*] All the laying and hatching. [*Pause.*] Just one great squawk and then...peace. (179)

Mary Bryden writes that "Mrs. Rooney is merely reflective, not mournful, about the abrupt death (and thus enforced sterility) of the previously prolific hen." Bryden is certainly correct in placing this in the context of sterility, which, she says, is "part of the natural order." Bryden goes on to suggest that "[s]exual activity has become impossible and in the most part unlamented"[6] in the drama of the 1950s and early 1960s, and that procreation is viewed as one of the "intrinsic dangers" of sex.[7] The dangers here inevitably refer beyond the individual to the continuance of the species itself. The reference to "all the laying and hatching" might merely bear witness to Maddy's own preoccupation with reproduction, and even to a not entirely wholehearted regret for the passing of her sexual salad days, but it also serves to emphasize the notion that death of the individual means, in one case at least, the death of the drive toward a new generation: "*All the* laying and hatching."

Schopenhauer suggested that reproduction should be eschewed on the grounds of pity for the unborn, as argued in the Introduction. Such a pity exists within Beckett's world, but it is more often reserved for those that have already been born, and is expressed across the works, finding its place in *All That Fall* as Mr. Tyler curses "the wet Saturday night of [his] conception" (175). Feeling pity for that which does not exist might well be felt to fall short of a "purely rational" consideration of which Schopenhauer speaks, but the prevention of future suffering and death through the refusal to reproduce, or, if necessary, through a process of judicious culling, can be seen as a purely rational, if pitiless, form of fatally wounding fatality. Dr. Piouk in *Eleutheria* is Beckett's most overt exponent of the necessity of sterility and euthanasia:

> I would ban reproduction. I would perfect the condom and other devices and bring them into general use. I would establish teams of abortionists, controlled by the State. I would apply the death penalty to any woman guilty of giving birth. I would drown all newborn babies. I would militate in favour of homosexuality, and would myself set the example. And to speed things up, I would encourage recourse to euthanasia by all possible means, although I would not make it obligatory. Those are the broad outlines. (*E* 44)

New life, then, is to be prevented or ruthlessly cut short, but for those already in existence, euthanasia is only a possibility and not an obligation. In effect, new generations are prevented, while the present generation is allowed to continue on as best it might. Ironically, Dr. Piouk is not himself able follow his own plan. Seemingly unaware of his own hypocrisy, he states the reasons for his wanting a child as "*primo,* to entertain me in my leisure hours, which are forever becoming briefer and more desolate; *secundo,* so that he can receive the torch from my hands, when they are no longer strong enough to carry it" (45). Piouk's self-interest, and his need for continuance by proxy, outweighs his disinterested desire to bring humanity to an end, suggesting that, if even the most enthusiastic exponent of the end of reproduction cannot follow his own dictates, then humanity will be condemned to continue its guilty, problematic existence. Nevertheless, Dr. Piouk's radical and logical solution is, frankly and clearly, a method to bring humanity, with all its sufferings and difficulties, to an end.

Vivian Mercier clearly states that in *Endgame*, "Hamm and Clov want to ensure the permanent extinction of the human race."[8] Undoubtedly, procreation, for procreator or for the unfortunate child, is seen in the play as an evil best avoided if possible. Nagg is indeed an "accursed progenitor" (*CDW* 96), in that he passes on the curse of living and so the curse of suffering to his progeny. Thus, any possibilities of regeneration are to be nipped in the bud, whether they be crab-lice ("But humanity might start from there all over again!") or the once bonny Mother Pegg ("...naturally she's extinguished" [108, 112]). However, the play is ambivalent toward any responsibility to bring humanity to an end. The small boy, who is described by Clov as a "potential procreator," is not murdered by a gaff-wielding Clov, and Hamm seems curiously noncommittal: "If he exists he'll die there or he'll come here" (131). For someone so concerned that humanity might sprout from a louse,

Hamm's laissez-faire attitude is at best inconsistent. Of course, Clov exaggerates somewhat, for the boy might be a potential procreator but with whom would he procreate? Nevertheless, the boy offers a means of continuation *free from the business of sexual reproduction*, and, in this, the desire for continuance, as hypocritically exemplified by Dr. Piouk, is negotiated without the necessity for the continuance of the species itself through reproduction. As with Clov before him, the boy offers Hamm the possibility of continuance through the fictional paternity of adoption. Paul Lawley has perceptively identified the importance of the adoption trope in the play when he writes that "adoption is the figure for the fictional process itself, the only acceptable means of self-perpetuation for characters who reject the processes of nature."[9] It is the status of this fictional, rather than natural, means of continuance that is of crucial concern. Thus the child, as Clov before him, will ensure the continuance of Hamm through an adoption that is predicated on the blood-ties of paternity being severed. The cycle of "birth to into death" (*MD* 114) will therefore be broken while Hamm will be in a position, in Dr. Piouk's terms, to pass on his torch to a fictional second generation.

As adoption functions as a form of fictional regenerative continuance within the play, so fiction itself, or aesthetic reproduction, similarly offers a means of going on while eschewing procreation. Hamm, who offers a paradigm of just such a peopling of the world through aesthetic reproduction, imagines himself alone in the refuge at last, mother and father dead, and Clov finally gone: "Then babble, babble, words, like the solitary child who turns himself into children, two, three, so as to be together, and whisper together, in the dark" (126). Out of nothing, the child reproduces himself in a form of aesthetic genesis that ensures that the means for continuance are generated without recourse to that kernel of the will-to-live, the genitals. As such, a sterile form of aesthetic continuance replaces the reprehensible fecundity of sexual reproduction. Clas Zilliacus noted that *All That Fall* is a "more densely populated canvas than any other Beckett play."[10] The population of that canvas amidst the barren sterility that dominates the radio play (which is just sound coming out of nothing) is an indication of the trope that was to be played out through much of Beckett's oeuvre in which sexual reproduction is replaced by aesthetic regeneration as a means of creating out of nothing, quite literally out of thin air and out of the dark, a peopled world.

Krapp and the Relation of Sex and Aesthetics

The efficacy of aesthetic forms of reproduction, and whether the ethical difficulties of actual procreation can be avoided, are issues to which Beckett repeatedly returns in both the plays and prose of the 1940s and 1950s. *Krapp's Last Tape* is well-placed to initially address the difficulties of the relation between aesthetic creation and the physical, sexualized world. The most common interpretation of that relation is one whereby sex is renounced in order to pursue a nonsexual and therefore more spiritual pursuit of art. (One wonders, by way of digression, why art is so often assumed to be a spiritual pursuit; as Malone alone demonstrates, the materiality of writing is often a pressing concern.) As the Introduction noted, this renunciation can be figured within the supposed dualism of Manichaeism, whereby the "light" of the spirit attempts to free itself from the "dark" of matter, with which sex and the female can be associated. This light/dark polarity would seem to be clear cut, yet the two critics who put Manichaeism at the heart of *Krapp* somewhat surprisingly differ on what belongs to the light and what to the dark. For James Knowlson, "Krapp is only too ready to associate woman with the darker side of existence and he clearly sees her as appealing to the dark, sensual side of man's nature, distracting him from the cultivation of the understanding and the spirit."[11] For S. E. Gontarski, however, the "struggle to control the body's needs (in Manichaean imagery the light or feminine side of his nature) by dedicating himself to spiritual or intellectual matters (the dark side of his nature) is Krapp's preoccupation."[12] To put this plainly, Knowlson associates woman with darkness and Gontarski associates woman with light, and "spiritual matters" are associated by Gontarski with darkness and by Knowlson with light. There can be little doubt that the light and dark imagery of the play is of crucial importance, yet this divergence of opinion over what Knowlson describes as a "fundamental dualism"[13] calls into question just how fundamental that dualism might be, both within Manichaeism and the play itself.

This divergence of opinion amongst two of Beckett's foremost critics might arise from a similar divergence on the nature of Manichaeism. Henri-Charles Puech, who, along with Julien Ries, has long been regarded as "the touchstone of the received wisdom in the study of Manichaeism,"[14] primarily considered the religion to be a "Gnosticism of an intellectual type"[15] but also essentially one of renunciation of the world in order to restore an *original* cosmic duality between light and dark that, in this world, has become mixed, with the light imprisoned within matter. "Accordingly," writes Puech, "the entire ethic consists in a single commandment: abstain, in order to acquire and preserve purity, a largely negative commandment." The Elect member of the religion must then devote himself (it is debatable whether women were allowed to be members of the Elect) to "renunciation, withdrawal, removal."[16] The Manichaean prohibitions (*signaculum oris, signaculum manuum,* and *signaculum sinus*) were, therefore, designed to facilitate this renunciation. In these terms, Krapp could be likened to a failed member of the Elect who cannot withdraw from the world sufficiently well, as his dependence on bananas, alcohol, and sex with Fanny would suggest. This is certainly the Krapp that Knowlson sees who "has attempted to separate the light from the darkness in his life in order to rise above the dark side of his nature and liberate the light of understanding..."[17] This Gnostic reading, of both the play and Manichaeism, interprets Krapp (as Belacqua long before him) as some form of "dud mystic" (*Dream* 186) who has not the will to renounce the pleasures of the flesh in favor of the pleasures of the spirit.

Recently, the work of Jason David BeDuhn has challenged this Gnostic model of renunciation by emphasizing the ritual practices of the Manichaeans and the vital role that the body played within those rituals. The light, or in BeDuhn's favored term the "Living Self," is trapped within all physical matter. The job of the Elect is then to release this "divine substance" through a process of alimentary distillation in the ritual meal that forms the center of Manichaean practice. So, "the disciplinary regimens are said to correct and perfect the deficient human body [of the Elect], rendering it into an instrument that can actively assist in the liberation of the Living Self from its 'mixture' in the universe."[18] It is on these tenets that Augustine attacks the Manichaean, Faustus, claiming that "[a]ccording to your notion, Christ is confined in everything you eat, and is released by digestion from the additional confinement of your intestines."[19] The terms Augustine adopts may be unfair, but, according to BeDuhn, the process he identifies is at the core of Manichaean thought and practice. Rather than withdrawing from the world, then, the Elect act as a very physical mediation between this world in which the light and dark are mixed and the pleroma to which the liberated light ascends.

This shift in the Manichaean paradigm allows for a similar shift in the question of the relation between sex and aesthetic creation in *Krapp's Last Tape*. Rather than assuming that art is a purely spiritual affair, and therefore the younger Krapp necessarily distances himself from the distractions of the flesh in order to pursue his magnum opus, the play's light and dark imagery can be suggestive of the mixed nature of the world from which art is then distilled, thus making the relation between mind and body the crux of aesthetic creation. The world to which Krapp has reduced himself certainly attests to the mixed nature of the world, with his clothes incorporating both white and black, and the contrasting dark shadows and pool of light of the room, which, of course, entails a great deal of gray rather than a strict demarcation from light to dark. This mixing of the opposites of light and dark is maintained in the figures of the loves that Krapp recounts. So, Bianca (white) lives in the dark of "Kedar Street," and the nursemaid who pushes a funereal perambulator is a "dark young beauty" dressed in "all white" (219). The play of light and dark in the scene on the punt is particularly well balanced. The woman's eyes are closed against the glare of the bright day, and it is only when Krapp "bent over her to get them in the shadow [that] they opened" (221). Krapp here provides the darkness necessary for the eyes to admit him into their darkness, for one looks into the depths of the pupils, not to the relative lightness of the iris. The phrase "Let me in," as Vivian Mercier long ago pointed out, can be read as the sign of success—the eyes opened and Krapp was let in to their depths—but, in the English version of the text, it can equally be plausible as a plea to be let in, both in a spiritual and a sexual sense.[20] The two possibilities, the "light" of spirituality or the "dark" of sex, here coalesce and indicate how these poles are merged throughout the play.[21]

It is this coalescence that might also account for the confusion regarding whether Krapp's art should belong to the light or the dark side of the equation. The artistic epiphany on the pier that Krapp undergoes is associated directly with darkness and yet results in what appears to be a Gnostic luminous insight: "...clear to me at last that the dark I have struggled to keep under so long is in reality my most—[*Krapp curses, switches off, winds tape forward, switches on again*]—unshatterable association until my dissolution of storm and night with the light of the understanding and fire..." (220). Knowlson and Gontarski can both find reassurance in these lines, but the fundamental dualism that both assume has possibly obscured the Manichaean *process* that is described. The dark and light are not here incompatible, but the beginning and end of a process of distillation. In aesthetic terms, the material of art comes from the mixed world of matter, replete with sex, the body, and attendant psychological difficulties. From this material, the art is refined into a light of communicable understanding, as if an essence were achieved that is then to be passed on in a pure form. The lyrical passage of the girl on the punt immediately follows this description of Krapp's aesthetic revelation and may function as an example of that aesthetic principle in which an everyday physicality—"my face in her breasts," the "scratch on her thigh" from picking gooseberries—is distilled into the possible promise of her eyes and the abstract musicality of "under us all moved, and moved us, gently, up and down, and from side to side" (221). Indeed, the distillates of the mixed world are stressed throughout the play: the relationship with Bianca is refined into a "girl in a shabby green coat, on a railway-station platform" (218); the nursemaid is refined into the "chrysolite" eyes (220); and the death of the mother is reduced to the essential of the small, black rubber ball.

The girl in the shabby green coat should remind one of the Smeraldina in *Dream of Fair to Middling Women* and the masturbatory aesthetics of that novel are again pertinent here. Gontarski has identified the importance of masturbation for the play when he records a notebook entry of Beckett's that stated "recorder companion of his solitude agent of masturbation," which allows Gontarksi to gloss Krapp's final, still stare as "a postcoital, rather postmasturbatory, emptiness and loneliness..."[22] It might be preferable to take the word "agent" in Beckett's note a little more literally, though. Rather than an aid to sexual reminiscence, the tape recorder is active in the process of distilling the essence of art in similar fashion to Belacqua's masturbatory paradigm for artistic apprehension. The tape-recorder allows for the separating of the "grain from the husks" when the grain is that essential element "worth having when all the dust has [...] settled" (217). Although the essential is achieved through the discarding of the husks, or the art achieved and the sexual moment thrown away, nevertheless the process is one in which the initial sexual object is the beginning, and the material from which that art is achieved. As the drafts of *Krapp's Last Tape* demonstrate, Beckett was initially unsure how to treat the sexual and aesthetic relation in the play. An early version has a 31-year-old Krapp thinking that "what would help me more than anything, I think, is a [...] fuller [...] more engrossing [...] sexual life" and this was maintained through the first three drafts before a reversal occurred. Beckett then tried a "less exhausting," then a "less wearing" sex life before adopting the final version of "less engrossing."[23] Of course, the evidence suggests a turning away from sexual activity, but the circularity of Beckett's thinking—he ends with the word "engrossing" with which he started—may also suggest a struggle to attain the precise wording needed. "Engrossing" does not necessarily entail a complete turning away from sex, but might rather mean adopting a certain indifference to sex. In Manichaean thought, the term has a particular resonance in that the spirit would become "engrossed," or imprisoned within the flesh, as a result of sexual intercourse. Sexual activity may then be maintained as long as the threat of making the spirit gross is avoided or, alternatively, sex may continue as long as the aesthetic distillation reverses the process of engrossment.

The aesthetic paradigm that has been derived from *Krapp* would see the essence of art transcend its dependence on the mixed material of its origin. Yet it is necessary to ask whether this transcendentalism is achieved by Krapp or whether such hopes for aesthetic consolation are ironically undermined in the play. Certainly, Krapp's magnum opus is a commercial failure, but this was something Beckett himself was used to in the fate of his prewar fiction. The possible failure of this aesthetic paradigm depends rather more on the quality of the distillates and their effects; in particular, whether or not admittance into the eyes of the lover transcends the moment and releases the promised light of understanding. That the 39-year-old Krapp feels regret at trying to retain the grain and discarding the husk of the moment on the punt can certainly be inferred from his insistence that his "best years are gone. When there was a chance of happiness. But I wouldn't want them back. Not with the fire in me now. No I wouldn't want them back" (223). He has apparently sacrificed happiness in the name of art, and art has not offered a worthy consolation for such a loss. Further, the motif of gazing into the eyes across Beckett's works suggests that any such gaze will end in failure. When Murphy stares into the eyes of Mr. Endon in the hope of gaining access to the perfection of insanity, as Murphy styles it to himself, all he actually sees is his own reflection and Mr. Endon remains utterly impervious to Murphy's presence (*Murphy* 156). It is in *Eh Joe*, however, that the Manichaean light and dark relation and the eyes of the loved object are revisited. Joe's reported description of the eyes of his beloved are "spirit made light," yet rather than attraction to this light, Joe rejects both the light and the beloved, who commits suicide. Sex and suicide merge in the final apostrophe to "the green one....The narrow one....Always pale....The pale eyes....The look they shed before....The way they opened after....Spirit made light" (*CDW* 366). The rejection of both love and light, together with Murphy's inability to connect with Mr. Endon, suggest that the motif is one of failure rather than success. One may look into the eyes of another, but that does not mean a connection is formed; rather one becomes aware of the inability to connect and of the solitary nature of one's existence. The eyes may appear to offer happiness or aesthetic consolation but only ultimately make one aware of one's solitude and the suffering inherent within life. Indeed, rather than aesthetic consolation, for the 69-year-old Krapp the eyes of the beloved only reveal "everything on this old muckball, all the light and dark and famine and feasting of [...] the ages!" (222). The suffering of and in the world cannot be assuaged by art or the happiness of a loving relation. Beckett's pessimism and his belief in the impossibility of human connection are attested to by an otherwise curious comment he made to Pierre Chabert: "I thought of writing a play about the situation in reverse. Mrs. Krapp, the girl in the boat, would be prowling around behind him, and his failure, and his solitude would be just the same."[24] They would be the same because actual or spiritual communication between two people is impossible and, therefore, an aesthetic based on the communication of two people distilled into an essential communicable aspect would be doomed to fail.

Krapp's aesthetics, and the consolation that might be derived from them, can also be seen to fail when one considers the fate of those "essential" elements, or epiphanies, that his art has so far produced. This is to propose a Joycean inflection to the aesthetics adopted by Krapp. P. J. Murphy— conflating Krapp and Beckett, to a certain degree—has argued that

"Beckett's 'dark' revelation is nothing less than his own version of Joyce's epiphany and that Beckett's artistic vision is in many ways complementary to Joyce's rather than being diametrically opposed."[25] Murphy's suggestion that it is the Joyce of *A Portrait of the Artist as a Young Man* to which Beckett repeatedly returns in his career, rather than to *Ulysses or Finnegans Wake*, certainly reopens the argument concerning the relation between the two authors, and, from the perspective of the current volume, offers new possibilities of Beckett complementing Joyce in terms of the sexual and aesthetic nexus. In the latter stages of *Portrait*, Stephen Dedalus repeatedly makes an overt connection between sexual and aesthetic reproduction as he attempts to formulate his own aesthetics. He speaks of "artistic conception, artistic gestation and artistic reproduction...,"[26] and, in a comment that parallels the more Manichaean transformations this chapter has discussed, sexual stimulus and the figure of the female is seen as the material from which a transcendent art might be formed, with the artist acting as a rival to the priest and "transmuting the daily bread of experience into the radiant body of everliving life."[27] This rivalry with religion in the creation of an eternal transcendence out of the "gross earth"[28] of experience is, as with Christianity itself, shadowed by a fear of the dangers of procreation in the perpetuation of sin and death. Thus, Stephen imagines for his own art a form of aesthetic immaculate conception as "in the virgin womb of the imagination the word was made flesh."[29] The ultimate aim for this aesthetic creation is to go beyond the gross world of desire and to lose oneself and one's will in the "luminous silent stasis of esthetic pleasure..."—a concept that Stephen associates with the aesthetics of English Romanticism and, in particular, Shelley's concept of the "enchantment of the heart."[30]

For Stephen, as for Krapp, the process of art is the distillation of the radiant, essential, and ever-living from the engrossing, temporal world. For Krapp, though, the essential distillates, the epiphanies, fail to offer access to any form of transcendence. The "memorable equinox" is not remembered by Krapp at all when he reads his index of the tapes. Perhaps even more telling is his inability to remember the "black ball" (217), which he swore he would remember to his "dying day" (220) and which the tape reveals to be poignantly associated with the death of his mother. Indeed, transcendence is replaced by a mechanical form of repetition. Rather than the epiphany transcending time, the business of the tape recorder seals those epiphanies within their moments of creation as Krapp does not remember, but the mechanism of repetition he bends over does. Once again, Beckett's skepticism concerning the consolations of art, particularly a Romantic or Romantically inspired conception of such a consolation, is very much in evidence. One might wish to argue that Beckett is hereby distancing himself from Joyce and that the aesthetics of *A Portrait* are found to be naïve. This would certainly seem to be the case. However, this is complicated by the question of how much Joyce himself adhered to Stephen's aesthetic means and aims, or whether the author repeatedly undercuts his artist as a young man and treats him ironically. (My use of "Stephen" rather than "Joyce" in the description of the aesthetics outlined in *A Portrait* is in recognition of this possibility.) If the latter is the case, then Beckett is following Joyce closely; if the former is more likely, then indeed Beckett is marking a difference between himself and his precursor. To pursue this would be to take too great a digression from the aims of this book, but whether Beckett was faithful to Joyce or parodying him, it is clear that what is objected to is the claim that art can function as a pure, disinterested form of consolation for the material suffering of the "gross earth," to use Joyce's terms, or this "muckball," to use Beckett's.

The failure to assuage the suffering inherent in this "muckball" in *Krapp's Last Tape*, whether through aesthetic or physical means, is supported by the activation within the play of elements that we have already seen as crucial within "First Love." Krapp's fatal fondness for bananas and his consequent constipation is often taken to be a primarily comic underlining of his inability to live free of his desires; desires that would encompass forms of autoeroticism that may be inflected with homosexuality. In Manichaean terms, one might suggest that Krapp's alimentary condition means he is unable to transform the mixed matter of this world into the pure light of the "Living Self," as if the digestive alchemy envisaged within the ritual meals of the Elect has been quite literally stopped by Krapp's fecal retention. In addition, his constipation is explicitly related to the death of his father. The 39-year-old Krapp summarizes a tape of some ten years before: "Last illness of his father. Flagging pursuit of happiness. Unattainable laxation" (218). The association of the death of the father and constipation were key elements in the psychological motivations of the protagonist of "First Love." As Chapter 3 argued in that regard, constipation is figured as an unconscious desire for the father and an inability to compensate for the trauma of birth through the partial return to the womb offered in heterosexual vaginal intercourse. Rather than entering into the economy of heterosexual intercourse through the fear of castration, the constipated man maintains the wish to entirely reenter the womb. In this sense, sex is no consolation for the fact of having been born. In *Krapp*, all this is figured by and through Krapp himself. He takes some satisfaction in retreating to his womb-like den, and this is immediately followed by the admission that he has just eaten three bananas thus maintaining his constipation (217). When he does return to the darkness of his womb-room it is inevitably to himself (and to the burden of being oneself) that he returns: "With all this darkness around me I feel less alone. . . . In a way . . . I love to get up and move about in it, then back here to . . . [*hesitates*] . . . me. [*Pause.*] Krapp." (217) Krapp then retains crap and is retained as crap in a suffering that he fails to assuage by aesthetic creation and human relations as the only true end to suffering would be ceasing to be Krapp at all. Instead, he must "be again, be again. . . . All that old misery." (223)

The Art of Reproduction: Malone and Schopenhauer

Krapp's art fails to provide consolation for the misery and suffering of life. This attests to a certain skepticism on Beckett's part whereby forms of Romantic aesthetics, in which art transcends the gross materiality of the world as experienced in time, are seen to fail. This skepticism is nowhere more in evidence than in the repeated failures of another solitary artist: Malone. Malone's aesthetic project of telling stories while waiting for death necessarily means the creation of viable scenarios and the characters to populate them from out of nothing more than his own solitary condition. His ability to invent further characters to allow him to continue is cast both in terms of play and in terms of nonreproductive sexuality, associated, as with Krapp and Belacqua, with masturbation. So, toward the beginning of the novel, Malone recalls the ease with which he once peopled his imaginative world: "If I said, Now I need a hunchback, immediately one came running, proud as punch of his fine hunch that was going to perform. It did not occur to him that I might have to ask him to undress. But it was not long before I found myself alone, in the dark" (*MD* 4). The sudden appearance of a further character to add to his tale, and so a further character to keep him going, is set against Malone's abandoned, lonely state. Yet even from the dark, something can be made to issue: "Perhaps as hitherto I shall find myself abandoned, in the dark, without anything to play with. Then I shall play with myself. To be able to conceive of such a plan is encouraging" (4). The less than subtle puns suggest that safe nonreproductive sexuality, in the form of masturbation, once again offers the metaphoric means to indulge in a sterile form of conception as fictional creation. In a form of autogenesis, Malone will create a means of going on out of the nothing of his own darkness.

However, the success of this aesthetic project is open to the same doubts as the aesthetics of Krapp. In the case of Krapp, aesthetic creation fails to compensate for the suffering of continuing life. This "failure" of art, whereby an epiphany does not reveal the "spirit" within the world, nor transcends the suffering of that world, in turn raises doubts as to the degree to which Beckett follows Schopenhauer in all the facets of his philosophy, and this doubt is most clearly discernible in the creative life of Malone. The masturbatory aesthetic model used by Krapp and, as seen above, by Malone himself, suggests that natural procreation is being replaced by a form of fictional generation. It would then be hoped that these creations would not fall prey to the will-to-live that Schopenhauer and Beckett see as the guarantee of existence and suffering. Given that Beckett follows Schopenhauer in his reaction against the procreative nightmare of sexual intercourse, it would therefore be reasonable to assume that he might follow Schopenhauer in his assertion that one effective, if momentary, way of overcoming the will is through the aesthetic attitude and aesthetic creation. Within Schopenhauer's aesthetic attitude we "consider things without interest, without subjectivity, purely objectively" and then:

> ...all at once the peace, always sought but always escaping us on that first path of willing, comes to us of its own accord, and all is well with us. It is the painless state [...] for that moment we are delivered from the pressure of the will. We celebrate the Sabbath of the penal servitude of willing; the wheel of Ixion stands still.[31]

The question for Malone then becomes whether his aesthetic creations can avoid the pitfalls of actual physical procreation and painlessly suspend the will-to-live or, like Krapp, will aesthetics fail to provide any consolation at all. Malone fully realizes that aesthetics are precisely at issue: "Aesthetics are therefore on my side, at least a certain kind of aesthetics," (6) he comments. Thus, torn between the paths of earnestness and play, Malone lays claims to have at least some form of aesthetic theory underpinning his choice and its significance. In "On the Will in Nature," Schopenhauer writes of the relation between play and "dull seriousness,"[32] but the more precise terminological analogue may be found in Schopenhauer's forerunner, Friedrich von Schiller. Beckett had the opportunity to encounter Schiller on a number of occasions, not least in the pages of Windelband's *A History of Philosophy* in which Schiller is seen as a poet-philosopher who acts as a bridge between Kant's *Critique of Judgement* and the aesthetics of Schopenhauer. Given that Beckett was already enmeshed in reading Schopenhauer during the period of the composition of *Proust*, it seems likely that he would have pursued the lineage of aesthetic ideas back to Schiller himself. Windelband not only stresses Schiller's connection to Schopenhauer but he also emphasizes the link between play and the ablation of desire. He summarizes: "In the aesthetic life the *play impulse* unfolds itself; every stirring of the will is silent in disinterested contemplation."[33] Schiller, particularly in relation to Goethe, is also given prominence in Robertson's *History of German Literature*, which, as Mark Nixon has pointed out in the essay "Scraps of German," Beckett used as a synchronic reading guide in the 1930s.[34] Moreover, Beckett's biographer James Knowlson relates that Beckett was sufficiently interested in the figure of Schiller to visit and then take notes on his house in Weimar.[35] Beckett's claim that "the theatre is not a moral institution in Schiller's sense,"[36] made in 1961, also speaks to some form of continuing engagement with Schiller beyond his reading of the 1930s. Although Windelband stresses the continuity of thought between Schiller and Schopenhauer, Beckett's notes on *The History of Philosophy* suggest that Beckett was somewhat exasperated by aspects of Schopenhauer's predecessors. Included within the notes are barbed asides from Beckett, directed at, for example, Schiller's aesthetic contemplation in the creation of the state of *schöne Seele*.[37] Beckett later dismisses Schlegel with a single "pfui!"[38] These frustrations with the possible consolations of aesthetic contemplation suggest an unwillingness to accept the more optimistic attributes of Romantic thought, as shall be made apparent in due course. However, for the time being, the degree of terminological and conceptual similarity between the "play" passages of *Malone's Dies* and Schiller's *Letters on the Aesthetic Education of Man* indicates that a case for a Schiller and Beckett relation might be raised not only on the basis of Beckett's notes but also on the internal, literary evidence.

Malone presents two possible poles: play or earnestness. Play is conceived of in terms of aesthetic creation, so, when in need of a hunchback one immediately appears, ready to "perform" (4). Yet these efforts at play unerringly fail, and "it was not long before I found myself alone, in the dark." It is in this darkness that Malone interrogates himself. "Such is the earnestness from which [...] I have never been able to depart. From now on it will be different. I shall never do anything any more from now on but play" (4). Earnestness, as a form of threatening and anterior force, is stressed in precisely those terms on numerous occasions within the opening pages. During the "live and invent" section of the novel, Malone's pendulum moves repeatedly between earnestness and play. Earnestness is portrayed as a "wild beast padd[ing] up and down, roaring, ravening, rending", while "play" is a form of clowning escape from that earnestness: "I turned till I was dizzy, clapped my hands, ran, shouted, saw myself winning, saw myself losing, rejoicing, lamenting." Unable to remain within play, Malone throws himself on his play things for, as he puts it, "I was already in the toils of earnestness" and so he inevitably relapses to "darkness, to nothingness, to earnestness, to home..." (20).

H. Porter Abbott relates the wild earnestness of Malone to the Wildean importance of being earnest,[39] but, rather than Wilde, an alternative earnestness is a crucial part of Schiller's aesthetics as the dichotomy between play and earnestness is precisely that which is focused upon by Schiller in the twenty-seventh of his *Letters on the Aesthetic Education of Man.*

> From the compulsion of want, or *physical earnestness*, [Nature] makes the transition via the compulsion of superfluity, or *physical play*, to aesthetic play; and before she soars, in the sublime freedom of beauty, beyond the fetters of ends and purposes altogether, she makes some approach to this independence, at least from afar, in that kind of *free activity* that is at once its own end and its own means.[40] (emphasis in the original)

Play is in Schiller a movement away from *physical earnestness*, as, in Beckett, "play" is an escape from the "earnestness" that afflicts Malone. This physical earnestness is connected to the dictates of the will and inspired by want: "An animal may be said *to be at work* when the stimulus to activity is some lack; it may be said *to be at play* when the stimulus is sheer plenitude of vitality, when superabundance of life is its own incentive to actions."[41] In order to fulfill lack, the animal sets to work; where there is a lack of lack, the animal is at play. Such play as aesthetic ideal has the potential to overcome immediate physical need and, therefore, to overcome the overarching dictates of time under which the will operates. Taking a pseudo-historical overview of the development of the aesthetic sense, Schiller writes:

> Not just content with what satisfies nature, and meets his instinctual needs, [man] demands something over and above this: to begin with, admittedly, only a superfluity of *material things*, in order to conceal from appetite the fact that it has limits, and ensure enjoyment beyond the satisfaction of immediate needs; soon, however, a superfluity in *material things*, an aesthetic surplus, in order to satisfy the formal impulse too, an extended enjoyment beyond the satisfaction of every need. [...] when he lets form enter into the his enjoyment, and begins to notice the outward appearance of the things that satisfy his desires, then he has not merely enhanced his enjoyment in scope and degree, but also ennobled it in kind.[42] (emphasis in the original)

It might be fruitful to consider Malone's possessions in the light of Schiller's material things, but, for the present, the necessary focus is on the "aesthetic surplus" and its relationship with time. Once the material object has been freed from the "satisfaction of immediate needs" the possibility of the strictly useless contemplation of the object is also freed, and time itself is momentarily "transcended." The final phase is for the object to be appreciated not in its relation to needs and therefore use, but in its formal aspects alone. At this stage, one assumes, time itself can be transcended altogether. Within the trilogy, there is just such a moment of the contemplation of a material thing shorn of the outward appearance that satisfies desires; Molloy and the curious object that he has stolen from Lousse's house: "For a time it inspired me with a kind of veneration, for there was no doubt in my mind that it was not an object of virtue, but that it had a most specific function always to be hidden from me. I could therefore puzzle over it endlessly without the least risk" (63–64). No longer a knife-rest designed to satisfy an immediate need, the object is contemplated for its formal, aesthetic nature. That Molloy can puzzle over this "endlessly" attests to the aesthetic surplus transcending the immediate moment, if not time altogether.

In contrast, the earnestness of which Schiller writes is that of the individual trapped within the materiality of the world and at the whim of need, from which play offers a momentary escape, and such a scheme reflects Malone's creative project most precisely. Resolved to "play," Malone begins with a story concerning a boy, Saposcat. The creation of the story and character of Saposcat is, as far as Malone is concerned, an attempt not to look at Malone as he actually is, trapped within time and the will—"That is just what I wanted to avoid," he says—however that is precisely what he finds himself continually falling into, for, as he puts it later, he is prey to "the desire to know what I am doing and why" (19). He inevitably returns to himself despite his best efforts to play in a world unsullied by his presence.

If it is the case that Malone inevitably falls into such an earnestness, why is such a failing inevitable? If Schiller is correct, then the aesthetic contemplation should be an opportunity for the transcendence of the moment and of the self-in-time at the mercy of lack and want. Of crucial concern to Malone—and to Schiller, as will become clear—is that Saposcat should bear no relation to Malone. "Nothing is less like me than this patient, reasonable child [...] Here truly is the air I needed, a lively tenuous air, far from the nourishing murk that is killing me" (18). In order for play to work, Sapo must be as far removed from Malone as possible; he must be a pure creation uninfected by the author. To put this into terms of procreation and genealogy, Sapo must be a child of Malone who has no filial relationship to Malone.

When one considers the moments of collapse in the early stages of the Sapo story, then the inability to create a pure aesthetic object with no relation to the author becomes decisive. On the matter of why Sapo wasn't expelled from school for throwing a cane through a window, Malone worries that he cannot find a credible solution. The problem is important, for once the fabric of the Sapo tale has been torn in such a way, the darkness in which Malone toils earnestly begins to beckon: "For I want as little as possible of darkness in this story. A little darkness, in itself, at the time, is nothing. You think no more about it and you go on. But I know what darkness is, it accumulates, it thickens, then suddenly bursts and drowns everything" (14). The darkness that Malone inhabits then intrudes into the story, and Sapo begins to become a creature too like his creator for comfort. Sapo, who is often associated with light, must be different from Malone floundering in his darkness. Similarly, on two occasions Malone falters when he writes of Sapo's eyes. In an image of the disturbing notion of filial similarity, which is analogous to Malone's fear of creating not a Saposcat, but a disguised Malone, we are told that Mr. Saposcat "could not endure the look in Sapo's eyes [...] He has your eyes, his wife would say. Then Mr. Saposcat chafed to be alone, in order to inspect his eyes in the mirror. They were palest blue. Just a shade lighter, said Mrs. Saposcat" (15). As the fictional father of Sapo is perturbed by the likeness between himself and his son in those eyes of palest blue, so Malone, the aesthetic father of Sapo, is perturbed by "...those gull's eyes. [...] I know it is a small thing. But I am easily frightened now. I know those little phrases that seem so innocuous and, once you let them in, pollute the whole of speech. *Nothing is more real than nothing.* They rise up out of the pit and know no rest until they drag you down into its dark" (17; emphasis in the original). The seemingly innocuous blue eyes of Sapo that so perturb Malone create a complex relation between Sapo, Malone, and Beckett himself. Sapo's eyes, in short, are disturbingly like Beckett's. Knowlson cites a Portora school friend on Beckett's "piercing eyes" and comments himself that he "had bright blue eyes and a piercing stare."[43] Similarly, the *Observer* feature writer noted Beckett's "pale blue eyes" in 1958.[44] The relation between the aesthetic object and the author-subject, via Malone, is just the merest hint of a connection, yet even so slight a relation is enough to raise the possibility of the created becoming like the creator, of the filial procreative model of artist and his work, with all that that might entail, becoming operative. In such a way, Mr. Saposcat's concern that he has the same eyes as his son amounts to a condensed exposition of the paradoxical joy and fear that haunts fatherhood—the son will in fact be as the father—a key feature in Beckett's misoepdia, as Chapter 3 argued. As Mr. Saposcat is concerned that Sapo might be too much like him, so too is Malone, whose play is dependent on Sapo remaining removed from his author, on the creation remaining in the light of play, far from the dark of earnestness.

Aesthetically, Malone's inability to keep Sapo sufficiently separate from himself is a serious failing. Schiller makes this point abundantly clear:

Only inasmuch as it is *honest* (expressly renounces all claims to reality), and only inasmuch as it is *autonomous* (dispenses with all support from reality), is semblance aesthetic. From the moment it is dishonest, and simulates reality, or from the moment it is impure, and has need of reality to make its effect, it is nothing but a base instrument for material ends, and affords no evidence whatsoever of any freedom of spirit.[45] (emphasis in the original)

The slightest resemblance between Sapo and Malone means that the aesthetic object is not autonomous and therefore cannot access the sublime. The unfortunate "support from reality" that is Sapo being based on Malone, entails Malone's inability to remain within aesthetic contemplation and therefore beyond the pulls of the will in time. He will not be able to enjoy the gift of the sublime that is "freedom of spirit." Malone puts it rather more succinctly: "I wonder if I am not talking yet again about myself? Shall I be incapable, to the end, of lying on any other subject?" (13). To characterize this as an aesthetic failure on Malone's part is to recognize that the creations of Sapo and Macmann fail in the objective to free Malone from time and the will. He is trapped within the materiality of the world, and art is no consolation for that. There appears here to be an interrogation of notions of the Romantic aesthetic attitude and its benefits within Beckett's work that demonstrates that while art may be capable of many things, it will not, as Schiller suggested, be a mode of access to the "freedom of spirit" or the ablation of desire, for, as Schiller writes, "for as long as necessity dictates, and need drives, imagination remains tied to reality with powerful bonds; only when wants are stilled does it develop its unlimited potential" (166).

The relation between Beckett and Schiller as seen through Malone's failed aesthetic projects perhaps sheds light on Beckett's frustration vented in his philosophy notes that is aimed at the possibility of aesthetic contemplation leading to a supposed moral benefit while also dismissing Schlegel precisely on the matter of ironic play. For Malone, the failure of aesthetic creation and contemplation necessarily means playfulness and moral benefit are both equally improbable. Certainly, the tone of Schiller's thought is unerringly redemptive—and in the "The Stage Considered as a Moral Institution" also nationalistic—with the aesthetic exceeding the role of the religious inasmuch as within the viewer's "breast there is room for only one sensation: the awareness that he is a human being" and that such a revelation is meant to be positive.[46] Beckett's notes follow Windelband in claiming that Schopenhauer removes the "religious element" and that "dear Arthur" thereby shows the "absolute unreason of objectless will. [...] and since world is nothing but self-revelation (objectivation) of the will, it must be a balls aching world."[47] Obviously, Beckett is attracted to such apparent pessimism in contrast to his disapproval of the overt optimism of Schiller. Yet, the question remains whether or not this mistrust of aesthetic benefits is transferred onto the different, yet arguably equally transcendent, claims of Schopenhauer. That question is perhaps best addressed by the specter of procreation that haunts Malone's attempts at aesthetic reproduction.

In this matter of the relations between Malone and Sapo, between creator and object, a form of aesthetic creation has become infected by modes more proper to sexual procreation. In this respect, Mr. Saposcat, rushing off to check his eyes in the mirror for fear that he resembles his son, is a hint toward a further troubling aspect of sexual procreation. His joy and fear that Sapo will resemble him and so be and act like him, is represented in mythic terms later in the same novel. Momentarily, Malone casts himself in the mould of Cronus: "Yes, a little creature, I shall try and make a little creature in my image, no matter what I say. And seeing what a poor thing I have made, or how like myself, I shall eat it. Then be alone for a long time, unhappy, not knowing what my prayer should be nor to whom" (53). Malone's Cronus figuration played a key symbolic role in the rationale for the misopedia of the novel (see Chapter 3), and here it marks a key shift in the aesthetic practice that Malone adopts. That Malone should invoke Cronus at this precise juncture in the novel is significant for, immediately after, Saposcat is rediscovered—"I have taken a long time to find him again, but I have found him" (53)—but now transformed into the much more Malone-like figure of Macmann. Therefore the Cronus figuration marks the turning point from the story of Saposcat to that of Macmann and introduces a different mode in the aesthetic creations of Malone. Whereas, with Saposcat, the aim had been to create an aesthetically pure object unlike his creator, now the aesthetic paradigm is one already informed by sexual reproduction and the fear of filial usurpation.

The adoption of the Cronus model of aesthetic creation, which is one already infected by the consequences proper to sexual reproduction, again leads to a failure of creation to act as consolation and to remove Malone from the will and time. The Cronus model is itself dual, and each aspect will be taken separately. First, contained within the model is the need for the child to act as a continuation of the father, based on resemblance between the two, just as Malone creates Macmann in his own image. As a grounds for an aesthetic relief from the will-in-time, this is flawed. As Schopenhauer suggests, the true artist is equipped with the "gift of genius" where genius "is the capacity to remain in the state of pure perception, to lose oneself in perception, to remove from the service of the will the knowledge which originally existed only for its service."[48] This aesthetic ideal is incompatible with sexual reproduction, or, as the case here, with aesthetic modes *infected* by sexual reproduction. Procreation, Schopenhauer claims, "goes beyond the affirmation of one's own existence that fills so short a time," but this is not to claim that individual continuation is assured through sexual reproduction, but rather that procreation "affirms life for an indefinite time beyond the death of the individual."[49] He goes on to assert the dual, Cronus-like nature of the reproductive process:

> The begotten appears before the begetter, different from him in the phenomenon, but in himself, or according to the Idea, identical with him. It is therefore by this act that every species of living things is bound to a whole and perpetual as such. [...] With that affirmation beyond one's own body to the production of a new body, suffering and death, as belonging to the phenomenon of life, are also affirmed anew, and the possibility of salvation, brought about by the most complete faculty of knowledge, is for this time declared to be fruitless.[50]

The child might appear different from the parent, but in reality, and as phenomenal expression of the will, they are identical, so the child replaces the parent and acts as a continuation of the will, but not of the parent. The will-to-live is hereby affirmed, not ablated, the procession of death and suffering continues, and the possibility of salvation through proper knowledge, which art can supposedly momentarily deliver, is, in a pregnant phrase, "fruitless." Malone's creation of Macmann as creation-child is, therefore, merely a further phenomenal expression of the will, rather than a momentary escape from the will.

Yet, in the second aspect of the Cronus model, the progeny is consumed. Can Malone also consume his own creation, Macmann? The fact that the ends of the narratives of Macmann and Malone *appear* to coincide would lend some support to the idea that Malone successfully consumes his own progeny. However, this is undermined by Malone's reactivation as one of the Unnamable's avatars in the subsequent novel in which Malone resurfaces but with "little trace" of his "mortal liveliness" (*U* 2). Even if he were to consume Macmann successfully, what end would be served and would the aim of aesthetic creation, the respite from the ravenings of the will, be achieved?

An answer to this question might arise from one of the most common misunderstandings of the Cronus myth, a misunderstanding into which even Jung fell. The misunderstanding asserts that Cronus represents the all-devouring nature of time, or as Jung put it: "...Chronos, the god who ate his own children, the word having the meaning of time."[51] Etymologically, there is no link between the god's name and the Greek for time, but nevertheless the myth of the myth has long been perpetuated. The popular conflation of Cronus and Khronos (the authentic representative of time) leads to a rather paradoxical reading of the Titan myth, whereby Time consumes his children in an attempt to stop time's progression and ensure his own survival, and yet is defeated by time's natural progression as Zeus defeats his father and the progeny are vomited forth. In this reading, time is rather confusingly defeated by time. Within Schopenhauer's thought, time and the will, which, although timeless, can only be phenomenally exhibited in time, can be momentarily suspended through the aesthetic attitude. Art, he writes:

> ...plucks the object of its contemplation from the stream of the world's course, and holds it isolated before it. [...] it stops the wheel of time; for it the relations vanish; its object is only the essential, the Idea. We can therefore define it accurately as *the way of considering things independently of the principle of sufficient reason*."[52] (emphasis in the original)

Malone's Cronus-like creativity displays precisely the opposite, for, no matter what he does, the creator is bound within time. Schopenhauer here invokes Ixion once again, and no doubt has in mind that only when Orpheus sang and played his lyre was the wheel on which Ixion was bound momentarily stilled. He does not remind his reader of *why* Ixion was condemned to spin upon a wheel of fire for all eternity. His fault was sex. So strong was Ixion's lust for Hera, that he copulated with a cloud Zeus had formed into his wife's replica. If the focus of the affirmation of the will to live is the genitals, then Ixion, condemned to suffer eternally, is its perfect embodiment.

But what of the respite offered by Orpheus? In *Malone Dies,* aesthetic reproduction fails to lift the creator out of time and the will. The aesthetically pure creation of Sapo becomes infected by the paradigm of sexual reproduction that is the means by which the will perpetuates itself. Malone then attempts the Cronus model of self-fashioning and self-consuming, but again the procreative paradigm indicates that there is no escape from time and therefore the will. Beckett's art is then a failure in terms of the aesthetic attitude as espoused by Schiller and Schopenhauer, albeit with different emphases. Beckett's novel demonstrates that one of the few consolations offered as a palliative for existence by Schopenhauer, the momentary quieting of the will in the aesthetic attitude, is no consolation at all. Erik Tonning has suggested that Beckett rejected the "'way out' suggested by Schopenhauer (partly inspired here by Hindu and Buddhist thought); namely, the ascetic denial of the will-to-live."[53] This rejection can then be seen to have its roots within Beckett's mistrust of the supposed temporary benefits of aesthetic contemplation and reproduction. In "Scraps of German," Mark Nixon records Beckett's friend, George Reavey, noting in his diary: "Sam. Beckett = Proust + Pessimism"[54] where the pessimism is provided by Schopenhauer. We might now wish to add a further term to the equation: "Sam. Beckett = Proust + Pessimism + Pessimism" for Beckett appears to be pessimistic of the optimistic power of art in Schiller, Schopenhauer, and Romantic aesthetics.

Malone Dies and *Krapp's Last Tape* reveal a profound ambivalence toward the consolatory possibilities of aesthetic creation and whether that creation can ever free itself from a dependency on the world and the will it is meant to transcend. Moreover, there are further grounds for pessimism, for Beckett also seems to be aware that, if aesthetic creation cannot free itself from the will-in-time, then the suffering inherent within sexual pro-creation may be recreated within the aesthetic realm. The Lynch family of *Watt* are undoubtedly a grotesque satire on the will-to-live and sexual reproduction, yet, it must not be forgotten, they are at the same time *not real*. They have no existence beyond the supposed necessities that Watt believes must be in play for Mr. Knott's leftovers to be eaten by a famished dog. C. J. Ackerley is correct when he points out that what begins as a hypothetical imperative engenders a substantive result: the dog was Kate and there she is eating from the bowl. Ackerley's description of what occurs to allow the Lynch family to appear and procreate is itself pregnant with procreation: "each premise yet fresh premises begetting,"[55] until the Lynch family in all their diseased glory are as real as anything else within the novel. The Lynches are then the product, seemingly born out of necessity, of a fictional reproduction on Watt's part that are then used to satirize sexual reproduction. Once born into a fictional realm, however, suffering and death are also reborn and even exploited by the artist. The method of reproduction may now be aesthetic, but the suf-fering of these fictional generations is no less than those of the populace of *All That Fall* who were similarly generated out of nothing. As father to his works, can Beckett be free of the accusation of being an "accursed progenitor"?

CHAPTER 6

Aesthetic Reproduction across the Oeuvre

Beckett's prose and drama of the 1950s and subsequent decades moved toward greater levels of abstraction. To trace the role of aesthetic reproduction across these later works is less a matter of interpreting sexual scenarios. As Beckett moves away from some of the more sexually explicit aspects of *Molloy* or *Malone Dies,* he yet retains the trope of aesthetic reproduction in structural and thematic terms, just as was the case of the Lynch family of *Watt,* who, as we have seen, are a fictional generation born out of apparent logical necessity upon whom the horrors of sexual reproduction are visited. This unfortunate ethical dimension—the suffering of the created beings—remains in Beckett's later works, and Ulrika Maude is certainly correct to assert that "the Beckettian characters' experience of the world is a markedly physical, bodily experience."[1] As shall be seen, the creation and possible exploitation of such necessary bodies, even in the most abstract prose and dramas, is precisely at issue in the deployment of aesthetic reproduction.

Out of Nothing: Texts for Nothing *and* How It Is

H. Porter Abbott has argued that *Texts for Nothing,* "far from being detritus from *The Unnamable,* cobbled together in a pseudo-text, is arguably Beckett's first full and thoroughgoing deployment of an aesthetic recommencement."[2] The thematics and techniques of recommencement within *Texts for Nothing* offer further examples of Beckett's replacement of sexual reproduction with aesthetic reproduction. Admittedly, there is little actual sexual activity within the *Texts* themselves upon which to draw, as Beckett's work grows more abstract. Yet, the paradigms of aesthetic reproduction established in Chapter 5 can be seen to inform, or indeed form, the individual texts of *Texts for Nothing* as each focuses on the seemingly impossible task of continuance, which, of course, means the continuing authorial task of production out of nothing.

The turn away from the heady sexual brew of a Molloy is signaled by a brief moment of regret in Text 9 that such avenues are no longer available: " . . . what a shame I am not appearing anywhere as testicle, or as cunt, those areas, a female pubic hair, it sees great sights, peeping down, well, there it is, can't be helped, that's how it is" (*CSP* 145). Instead, the texts begin with the now familiar trope of expulsion, which, as "First Love" demonstrated, is a figuration of the expulsion from the womb in birth. So, the narrator relates that "someone said, you can't stay here" (100) and so must leave the security of the quag into which, in a foreshadowing of *How It Is*, the narrator seems to want to sink. This expulsion *from* "home" is also, paradoxically, an expulsion *toward* home: "All you had to do was stay at home. Home. They wanted me to go home. My dwelling place" (101). This apparent paradox can perhaps best be explained as a need to achieve a proper birth in order to attain a proper death. Such a concept is expressed across the texts, from Text 5 where the narrator admits that "one is frightened to be born, no, one wishes one were, so as to begin to die . . ." (117), through to the desire "to make possible a deeper birth, a deeper death . . ." in Text 12 (129). Text 9 expresses a similar desire:

> The graveyard, yes, it's there I'd return, this evening it's there, borne by my words, if I could get out of here, that is to say, if I could say, There's a way out there, there's a way out somewhere, to know exactly where would be a matter of time, and patience, and sequency of thought, and felicity of expression. But the body, to get there with, where's the body? (139)

Abbott notes of this passage that "the graveyard becomes a nostalgic locale where the price of admission is a body"[3] and thereby captures the womb/tomb logic of the piece; one must be born properly in order to properly access the womb-like quiescence of death. What should also be emphasized, though, is the necessity of embodiment within this process. It might be tempting to read the texts, as I have done previously,[4] as being exemplary of the postmodern, postessentialist strain in Beckett's work, whereby everything is generated by and of words that do no more than refer to themselves. Yet, as this passage amongst others makes clear, those words are expected to "give birth to" a distinct physical form, albeit one that is necessarily expressed in words;

an emphasis contained within the homophonic pun of "borne": "The grave-yard, yes, it's there I'd return, this evening it's there, *borne* by my words..." The creation of a body is continually stressed throughout *Texts for Nothing*: "Start by stirring, there must be a body, as of old..." (109) and "I'll be man, there's nothing else for it..." (110), or, with a hint of a postmortem twist: "I'm under the ground, or in my body somewhere, or in another body..." (144–5). Although only "the words break the silence" (131), those words ultimately, for good or ill, become "bedded in the flesh" (113), and, as Text 3 suggests, this embodiment is at once out of nothing and at the prompting of the mind: "It's enough to will it, I'll will it, will me a body, will me a head, a little strength, a little courage, I'm starting now..." (109).

An embodied life appears within the *Texts for Nothing* as an inevitable corollary of speech, for "once there is speech, no need of a story, a story is not compulsory, just a life..." (116). The words of which speech is built, and out of which the embodied life is engendered, are offered up as both a possible means of ending and a means of creation: "Me, here, if they could open, those little words, open and swallow me up, perhaps that is what has happened. If so let them open again and let me out, in the tumult of light that sealed my eyes, and of men, to try and be again" (132). Words here are very much figured as a site of passage; as a vagina, through which the word becomes flesh and takes its place among men, in order for the true "end" to be achieved, or as an anus, expelling fecal matter into a world of waste. As the man who actually wrote the words on the page that we read, Beckett might be seen as transforming himself into a maternal, creating presence.

Yet, ultimately, the paradigm of words giving birth to an embodied life in which to then die fails within *Texts for Nothing*. Text 3 first posits this failure by undoing the life-filled details of the text. These imagined details encompass not only a figuration of the narrator himself as a childlike, older man but also a Nanny, whom he will name Bibby, and a fellow crony, Vincent, whom he meets beside the canal or outside Duggan's bar; two further lives are therefore created out of the words designed to grant the narrator an existence. Of that existence, the narrator never fails to return to a body, no matter how reduced or dismembered: "I'll sprout a head at last, all my very own, in which to brew poisons worthy of me, and legs to kick my heels with. [...] Just the head and the two legs, or one, in the middle, I'd go hopping" (113). All this existence is finally cancelled out as the narrator claims that there "is no flesh anywhere, nor any way to die" and that the voices that urge him on "wherever they come from, have no life in them." The text—which does not amount to a story—closes with a renunciation of what has been created in accordance with the paradigm of

aesthetic reproduction, that where there is speech there is life. The lifeless-
ness of the voices, and hence of words themselves, ensure the failure of the
aesthetic program to bring life and hence death to the narrator. This is
returned to at the close of Text 12 in what is a striking foreshadowing of
How It Is. In order to "be" and therefore end

> all the peoples of the earth would not suffice, at the end of the billions
> you'd need a god, unwitnessed witness of witnesses, what a blessing it's all
> down the drain, nothing ever as much as begun, nothing ever but noth-
> ing and never, nothing ever but lifeless words. (151)

The passage amounts to a reversal of the creative forces that have generated the text up to this point. In order for the figure of the texts to "be" he
must first be embodied, a new form must be born, and then witnessed by
some third person in order for that embodiment to be validated. Logically,
this process might have no end, as he who witnesses would then need to be
witnessed. The process is very similar to that of the Lynch family in *Watt*:
in order to solve the problem of existence, the hypothetical imperative of
"there must be a body" in turn necessitates the generation of further bodies,
further lives, until the world is reconstructed. Yet this is unacceptable and
all is washed away down the drain as excremental waste for the text to return
to the "lifeless words."

Texts for Nothing, then, extends the paradigm of aesthetic reproduction
we have already encountered in *Watt* and *Malone Dies* and that informs
Hamm's babbling creativity in *Endgame,* and the generation out of silence
of the radio play *All That Fall.* Although one should fear being oversche-
matic, the elements of this paradigm might be summarized as: aesthetic,
rather than sexual, generation of an embodied figure as if out of nothing;
the multiplication of other "beings" (be they other characters, animals, or
just feasible scenarios dependent on the creation of a material world) to vali-
date this figure; the final renunciation of this attempt at aesthetic creation
and validation.

This paradigm and the end of Text 12 were reactivated by Beckett in
fuller form in *How It Is.* As Chapter 4 noted, that text ends with a renunciation of all that has gone before and it may be argued that if any relation
between subjects is possible, it is only in a shared fate to be expelled as
excrement into an excremental world. Part Three of *How It Is* fleshes out
the sketch with which Text 12 of *Texts for Nothing* ends in the creation of
millions of figures crawling in the mud and a divinity to arrange the sacks
and witness it all. This process, I would argue, is the same in kind as that
of *Texts for Nothing* in that, from an initial fictional birth into "being," an

entire world of suffering beings is fictionally generated. Hugh Kenner long ago realized the importance of this novelistic principle of generation:

> In obedience to purely logical laws, by the time the book is two-thirds over, the empty world is filled with an infinite number of beings, with social rituals, with memories, with educational processes and private lives, with mountains of tinned fish, millions of sacks, and even scribes, whole hierarchies of scribes. There is not a flaw in the process by which all this is generated; it fills the recumbent narrator with consternation, and he is reduced to waving it all away as illusion.[5]

All that is generated in the novel is renounced as "illusion" yet this should not detract from the fact that when individual illusions, or characters, are encountered in the novel they are not presented as illusion, but as corporeal, suffering beings. Chapter 4 dealt with the physical, suffering figure of Pim at some length, but even the figures of the scribes Krim and Kram, who are devised by the protagonist in order for him to be witnessed, are not immune from the process of generational decay. So, Kram recalls "Kram the Seventh at his last gasp perhaps his face whiter than the pillow-slip and me still a shitty little chit…"(71). One should note that Kram is here not exempt from the excremental, and that Kram the Seventh is not immune from suffering. Indeed, the Krams offer almost as unfortunate a catalogue of generational suffering as the Lynches, stretching back at least 13 generations and "who knows how long how many other dynasties" (72). Kram the Ninth was "raving mad before the limit brought up by force trussed like a faggot" (71), and it is clear that the scribes are present only through compunction and fear of punishment, so it is "forbidden to take our eyes off him" and "forbidden to touch him" (72) and the scribes must uphold "the honour of the family" before a nameless authority. As much as any other Beckett being, Kram wishes for release with little hope of his wishes being granted: "two more years to put in a little more then back to the surface ah no lie down if I could lie down and never stir any more…" (72). This is all generated out of nothing more than the protagonist's need to be witnessed: "all alone and the witness bending over me name Kram…" (69). Once Kram is willed into being in such a way, his predicament and the suffering ancestors are brought in to assert the feasibility of the fiction. In order to gain verisimilitude, even in this apparently abstract, fictional world, the beings created must be seen to be prey to the suffering inherent within life. This process is captured in miniature by the figure of the dog, Skom Skum. The dog only appears in a single verselet, yet this is long enough for it to be "run over by a dray" and for its spinal column to be broken (74). As soon as a being appears, it suffers.

But who is responsible for the suffering occasioned by the aesthetic generation of the figures of *How It Is* or *Texts for Nothing*? If Beckett is taking upon himself the maternal role of creation and giving birth to suffering worlds through words, then it is tempting to lay the blame at the door of the author himself. But this would only beg the question of what is meant by "Beckett" and "author." As the *Unnamable* suggested, it might rather be a question of "voices" and from where such voices originate. The protagonist in *How It Is* repeatedly claims to "say it as I hear it" (3). Similarly, *Texts for Nothing* is frequently troubled by a sense of "who says this?" (114), and the narrator seems to respond to "the weak old voice that tried in vain to make me...." (152). The manner in which the texts are transmitted is in doubt, and the questions of who is speaking, and, therefore, who is the *authority* of the text remain open. Addressing the question of who speaks in the "trilogy," Blanchot claims that we "might say it was the 'author' if this name did not evoke capacity and control..."[6] That the voice that is quoted in *How It Is* may be one of "capacity and control" is precisely at issue, given that the protagonist seems to have no choice but to "say it as I hear it" and that the quoting of the voice generates the embodied suffering of the text. This possibility of a controlling, competent voice is alluded to by J. E Dearlove, who suggests that the voice might be viewed as that of a divinity: "[The protagonist] uses the externality of the voice as the first premise in the proof of its divinity. If the voice is other and is the source of words, it may be the source of the murmurings of all the Pims and Boms. The voice is prime matter and prime mover."[7] She goes on to argue that the protagonist "construct[s] a universe over which such a voice would be the divine intelligence, only to end by acknowledging the errors of his system and his own responsibility for the voice." Dearlove is right to place responsibility at the center of the issue, and no less right to consider the competence and, indeed, *potency* of the voice at the behest of which an entire "universe" is constructed.

The protagonist initially refers to this voice in quasi-mythic terms: "Voice once without quaqua on all sides then in me when the panting stops tell me again finishing telling me invocation" (3). Such an invocation places the text within a classical, epic tradition (as Abbott has pointed out, albeit with a different emphasis[8]) with the protagonist calling on one of the muses to aid him in his relation. Previously, the muse had functioned in Beckett's fictions as little more than an excuse for a regrettable lapse in decorum; when Molloy is talking of his "arse," he blames it on the will of the muse, for example (*M* 80). The external/internal nature of the voice, to which Dearlove alludes, is embedded within the structure of the invocation itself. The voice is "without" and then "in me," while the phrase "telling me" delicately suggests both the protagonist as the subject of an imperative voice—"telling me what to do"—but also the protagonist as the material from which the voice takes its subject—"telling *of* me." This same external/internal nature is also evident in that most famous of invocations that begins Milton's *Paradise Lost*. The "heavenly Muse" is asked to "Sing" and first figured as an external, almost eternal inspirational force, or, if one prefers, a dictating voice. Yet, subsequently, the poet invokes "thy aid to my adventurous song," which implies that the "song" is part of the poet and only needs the help of the muse to bring it to the fore. As this classical muse changes into an invocation of the Holy Ghost, these two possibilities are retained:

> Instruct me, for thou know'st; thou from the first
> Was present, and with mighty wings outspread
> Dove-like sat'st brooding on the vast abyss
> And madest it pregnant: what in me is dark
> Illumine, what is low raise and support;
> That to the highth of this great argument
> I may assert eternal providence,
> And justify the ways of God to men.[9]

It may be tempting to see this brooding presence bringing creation out of the "vast abyss" as bearing more than a passing resemblance to the voice of *How It Is*. In the present context, however, the potency of the muse's voice is at once independent of, and drawing upon, the figure of the poet himself. The muse "know'st" (a sure indication of competence) and has the role of bringing light to bear on the darkness of the poet. One also notes that the muse is invoked to "make pregnant" the abyss in a recognition of the parturition of poetic creation.

If the voice of *How It Is* is invoked in such a classical manner, then it is already presented as being both external and internal to the figure in the mud. The inability to locate the voice has the subsequent effect of making the location of the "life in the light" images equally doubtful: they may be "memories" or "dreams" of the mud-bound figure, or they may be images whose source is within an external voice. Rather than trying to tie down these images to a definite locale, it might be better to recognize that the inability to do so effectively disperses the power relations implicit within the creation of those images and the world of *How It Is* itself. If the protagonist is only obeying the dictates of the voice, then he is a victim of a powerful imperative; if, alternatively, he is the source of the voice itself, then he is the dictatorial voice creating all. The text, though, does not allow one to rest on either of these solutions.

For J. M. Coetzee, this difficulty of locating the voice of authority in Beckett has been a feature of the works from a very early stage. One of the published essays that arose from Coetzee's PhD on Beckett, "Murphy" of 1971, appears to be a rather dry account of the variety of sentences that Beckett adopts in the novel. Yet the core issue is how the style of the prose deals with the question of authority, or, to put it another way, with the question of deployment of authorial power. He writes:

> As author, Beckett (or "Beckett") lends his authority to these sentences by printing them under his name; he also delegates this authority to his narrator, who on occasion delegates it in turn to various of the characters [...] For the reader to assign an authority to each sentence is thus a potentially complex task.[10]

The process that Coetzee describes is one in which authority is dissipated through the prose of the novel. Even the source of that prose, the historical figure of Beckett "himself" is already within those scare quotes functioning as a plurality of possibility, a double entity rather than a strong, singular authoring presence. Who is talking in *Murphy?* It is indeed difficult to decide as authorial presence slides between the overt, the mediated, and the occluded. In *How It Is* the same dispersal of authority occurs, albeit to an even greater degree. It is as if "Beckett" were shedding himself of the very power inherent within aesthetic production in the knowledge that any such production entails the suffering of beings just as if they had been subject to actual sexual reproduction. Such a shedding of authorial power would also amount to a shedding of authorial responsibility.

For this reason, the renunciations at the close of the novel are of crucial importance. Not only are the "fictions" of the text renounced as "all balls" but so too is the feint of a voice that is quoted: "my voice yes mine yes not another's no mine alone yes sure yes..." (128). And so the final verselet also necessarily means the "end of quotation" as the protagonist's voice takes sole responsibility and, once having done so, ends the text (129). This acceptance of responsibility may also be seen as an acceptance of the power within aesthetic production. Rather than a form of pure, disinterested manipulation of abstract notions, aesthetic creation demands "feasible" worlds and recognizable, that is, suffering beings who must be then witnessed by further beings. No matter how much Beckett tries to disperse the power and responsibility behind this creativity, that power retains its potency, leaving the cessation of the creation the only ethical alternative. This would be to reframe the debate over Beckett's "aesthetic of failure" and to suggest that Beckett, despite his best efforts, finds that aesthetic creation fails to fail enough.

Writing in the Womb

As even the relative minimalism of *How It Is* still succumbed to the potency of aesthetic reproduction, Beckett's attempts to "fail better" saw (to put it paradoxically) an increase in lessness.[11] In the short prose pieces of the 1960s, the journeying of such texts as *How It Is* is replaced by closed spaces in which, as if in a womb, bodies are fixed and investigated. It could be argued that these texts are, in many ways, imaginings of an intrauterine experience, and yet it is open to doubt whether, by taking creation back to a stage prior to parturition, Beckett thereby avoids or compensates for the trauma of birth as theorized by Otto Rank. Much of Rank's *The Trauma of Birth* is less concerned with the trauma itself than with the trauma's intimate link with the rise of civilization and art. In this context, Otto Rank and the Unnamable could not be more divergent in their opinions concerning the figure of Prometheus:

> The artist [...], like Prometheus, creates human beings after his own image, that is, he brings forth his work in ever new, constantly repeated acts of birth, and in it brings forth himself amid the maternal pains of creation.[12]
>
> The fact that Prometheus was delivered twenty-nine thousand nine hundred and seventy years after having purged his offence leaves me naturally as cold as camphor. For between me and that miscreant who mocked the gods, invented fire, denatured clay and domesticated the horse, in a word obliged humanity, I trust there is nothing in common. But the thing is worth mentioning. (*U* 13–14)

For the Unnamable, the fact that Prometheus aids humanity is enough to condemn him. Yet for Rank, Prometheus offers a significant representation of the social, religious, and, most importantly, artistic development away from the mother-as-creator to the father-as-creator figure. The Promethean artist "repeats the biological and prehistorical act of becoming human, the severance from the mother and the standing upright from the earth, in the creation and perfection of its aesthetic ideal of the human body."[13] This act of creation is predicated on the difficult, but necessary, denigration yet also imitation of the mother. According to Rank, women are able to perform a "complete reproduction of the primal situation" from which all have been banished through the "actual repetition of pregnancy and parturition," whereas the male normally only has recourse to the simulation of a partial return to the womb through the act of sexual intercourse. As we have seen, such a partial return is repeatedly rejected as unsatisfactory within Beckett's works. However, Rank offers another possibility, whereby the male "has to create for himself a substitute for this [female sexual] reproduction, by identifying himself with the 'mother' and the creation resulting from it of cultural and artistic productions."[14] This form of aesthetic reproduction then functions in imitation of the mother without recourse to the mother figure, just as the maternally based "Asiatic" religions gave way to the Greek ideal of a male creator of humanity, according to Rank. He goes on to argue that art developed from a practical and maternal form—that of the vessel or pot— to focus more on the content of the pot in the form of a child who, eventually, stood alone as an art form independent of the vessel of which it was once so inextricably part: "And when the later real art, which, so to say, completely freed human beings from the vessel, produced complete human beings, as did Prometheus and the Greek sculptors, we have to recognize in it the tendency to avoid the birth trauma, the painful deliverance."[15] Art, then, is a way of compensating for the trauma of birth, but one undertaken within a male-dominated (one could argue phallocentric) scheme consisting of the denigration, imitation, and, ultimately, the replacement of the mother.

From this brief description of Rank's faith in the power of art as a consolation for, and avoidance of, the birth trauma, it may already be inferred that Beckett's form of aesthetic reproduction fails in those terms. As Romantic aesthetic ideals, be they from Joyce, Schiller, or Schopenhauer, have been seen to fail, so too Rank's aesthetics of consolation fail to compensate for the trauma of birth when put to work by Beckett. Certainly, Rank's faith in a Prometheus producing humans in his own image would seem to be contradicted by Beckett's lack of faith in the positive possibilities of a Cronus who only produces humans in order to consume them, as Chapters 3 and 5 demonstrated. Yet the relation between the trauma of birth and the creation of art is as fecund a thought in Beckett's relation to Rank, as we have seen it to be in Beckett's relation to Schopenhauer.

In many ways, the "rotunda stories" of the 1960s—particularly "All Strange Away" and "Imagination Dead Imagine"—could be seen as a reversal of Rank's notion of an artistic progression from the "vessel" of the womb to the ideal of the human body "standing upright from the earth." Indeed, the rigidly confined and enumerated spaces of these stories invite identifications with the womb as readily as some have identified them with the skull. (As shall be seen, these identifications are far from mutually exclusive.) In both stories, human figures are caught within closed spaces in which light and heat—apparently from no identifiable source—rise and fall and into which faint sounds can intrude (at least in "All Strange Away"). To rise and stand upright upon the earth would be an impossibility for any of the figures of the stories, and indeed the earth itself has been largely banished from the texts, as occurs explicitly at the start of "Imagination Dead Imagine": "Islands, waters, azure, verdure, one glimpse and vanished, endlessly" (*CSP* 182). The particularized descriptions of the figures within the rotundas, which most commonly focus on one aspect of the body rather than on the body as a whole, amount to a form of dismemberment rather than any celebration of the human body that Rank sees as the epitome of classical, Promethean, Greek art. Beckett, then, takes his artistic creation back into the womb under controlled and reasoned conditions. It remains to be seen whether this acts as a consolation or an exacerbation of the birth trauma.

A close reading of the opening of "All Strange Away" reveals that while Beckett can be seen to be undoing Rank's optimistic theory of artistic progression—the body is now back in the "vessel" from which Promethean art had "freed" it—he may also be making more positive use of facets of Rank's aesthetic thought. As "Imagination Dead Imagine" after it, "All Strange Away" initially boldly cancels out all signs of life or art that had preceded it:

> Imagination dead imagine. A place, that again. Never another question. A place, then someone in it, that again. Crawl out of the frowsy deathbed and drag it to a place to die in. Out of the door and down the road in the old hat and coat like after the war, no, not that again. Five foot square, six high, no way in, none out, try for him there. (169)

This cancellation encompasses the tropes of Beckett's prose up to this point. The familiar quests of *Mercier and Camier, Molloy,* and (through the imagination of its protagonists) of *Malone Dies* and *How It Is* are to be replaced by a single, immoveable site. This cancellation recalls *The Unnamable* in which the question of place and being is of crucial concern: "It would help me, since to me too I must attribute a beginning, if I could relate it to that of my abode. [...] I shall say therefore that our beginnings coincide, that this place was made for me, and I for it, at the same instant" (6). The Unnamable's hypothesis is now given a literal depiction in the framing of "All Strange Away" as a place and a figure are willed into existence in an act of imagination. This renunciation of the quest, which amounts to what H. Porter Abbott has described as "narraticide," or the killing of sequential progression, focuses the beginning of the story on the initial creative moment itself.[16] As with the radio play *All That Fall*, the beginning of the story is enunciated out of nothing; in the case of the story, out of the whiteness of the page that precedes it and out of the "meremost minimum" of imagination, to use the phrase from *Worstward Ho*. (C 82) The imagination's first act is the creation of space, or the creation of the vessel into which the human figure can be placed. In this respect, Beckett places the narrative voice as one that creates both womb and fetus.

As Rank suggested, the narrative voice as aesthetic creator imitates the natural creative role of the mother, which should then entail an avoidance of, or consolation for, the trauma of birth in aesthetic and cultural production. Yet this is belied by the discomfort of both the male and subsequently the female figure within the rotunda, as the floor of the space burns his feet, and she, Emma, writhes in what little space she has. It is similarly belied by the manner in which the narrative voice worsens the situation in which the figures are trapped. From a space of "five foot square, six high," the initial cuboid is reduced to the final dimensions of the rotunda as "two foot across and at its highest two foot high," which are made still worse by the "full glare" of the light that torments the lashless eye of the enclosed figure. The womb-like space of the rotunda is less a place of peace than a site of slow physical and mental suffering ("faint sighing sound for tremor of sorrow at faint memory" [181]) as the narrative voice manipulates the enclosed figure. Similarly, Emma is not granted the boon of being beyond the will in this intrauterine state, but is still prey to desire and the frustration of desire. She is said to wish for "sweet relief" from her present condition and to be "longing for it again and to be gone again a folly to be resisted again in vain" (180). The womb is not then figured as a place of rest before the tragedy of being truly begins, but a site in which suffering and the will are already active.[17]

There then appears to be a contradiction. The previous chapters have argued for a desire within Beckett's art to avoid suffering engendered by the will by the hope of access to a quiescent womb-like state. Yet when such wombs are encountered, as in "All Strange Away," the same suffering and vain desiring pertain. However, just as the consolation offered by Romantic aesthetics was rejected in *Malone Dies* as purely aesthetic modes of creation came to be infected by the unfortunate consequences of sexual reproduction, so in "All Strange Away," the apparently pure methods of aesthetic creation are compromised as being imitations of natural processes. If the creator assumes the role of the mother, to use Rank's paradigm, then the creator is as guilty as the mother as they both perpetuate the will and suffering, albeit through different means. Once in existence, both real and imagined creations are inflicted with the suffering of being. This again directs us toward a profound pessimism within the works concerning their own consolatory possibilities. This pessimism is played out in "All Strange Away" both within the supposed "mind" of the Emma figure and also within the aesthetic assumption of the story as a whole. Emma's desire for relief from her situation leads her to punctuate the silence with "she's not here, for instance if in better spirits or, Fancy is her only hope..." (175). Placing hope in "Fancy" is to imagine a boon derived from the imagination. This hope is placed alongside further scraps of impotent consolations: "She's not here, Fancy is her only, Mother mother, Mother in heaven and of God, God in heaven, Christ and Jesus all combinations, loved ones and places, philosophers and all mere cries..." (180–81). Mother, religion, and philosophy are not offered as effective means of assuaging suffering, but are reduced to "mere cries." As these poor consolations are sloughed off as the story winds to a close, so too the hope in fancy is replaced by the assertion that: "Fancy dead" (181). As James Knowlson has argued, "Beckett [...] resuscitates the category of Fancy that the great Romantic poets considered decidedly inferior to Imagination, reminding us implicitly that he is a good deal less interested in the Sublime than they were."[18] This categorization of Fancy was most clearly expressed by Coleridge, for whom the essentially vital attributes of primary and secondary imagination contrast with Fancy which "has no other counters to play with, but fixities and densities." For him, "Fancy is indeed no other than a mode of memory emancipated from the order of time and space; and blended with, and modified by the empirical phenomenon of the will, which we express by the word choice."[19] The link between fancy and memory is certainly active within the text as Emma is prone to "sorrow at faint memory of a lying side by side" but this is renounced at the end of the story as "memory of lying side by side and fancy murmured dead" (181). Knowlson is certainly correct in suggesting that manipulation of Fancy does not give access to the sublime, yet the resuscitation of "Fancy" begs the question whether the imagination of the narrative voice is of the same or of a different order. Texts such as "All Strange Away" might often seem to be little more than playing with "fixities and densities," but throughout the story the Fancy of the figures in the text is counterpointed by exhortations to "imagine," as most famously, if oxymoronically, expressed in the opening sentence: "Imagination dead imagine." The paradox of the sentence is precisely what generates the story that follows, which is an attempt to relate without imagination, and thereby to reduce the imaginative faculty to that merely of Fancy. One notes the weariness of dealing with the "fixities" of a "place, then someone in it, that again," and how the text struggles to increase the fixity of the scenario that is described, until the figure of the woman in the rotunda is achieved.

Yet, no matter how much this process of reduction eradicates, a minimum obtains; a place, a body, scraps of thought uttered as "mere cries." The womb and the skull here coalesce as sites of imaginative creation and subsequent action on a body, which, like Pim in *How It Is*, is to be quickened into expression, even if that expression is, as here, the expression of the end of expression: Imagination dead imagine.

This process is encapsulated in *Worstward Ho*, some twenty years after "All Strange Away":

> On. Say on. Be said on. Somehow on. Till nohow on. Said no how on. [...]
>
> Say a body. Where none. No mind. Where none. That at least. A place. Where none. For the body. To be in. To move in. Out of. Back into. No. No out. No back. Only in. Stay in . On in. Still. (81)

The body is still an absolute necessity even when the fictional nature of that body is indicated: "where none." This body is intimately related to the act of speech, as were the bodies of *Texts for Nothing*, but the degree of intensity is now greater. Rather than an ambiguous external/internal voice, the body and the voice occur at the same moment with the first word of the text. "On" is at once an imperative of continuation and, through a pun on the Greek, "being" itself. In order to go "on" being is necessary. This imperative of onward being, as it might be called, is no longer mediated, but functions as a direct and powerful command. As soon as the body is commanded into existence through speech, a place for that body to inhabit becomes necessary. From nothing, the business of fiction is slowly, but inexorably, reconstructing a minimal world. Very soon it becomes apparent that the aesthetic creation of physical form is for pain to be inflicted:

> No bones but say bones. Say ground. No ground but say ground. *So as to say pain*. No mind and pain. Say yes that the bones may pain till no choice but to stand. Somehow up and stand. Or better worse remains. Say remains of mind where none *to permit of pain*. (82.; My emphasis.)

The causality here is somewhat surprising, perhaps, with pain the necessary precursor of a mind, bones, and ground rather than a result of being. The imperative voice creates an imagined world, later described as "hell of all" (101), in which suffering can function, seemingly in order for suffering *to* function. This demands a body and at the least a remnant of mind. This is of a different order to the suffering bodies of *Texts for Nothing* or *How It Is*, as there is no dispersal of the power inherent within the imperative voice.

When the voice of the text commands, the bones, the body and mind are immediately there for suffering to act upon.

This imperative aesthetic birth into suffering permeates throughout the late "trilogy" of *Company*, *Ill Seen Ill Said*, and *Worstward Ho*. The old woman of *Ill Seen Ill Said* is also brought into being with an imperative "on," but this time under the influence of the goddess of love:

> From where she lies she sees Venus rise. On. From where she lies when the skies are clear she sees Venus rise followed by the sun. Then she rails at the source of all life. On. (45)

The connection between Venus and "source of all life," the sun, is suggestive of the dangers inherent within love and sexual reproduction that this book has detailed, but this is now laid out in more abstract terms as the old woman is willed into being under the sign of erotic love with the promise of continuation of life following hard upon. This allusive opening to natural forms of reproduction—suns and sons keep rising—shadows the figure of the old woman who seems to come out of nothing, for Beckett does not allow art to transcend the reality upon which it depends, but rather repeatedly stresses the relation of the aesthetic to the real. So, the narrative voice opines:

> Already all confusion. Things and imaginings. As of always. Confusion amounting to nothing. Despite precautions. If only she could be pure figment. Unalloyed. This old so dying woman. So dead. In the madhouse of the skull and nowhere else. Where no more precautions to be taken. No precautions possible. Cooped up with the rest. Hovel and stones. The lot. And the eye. How simple all then. If only all could be pure figment. Neither be nor been nor by any shift to be. (53)

The language of family-planning—"despite precautions"—alerts us to how an attempt at pure aesthetic creation beyond the will-in-time is once again contaminated by the paradigm of sexual reproduction. Imaginings are not freed from the nature of being as suffering and so cannot be "pure figments." Despite precautions, life seeps into Beckett's prose no matter how minimal the aspects of that prose appear to be. The frustration that the meremost minimum is never minimal enough to exclude being occasionally takes hold of the narrative voice in a form of destructive panic: "Let her vanish. And the rest. For good. And the sun. Last rays. And the moon. And Venus. Nothing left but black void" (60). Only when such a void is reached will the narrator find "Home at last", or, to follow Rank, find a final, fatal compensation for expulsion from the womb. Yet that home is threatened by the power of creation: "Void. Nothing else. Contemplate that. Not another word. Home at last." As soon as words interrupt the void, the home it promises is destroyed. Beckett's art, then, cannot bring him into the silence that will compensate for life. It seems that the word will always become flesh.

It is in *Company*, however, that the ethics of aesthetic reproduction, and its dubious ability to offer consolation for the trauma of birth, is most clearly expressed. In details and structure, *Company* bears close resemblance to *How It Is*: the memories or dreams of "life in the light" are revisited in *Company* as spots of memories, which play tantalizingly across a biographical/fictional divide; in both texts a "voice comes to one in the dark" (3); at moments the figure in *Company* "crawls and falls" rather like the protagonist of *How It Is* (37) and in both texts, the text and company are renounced leaving the narrating voice "Alone" (42) at the close of novel. Yet *How It Is* is not the only presence, for *Company* is almost a repository of Beckett's prior fiction. So, the child asking how far away the sky appears revisits *Malone Dies* and "The End"; the creation of M and, subsequently W, in their "unnamability" (30) recalls Mahood and Worm of *The Unnamable*, if not also all the other *M*s of Beckett's fiction as well as Watt; the exhortation to "Imagine" and the figure "on his back in the dark" (3) recall the rotunda pieces of the 1960s. Somewhat more subtly, the scene, which initially was published separately as *Heard in the Dark 2*, of a tryst between two young lovers, which is punctuated by the memory of a child chuckling along with his father while reading *Punch*, captures a thematic that has been so strong in Beckett since "First Love": "I associate, rightly or wrongly, my marriage with the death of my father, in time" (*ECEFL* 61). In the memory, the child emulates the father in his chuckling and attention is drawn to the father's stomach. When the lover arrives, her own impregnated body merges with the father's distended paunch: "Your gaze descends to the breasts. You do not remember them so big. To the abdomen. Same impression. Dissolve to your father's straining against the unbuttoned waistband" (27). The Oedipal possibilities that I argued were pertinent to "First Love" are once again evoked here and the link between the figure of the father and sexual reproduction is clearly drawn. Indeed, it is through the figure of the father that the now-familiar trope of expulsion in birth is characterized, with its concomitant pattern of flight-and-return. The father flees home while labor is in progress to tramp along the mountain roads, returns in the evening to find the child has not yet been born and so flees once again to "the coach-house [...] where he housed his De Dion Bouton. He shut the doors behind him and climbed into the driver's seat. You may imagine his thoughts as he sat there in the dark not knowing what to think" (8). The flight from birth is followed here by an attempt to return to a womb-like quiet as he confines himself to the darkness of the car. He is on the verge of fleeing once more, when the news of the successful delivery comes and that "it was over at last. Over!" (8). In a further memory (or perhaps dream), the father exhorts his son to jump into the sea from a high board: "Be a brave boy. The red round face. The greying hair. The swell sways it under and sways it up. The far call again, be a Brave boy" (11). The father is again situated in a womb-substitute, this time the ocean, but the boy hesitates to join him.

The inclusion within *Company* of moments, motifs, and concepts from Beckett's prior fiction is augmented by apparently biographical details, which the account of the father during labor is purported to be. Such details include a birth date of "Easter Friday" (22); the child throwing itself from the top of a fir-tree (13); the death of a hedgehog the child had tried to save (18–19); the exhortation to dive into the Forty-Foot (11). These apparently biographical details have long been recognized and, as Daniela Caselli has pointed out,[20] Anthony Cronin for one has used them as direct real-life experience that then provide the "evidence" for the biographer to assert that the young Beckett was "physically adventurous and brave" but to such a degree that the "child psychologist might [detect] a certain level of disturbance."[21] James Knowlson is far more circumspect, partly because some of the scenes exist in Beckett's prior fiction, and partly because Beckett stated to Knowlson that he had "deliberately fictionalis[ed]" at least the pregnant lover scene. Knowlson goes on: "Yet it was clear in our discussion, not only that real-life incidents had been shaped and transformed to fit the fiction but that the scepticism that, as a young man, he had brought to his criticism of the role of memory in Proust (involuntary as well as voluntary) had been reinforced by the distance that separated him from his own past. Memory emerges here as very much like invention."[22] Knowlson and Abbott concur on the text's unwillingness, or inability, to function as biography. For Knowlson, traditional biography "relies on linear notion of time and on a causal view of human development. And Beckett breaks this mould by not presenting the memories chronologically and by deliberately ignoring any significant impact that they may or may not have had on a later self."[23] For Abbott, Beckett "repeatedly sabotages both the narrative character and historical authority of autobiography and [...] the 'figments' and 'imaginings' that emerge in the text are, as it were, unborn."[24] The supposed end-product of biography—a recognizable, explicable life—is not forthcoming in *Company* and, to use Abbott's pregnant phrase, the being in the text remains "unborn."

That this abortive life should occur in a text in which possible memories are restyled as "imaginings" once again points to the danger in the reproductive possibilities of aesthetic creation. In this respect, Abbott is surely correct to point out that the question of the generation of the text ("Can the crawling creator crawling in the same create dark as his creature create while crawling?" [34]) raises "the closely allied issue of paternity."[25] Of the father and lover scene, Abbott argues that "the voice aligns father, lover and the possibility of progeny in a spatial conflation of the master narrative of identity."[26] This master narrative and the father is then rejected by the close of the scene in which we see the young man with "eyes closed and [his] hands on [his] pubes." For Abbott, such moments of "narraticide," which also implies the rejection of paternity, suggest that "the whole structure of oedipal conflict undergoes erasure. The signs of originary force which so absorbed Beckett's attention throughout his life achieve a configuration, not within a dialectic of parent and self, but outside of it."[27]

There is an optimism to Abbott's account wherein Beckett's art successfully negotiates itself away from a procreative model—father passing on to son, and so on—and by so doing negotiates itself effectively out of time, and, therefore, beyond the Schopenhauerean will that expresses itself phenomenologically only in time. This may account for the text's refusal for the so-called memories to amount to a life, but the aesthetic process within the text when it concerns the figure in the dark and "devising it for company" still retains the dangers inherent within natural reproduction. Aspects of the paradigm that *Texts for Nothing* and *How It Is* developed—aesthetic creation of being leading to the inevitable suffering of being—are repeated time and again. One section is particularly clear in this respect:

> Why not just lie in the dark with closed eyes and give up? Give up all. Have done with it all. With bootless crawl and figments comfortless. But if on occasion so disheartened it is seldom for long. For little by little as he lies the craving for company revives. In which to escape his own. The need to hear that voice again. If only saying again, You are on your back in the dark. Or if only, You first saw the light and cried at the close of the day when in darkness Christ at the ninth hour cried and died. The need eyes closed the better to hear to see that glimmer shed. Or with adjunction of some human weakness to improve the hearer. For example an itch beyond reach of the hand or better still within while the hand immovable. An unscratchable itch. What an addition to company that would be! (*C* 36)

The narrative sequence beginning in that imperative of aesthetic creation, "If only saying…," is certainly brief, but it is nevertheless a sequence of the inevitable increase in suffering, or worsening. That worsening culminates in

a form of suffering that cannot be alleviated—the "unscratchable itch"—
which is compounded by the ironic use of Christ depicted at the moment
of greatest suffering, which has not yet been transformed into the promise
of the resurrection. Although, then, the "spots of memories" do not add up
to a life, the other figments of the figure in the dark repeatedly add up to a
brief history of worsening being. This, one notes, is almost met with joy on
the part of the narrative voice: "What an addition to company that would
be!" The ethical question that was raised in *How It Is* is here once again
pertinent. Is the creation of company on these terms acceptable? Weakness
and discomfort are added to the figure in the dark in order for that figure
to be more credible and therefore more effective as a source of company "in
which to escape his own" (36). The figure is then entirely at the disposal
of, and used by, the narrative voice in an attempt for that voice to alleviate
its own pain. Once again, Beckett's creating voice brings suffering being
out of nothing in order to act as a form of consolation. Once again, that
aesthetic consolation fails. The ambiguity of the phrase "figments comfort-
less" captures this dual operation: the figures within the figments are not
afforded any comfort, and the figments themselves do not ultimately offer
any comfort to the suffering-in-being of the narrative voice. Aesthetic creation, as the natural forms of procreation that it replaced in Beckett's work,
only succeeds in creating further suffering on the aesthetic plane. If the wish
"Oh never to have been" (*C* 12) is impossible in the text then the next best
thing is to cease to be and cease to continue the cycle of aesthetic creation:
"And how better in the end labour lost and silence. And you as you always
were. Alone" (42).

Out into the Theater

If, as we have seen, Beckett's late prose is marked by the regrettable power
relations inherent within aesthetic reproduction, then one way of avoiding
those relations might be through a change in media. Writing for the theater
must mean a change in the dynamics between creator and creation, not least
because the theater is already an embodied art form. No longer is the author,
or a form of surrogate voice within the text, entirely responsible for the generation of a suffering, embodied being as if out of nothing. Similarly, the voice
within the theater is already connected to a body that is directly accessible
to the audience and that can act as a guarantor for the words spoken. As
Steven Connor has summarized, "drama's claim to embody a 'metaphysics of
presence' rests largely upon two claims: that it represents human beings with
the actual bodies of human beings, and that it represents spoken words with
words spoken by those actual human beings."[28] In this way, it might be argued

that the power relations within aesthetic reproduction are already dispersed amongst different bodies and therefore the force of that power is dissipated.

However, the dispersal of authority within the theater might not be as simple a matter as the presence of an embodied voice might imply, and theatrical representation may also be implicated in the ethical problems of aesthetic reproduction. On one occasion, the reintroduction of a textual authority within Beckett's later plays verges on the perverse. In the sequel section of *Footfalls*, the pacing May changes tack in her monologue to refer to "Old Mrs. Winter, whom the reader will remember..." (*CDW* 403), which is then reaffirmed with "Amy—the daughter's given name, as the reader will remember..." (404). The reference to a textual origin (which does not appear to be the origin of the play on stage) creates a number of consequences, not least of which threatens the drama's claim to immediacy. As Stanton B. Garner Jr. puts it:

> On the more fundamental levels of perception and cognition, and in terms of narrative function, the author's presence is not felt in the theater as it is felt in so many ways in the printed text. The movement from script to performance liberates the play from its exclusively linguistic embodi-ment: language becomes speech, directions become mise-en-scène, implied presence becomes performance reality. Production realizes the play as something outside the printed text, and as such it stands on its own, shaped only invisibly by the text it seeks to embody.[29]

By reintroducing a printed text (although not necessarily *the* printed text), *Footfalls* is in danger of not standing on its own and, in effect, the process of "realization" threatens to be reversed, thus leading one back to the pres-ence of the author. And yet, as the text to which the reader, who does not exist, is referred is not the actual text of the play, a curious displacement of authority occurs. It is a displacement that Beckett had to address in the first German production of *Footfalls* at the Schiller-Theater Werkstatt, Berlin, in 1976. Walter D. Asmus, the director nominally in control of *That Time* and *Footfalls*, made detailed notes of events in rehearsal.[30] As might be expected, the actress playing May, Hildegard Schmahl, had some difficulties in get-ting her performance correct, and, understandably, she wanted some form of motivation for her character's words and actions, yet Beckett was famously chary of giving such tips. The Old Mrs. Winter difficulty and the question of the "reader" arises, and, in order to help, Beckett first tries to place the written text in terms of May's character. Beckett was reported as saying on Thursday, September 2, 1976: "One can suppose that she has written down everything which she has invented up to this, that she will one day find a reader for her story—hence the address to the reader." On Monday, September 6, Ms. Schmahl appears to be still unhappy, and Beckett tries a different tack: "It shouldn't give the impression of something already written down. May is inventing her story while she is speaking." This little insight into the instructions given to one of the many Mays is a curious slide in which Beckett gradually shifts his explanations with the possible aim of making them seem less upsetting to the theatrical context. Beckett seems to be aware that he must absent himself as author and authority if the actress is to perform theatrically. In the production in Berlin, this meant a tactical withdrawal on Beckett's part, as on Thursday, September 16, he told the increasingly frustrated Schmahl that "I will leave you alone for a few days." He duly did. Yet one also notices that Beckett's comments are an attempt to displace a "textual authority" away from the author and onto the character within the drama, as if May were quoting a text ("I say it as I hear it") of which she is the author. That this is done at the instruction of the actual author is not a little ironic.

The thematic of regrettable reproduction, both natural and aesthetic, and the subsequent suffering of life is as present in *Footfalls* as it is in Beckett's prose. The voice of the mother intones: "I had you late. [*Pause.*] In life. [*Pause.*] Forgive me again. [*Pause. No louder.*] Forgive me again" (400). Rather like Molloy, this is something that May/Amy cannot forgive; she is silent and resumes her pacing. The fact that a reminder of the expulsion into life is sufficient to get May moving on her repetitive, cyclical journey may be read as a microcosm of the expulsion-return-and-flight pattern that so many of Beckett's characters adopt in the face of having been born. That May has no choice but to "revolve it all" in her "poor mind" (403), where the "it" is ambiguous yet seems to have the force of "all this life," results in Beckett adopting the technique we have seen applied in *How It Is* and *Company*: he just stops, as the final section reveals a bare stage with no "trace of May" in a form of renunciation of all that has gone before (403).

That birth is the agent of suffering within the play has been attested to by Billie Whitelaw, who in turn quotes Beckett: "He told me this story of attending a lecture of Jung's. Jung brought in this girl, of about 21 [...] He said, 'The trouble with this girl is that she was never properly born.' I think perhaps Amy, May in the play was not properly born. That's all I needed to know."[31] Beckett is here recalling the Jung lecture he attended with Bion in 1935, which had already been put to use in *All That Fall*. As an ill-born being, May, like so many of Beckett's characters, seeks a womb-substitute in the room that she paces and that she appears not to have left for many years. What is also of concern here, though, is once again the question of authority and, therefore, responsibility. As we have seen, Beckett attempts to disperse the authority behind the play through the displacement-device of the "hidden" text being revealed and suggesting May herself is the author of this text, in some sense. Yet, Whitelaw needs only a brief anecdote from Beckett for the play to become clear to her and therefore performable. In this way, Beckett provides the necessary supplement for the text to become represented in the theater. It is then, one might argue, Beckett himself who is the authority of the play and hence the one responsible for creating a suffering, ill-born being in the figure of May.

Beckett's control within the theater during his lifetime has become somewhat legendary and, in the context of his attempts to disperse power within the prose and *Footfalls*, seemingly contradictory. Steven Connor has suggested

> that Beckett's power and prestige as a writer have come after his turn to the theatre means that his reputation is established within a discourse underwritten by a network of power relations, in which the authority of the author is always to some degree pitted against his medium.[32]

To trace these power relations is to trace the fluctuations of a voice. Connor notes that Beckett preferred to work with a small coterie of trusted actors and that "Beckett hears in these performers the voice that speaks to him when he is writing…" The result, Connor argues, is that "the actors' voices are no longer repetitions of Beckett's own voice, but rather of a deeper more authentic voice that speaks through him and his writing."[33] This would amount to Beckett utterly dispersing any authority. He is the "victim" of a voice that is distanced from him still further by that voice being realized as that of an actor who will ultimately embody that voice on stage. The end product—an actor on stage saying lines—is here being reconfigured as a point of beginning. In contrast, Connor argues that the result of the actors' voices functioning as muses for a "deeper voice" is that the actors become interchangeable and that this "helps restore the texts to the ownership of its central authorial voice."[34] Connor may well be correct, and if one traces the question of the "voice" in the process of the writing and performance of the late plays a complicated entanglement emerges. James Knowlson recounts how Beckett came to write *Not I*, saying of the "character" which would become Mouth: "I knew that woman in Ireland. I know who she was [...] And I heard 'her' saying what I wrote in *Not I*. I actually heard it."[35] Beckett is here placing himself in the same position as the protagonist of *How It Is*; he is only saying it as he hears it, or quoting from a preexisting voice. When Knowlson pushed Beckett for further details of the genesis of the play, Beckett referred him to *The Unnamable* who "had no voice but must speak." By referring to a prior work, Beckett would seem to be suggesting that *The Unnamable* is also a form of quotation of this preexisting voice that moves through, but does not originate in, Beckett. Yet, as Billie Whitelaw again demonstrates, Beckett's own speaking voice then becomes the arbiter of the voice that is heard on stage. Of *Rockaby*, which was supposedly written for Whitelaw,[36] the actress describes how first she rehearsed with Beckett over the telephone to get "from him an indication of the basic things, how fast, how slow" and that then, thereafter: "I can hear it in my head. I can hear him saying it. I imagine Sam saying it."[37] Whitelaw's dependence on this voice was such that she could not envisage performing his plays once Beckett was dead: "I've never been without him. I don't know what I would do without him. When he dies, I think that's it. I don't know how I would start without him."[38] From the theoretical position in which the absence of the author is necessary for theatrical performance to truly gain its own life, we have come to the situation in which that theatrical life, at least for one performer, is unimaginable without the presence of the author.

This question of the voice within Beckett's late plays is important not only as it seems to link with similar, troubling issues within the prose but also because it raises the question of how the voice effects the bodies within Beckett's theater. After all, the sufferings that are inflicted upon a Pim or an Emma of "All Strange Away" remain only within words, whereas, if such suffering is to be staged, then the body of the actor may become the site of that suffering. The forms of sadism which previous chapters have noticed take on a more embodied, and so possibly more troubling, actuality within the theater. In Beckett's late theater, the body is most often subjected to interrogation, manipulation, and dismemberment at the behest of a voice of dubious origin. If, as Connor claims, the immediacy of theater derives in part from "spoken words with words spoken by those actual human beings" then Beckett's theater marks a movement away from this identification in such plays as *That Time,* in which the link between the transfixed head and the three recorded voices is precisely not embodied, or *Rockaby* in which the overwhelming majority of the words in the play are offstage and recorded, or again in the television drama *Ghost Trio* in which a disembodied voice directs our gaze at a lone figure. Even when the onstage presence gives voice to words, it is uncertain whether all those words "belong" to that presence: the Reader of *Ohio Impromptu* takes his words from the book that he reads; in the sequel section of *Footfalls*, May speaks in the third person of Amy and adopts a form of playscript; Speaker in *A Piece of Monologue* again uses the third person and takes on the language of stage-direction ("Then slow fade up…Takes off globe and disappears. Reappears empty. [427]); and, of course, Mouth in *Not I* refuses to accept the first-person pronoun.

Indeed it is in *Not I* that the issues of the voice, the body, and aesthetic reproduction can be seen most clearly. The text of the play coincides with the birth of the subject of the monologue: "out...into this world...this world...tiny little thing...before its time...in a godfor—...what?...girl?.. yes...tiny little girl...into this...out into this...before her time...godforsaken hole...called...called...no matter" (*CDW* 376). The repetition of "this" and the suspension of "godforsaken hole" allow for "this" to apply to the theater space itself. Moreover, "this" and "godforsaken hole" are equally applicable to the mouth; a hole in which the girl is created and from which she is expelled.[39] Of course, this description is suggestive of Mouth as a vagina; a suggestion that has long been part of the reaction to the play. Knowlson, in *Frescoes of the Skull*, notes that *The Times* reviewer of the UK premiere suggested that "in isolation [mouth] could be any bodily orifice," and then Knowlson goes on to report that "Beckett displayed no trace of displeasure as, watching the BBC television version, he realized that Mouth had the appearance of a large gaping, vagina."[40] The lips of Mouth as labia has more recently led Ann Wilson to argue that the audience assumes a pornographic gaze and that "Mouth is an image of castration, for she is both castrated (marked by the absence of the phallus) and potentially castrating" and that such an image "cannot be construed as feminist."[41]

Whether or not the image of Mouth can be construed as feminist or trapped within the Order of the Father, the temptation to equate Mouth with the vagina is strong, and is not only sanctioned by Beckett's lack of "displeasure" at the thought but, more importantly, by the text itself as the "girl" and the words that constitute the play are pushed out into the world. This is reinforced, and perhaps complicated, by the stage directions that precede the words of the text. For someone so famed for reinventing the conventions of the theater, Beckett is curiously conservative about the nature of the preexisting physical aspects of the theater. This is no more evident than in his insistence on the opening of the curtain in *Not I*: "As house lights down Mouth's voice unintelligible behind curtain. House light out. Voice continues unintelligible behind curtains, 10 seconds. With rise of curtain ad-libbing of text as required leading when curtain fully up and attention sufficient into..." (376). And then the text "proper" begins with the word "out." The curtain then functions as another vaginal image, with the unintelligible words as a form of intrauterine activity, from which Mouth is herself expelled to then expel the play and the figure of the girl in what amounts to a succession of births: of Mouth, and then, through Mouth, of the play and the "She" of the text.

Ann Wilson has criticized Knowlson and Pilling in *Frescoes of the Skull* for describing a "textual economy within which feminine sexuality is erased" by a "slip" that "fuses the vagina and the anus."[42] As previous chapters have argued, the relationship between birth and excrement, vagina and anus, is far from being a slip, but is part of the sexual economy that Beckett developed and deployed across his works. We should now add to this economy the relation between the mouth and the anus. Yoshiki Tajiri has argued that "the most conspicuous displacement of organs in Beckett's work occurs between the mouth and the anus" and goes on to refer to *Texts for Nothing* that speaks of the "the head and its anus the mouth [...] slobbering its shit and lapping it back off the lips..." (*CSP* 104). The lines of displacement are deepened and strengthened by this link, whereby the mouth of *Not I* can at once be equated with the vagina and with the anus as channels of birth in the literal and figurative senses. We return to the idea of being born as shit into the shit. However, with the mouth now figured as anus and vagina, an extra element has come into play; the element, to use Keir Elam's word, of "wordshit."[43] Certainly, the words that the "She" of the narrative blurts out are equated with such a concept: "sudden urge to...tell...then rush out stop the first she saw...nearest lavatory...start pouring it out...steady stream...mad stuff..." (*CDW* 382). Wilson, who argues against the vagina/anus relation, prefers to view this moment in terms of menstrual flow. Such an interpretation is consistent with the mouth as a vagina but, in terms of the present argument, has the unfortunate implication of denying the reproductive thematic within the scenario. If the words of "She" are to be equated with menstruation then this would suggest fertility but that which is produced—the menstrual blood—would signal that conception has not occurred. With the words as fecal matter, the reverse becomes possible. The relation between feces and reproduction is attested to across Beckett's works, from the sexual stimulus of defecating horses in *Dream* and *The Unnamable* through to Molloy imagining himself born through the anus and his "first taste of the shit" that entailed being destined for "less compassionate sewers" (*M* 15). As "wordshit," Mouth's words are waste products, but in the dual sense of fecal matter to be flushed away and an offspring destined for a similar fate. Yet these words also constitute the play itself, so, when Mouth says, "out...into this world...this world...tiny little thing...," that little girl is generated by and in the wordshit and is herself waste, the "offscourings of fornication" (*MC* 31), to use Mr. Madden's words, from a relation with no love of any kind: "parents unknown...unheard of...he having vanished...thin air...no sooner buttoned up his breeches...she similarly...eight months later...almost to the tick...so no love..." (376). The girl is abandoned as just so much waste.

The connections and displacements between mouth/vagina/anus and words/child/excrement also, however, lead us back to the figure of Mouth itself as a site of creation and expulsion, engendering and then abandoning its products, but also as that which has been created and expelled. The opening of the stage curtain and the spot bearing down on Mouth make its appearance coincide with the opening "out." This connection facilitates and encourages the almost identification of Mouth with the "she" of the narrative and, when one hears of "she" giving way to her logorrhea, the narrative description mirrors the stage image:

> her lips moving...imagine!...her lips moving!...as of course till then she had not...and not alone the lips...the cheeks...the jaws...the whole face...all those—...what?...the tongue?...yes...the tongue in the mouth...all those contortions without which...no speech possible...(379)

Although, as the stage image does not encompass the cheeks, jaws, and whole face of the description, the identification of Mouth and She must remain provisional, yet the audience is left in little doubt that some form of connection obtains between the two, perhaps because of the theater's traditional dependence on an embodied voice. As the situation of Mouth is so extreme—merely a jabbering orifice—then the identification with "she" panders to the audience's need to understand why this situation pertains. The text warns against such "vain questionings" and yet the narrative still persists in asking them of "she" and, therefore, by association, of Mouth itself: "something that would tell...how it was...how she—...what?...had been...yes...something that would tell how it had been...how she had lived...lived on and on...guilty or not..." (381). The question of guilt is not specific, rather the text asserts that one is guilty and punished "for some sin or other...or for the lot...or no particular reason...for its own sake..." (377). As Knowlson long ago suggested only "the possibility that she is being punished unjustifiably for the original sin of having been born remains unrefuted."[44] The words/child/excrement axis reinforces precisely this point and, moreover, implicates the creator of words in the opprobrium which might more normally be directed at the creators of offspring.

This, of course, raises the issue of whose words one hears pouring out of Mouth. Again, the connection between Mouth and She encourages us to see Mouth as alienated from the words coming babbling from the lips, just as She speaks in a "voice she did not recognize" (379). Furthermore, Mouth, in her questions and qualifications, is clearly responding to some other voice: "...what?...not that?...nothing to do with that?...nothing she could tell?...all right..." (382) It might be tempting to link this to the "buzzing in the brain," as if Mouth were changing her monologue in order to bring it into line with what Simon Critchley has called the "tinnitus of existence." For Critchley, Mouth's babble, like that of the Unnamable, is a "narrative voice [that] approaches a void that speaks as one vast, continuous buzzing, a dull roar in the skull like falls..."[45] Yet, a different approach might be taken via the often overlooked figure of the Auditor, who raises and lowers his hands in a "gesture of helpless compassion" (375) on three occasions during the pause following "what?...who?...no!...she!" (379, 381, and 382). The Auditor has most often been seen as a mediator between the audience and the Mouth image and voice, and this might account for the ambivalent attitude Beckett has displayed toward this figure. Yet, although Auditor is obviously primarily a listener, I would suggest that the figure might be seen as a mediated presence for the author, Beckett, and precisely because the role is one primarily of a listener. This would be to take seriously Beckett's claim that "I heard 'her' saying what I wrote in *Not I.* I actually heard it."[46] In this case, the Auditor is still a mediator between audience and voice but rather more in the sense that an author is always already a mediator of the texts they produce, as if compelled by a voice or muse. As mediator, such an author takes no responsibility for the text other than a responsibility of fidelity to the inner voice that dictates that text. As the author is not responsible for the being that is created, no matter how limited, and the suffering that being experiences (and there may be two beings at stake: Mouth and She), the ethical position adopted must be precisely that of "helpless compassion." This was precisely the position Beckett *physically* took in an often repeated anecdote, here told by James Knowlson: "When Beckett's American director, Alan Schneider, questioned Beckett as to whether Auditor was a death figure or a guardian angel, the author shrugged his shoulders, lifted his arms and let them fall to his sides, leaving the ambiguity wholly intact."[47] By repeating the gesture of the Auditor in such a way, the link between that figure and Beckett may be hinted at. Certainly the attitude of impotence is shared by both, and, moreover, Beckett here seems to renounce knowledge and power over his own work. And yet, at the same time, Beckett refers the questioner back to the play as a site of knowledge in the very same gesture with which he disavows his own knowledge of that work. It seems that the "author" can do nothing to prevent the voice he hears from engendering being in the work, and must watch helplessly, just like the Auditor, at the consequences of that birth.

The relation between speech and birth in *Not I* is revisited in *A Piece of Monologue,* in which theatrical presence and the aesthetic creation of being are closely allied. Speaker (who once again speaks in the third person) admits from the start that "birth was the death of him" and yet is still obliged to try to bring a form into being "Again" (*CDW* 425). On the next occasion when being is aesthetically generated, Speaker comments: "Nothing. Empty dark. Till first word always the same. Night after night the same. Birth. Then slow fade up of a faint form. Out of the dark" (427). The use of the language of stage direction—of a play, moreover, which the audience does not see—is here allied precisely with speech as the agent of generation. As soon as one says "birth" a form, no matter how faint, is created out of the dark of nothing. On a later occasion in which Speaker speaks a form into being, oral, vaginal, and phallic images converge: "It gathers in his mouth. Birth. Parts lips and thrusts tongue between them. Tip of tongue. Feel soft touch of tongue on lips. Of lips on tongue" (428). The eroticized play of lips and tongue serves to equate this asexual, aesthetic generation with sexual reproduction, and, as the first words of the play demonstrated, to be born is to generate "the end"; to give death its power by entering into life. No wonder, then, that "never but the one matter. The dead and gone. The dying and the going. From the word go" (429). That "go" has a similar imperative force to the "On" of the late prose. As with *Not I,* however, the question of the voice is again crucial. Speaker certainly speaks, yet it is unclear if his speech is responsible for the aesthetic births within the text. Rather, it appears the Speaker is describing the process of aesthetic birth as experienced by the "he" of the narrative who must wait "for the first word" that "gathers in his mouth," seemingly of its own volition. The lines of displacement are such that the Speaker tells of a figure who speaks "birth" yet who seems to be merely a conduit for words—"The words falling from his mouth. (428)"— rather than in control of them. This places the Speaker at least two removes away from the point of potent annunciation; he is merely telling "how it is" rather than responsible for "how it is."

This question of who lays claim to the generating voice might best be approached through *Rough for Radio II* and *Cascando.* These texts may be exemplary primarily because they are plays for radio, and so the voice can be regarded as generating the aesthetic object and actually constituting that object. A secondary reason is that both plays have been taken to represent Beckett's creative process. Of *Rough for Radio II,* Martin Esslin has argued that it is "one of the clearest, least 'encoded' statements of Beckett's view of the artistic process or, at least, his own process of creation."[48] Esslin later elaborated this concept: "Beckett represents the process of his own creativity as a writer by an 'animator' and his secretary who takes down the utterances of a little man, who is usually gagged and blindfolded, but taken out each day and asked to speak."[49] Of *Cascando,* Michael Robinson has written: "For once, and only once, Beckett's own presence enters directly into his mature work. This is the sole comment he has allowed himself on the nature of the stubborn enterprise he has been engaged in for almost half a century."[50] A third reason for the importance of these radio plays, and the most interesting for the present volume, is the manner in which voice and aesthetic reproduction are thematically brought to the fore. In *Rough for Radio II,* Fox is tortured into uttering: "...my brother inside me, my old twin, oh to be he and he—but no, no no. [...] Me get up, me go on, what a hope, it was he, for hunger. Have yourself opened, Maud would say, opened up, it's nothing, I'll give him suck if he's still alive, ah but no, no no" (*CDW* 279). It is certainly tempting to see this as representing the writer bringing aesthetic life to some element of his own psyche—or, rather, precisely refusing to do so—and this birth metaphor is all the more compelling for the displaced, yet nourishing, mother-figure of Maud. A similar process can be seen in *Cascando,* albeit in more abstract terms: "Opener," who opens and closes the listener's access to "Voice" and "Music" does so in a metaphorically suggestive manner: "I'm afraid to open./ But I must open. / So I open" (302). Comparing these two moments, Paul Lawley has perceptively argued that they "combine the ideas of forced birth and forced utterance: utterance has gathered an ontological significance." Lawley goes on to argue that the "connection between the figure of the 'difficult birth' and the generation of the dramatic world is [...] more than merely fortuitous" and, indeed, that the "figure penetrates the dramatic medium."[51] Of course, the birth imagery is crucial here, but it begs a further question: who or what is the agent of conception? If one accepts that idea that these two plays are in some way representative of the creative process of the artist, is the artist in control of the engendering voice, or a victim of it?

The paradigm of artistic creation within *Rough for Radio II* suggests that all involved are victims. Of course, Fox as source of the voice and the subject of the torture inflicted by Animator, Stenographer, and Dick is the most obvious victim and the most obvious representation of the artist. In a departure from the displacements of the voice from an individual of which we have become aware, the life of which Fox speaks is unambiguously a "life of his own" (278), thus suggesting that he is responsible for the aesthetic output. Yet his words are only brought forth through the crude exertion of power, in a manner similar to the relation between the protagonist of *How It Is* and Pim, as if Fox would have remained silent had it not been for the application of torture. On the other hand, the torturers themselves may be viewed as victims. They are apparently under the strict control of a nebulous "they" who dictate the terms of the torture, and the Animator, Stenographer, and Dick will not be released from their roles until the right word has been uttered, but "of course we do not know, any more than you, what exactly it is we are after, what sign or set of words" (282). However, the allusive nature of the text suggests that the word they are looking for should in some sense be literary. The references to Dante and Laurence Sterne (the first a mainstay of criticism on Beckett, and the second a less frequent, but still familiar, point of reference for Beckett scholarship) suggest that what Fox says should be brought into a literary tradition and therefore recognizable as literary art. So, Animator admires the phrase "such summers missed" for its sibilant, and, therefore, aesthetic literary qualities. The irony of the end, in which Animator insists on the interpolation of "between two kisses" into the record of Fox's speech, is not only that Animator has failed to be faithful to the voice he has heard but also that he has "give[n] way to literature" (*M* 158), in the words of Moran, by adding an erotic element (here in italics) to the description: "Have your self opened, Maud would say, *between two kisses*, opened up, it's nothing, I'll give him suck if he's alive" (284).

This lapse into the literary on the part of the Animator should be placed in the context of the highly sexualized nature of the play itself. The Animator repeatedly leers after the Stenographer, and wishes himself thirty or forty years younger; Dick—whose name has clear phallic overtones—wields a bull's "pizzle" or penis, rather than a conventional whip, in his beating of Fox; the Stenographer is urged to kiss Fox "on his stinker of a mouth" as a further form of torture: "Till it bleeds! Kiss it white! [*Howl from* Fox.] Suck his gullet!" (282). And, finally, the fact that Maud offers to give suck to Fox's phantom twin means "someone has fecundated her [...] If she is in milk someone must have fecundated her" (283). The clear suggestion is that the guilty party must be Fox himself. The sexualized context leads us back to a main argument of this book that aesthetic creation cannot remain pure and disinterested but is continually being infected by the paradigm of sexual reproduction. The error that the Animator makes in his interpolation of "between two kisses" is the reintroduction of a sexually reproductive element into Fox's speech. This reintroduction then transforms Fox's utterances into aesthetic speech already informed by sex and, therefore, in Schopenhauer's terms, the will-to-live. In such conditions, it is highly unlikely that the torturers and their victim "may be free," as the Animator hopes at he close of the play. That this reintroduction is regrettable is made all the more plain by Fox's own form of reproduction not coming to fruition. He negates the possibility of opening himself and giving birth to his phantom twin with "no, no no," and the other moments of utterance suggest rather an ability to be born than a wish for it. As Paul Lawley suggests: "Fox's three utterances can be seen to construct a scenario of a self-birth attempted yet blocked."[52] In terms of aesthetic reproduction, the paradigm here is intriguing, with the artist (Fox) not wishing to aesthetically reproduce and yet an insistence upon the part of others (Animator, etc) that he does so, which leads to a sexualization of the aesthetic product. Whether one wishes to figure these others as critics, scholars, or a wider reading public, little matters; what is of concern is the inevitability of the inclusion of the sexual within the aesthetic product once it has been translated from an initial artistic vision. "Translation" is here the key word that takes us back to Beckett's Schopenhauer-inspired view of artistic genius in *Proust*. Following Schopenhauer closely, Beckett argues that the process of aesthetic production is one whereby once the "artist has acquired the text; the artisan translates it" (*Proust* 84). According to the interpretation of *Rough for Radio II* just offered, difficulties arise precisely in this exchange between artist and artisan, even if they are the same person. It is through the process of translation into a communicable aesthetic form that the problems of those forms becoming infected by the will-to-live arise. The translation, then, fails, and tortured and torturer will not be freed.

The role of "Opener" as representation of the artist in *Cascando* at first sight couldn't be more different from that of Fox. Rather like the Auditor of *Not I*, Opener is offered as a mediator of the voice. Although "they" identify Opener as the source of the voice—"He opens nothing, he has nothing to open, it's in his head" (300)—Opener insists that there "is nothing in my head [. . .] I open and close." As such, Opener is a "neutral medium for the transmission of sounds the content of which is beyond [his] control."[53] As Clas Zilliacus suggests, the "drawing together" of Voice and Music in the play, which the Opener mediates by opening and closing access to sound and voice, is predicated on the increasing abstraction of Voice's story. "The less Voix particularizes," writes Zilliacus, "the more Voix and Musique agree."[54] Voice's words, then, have the example of music to aspire to; an example informed by Beckett's very Schopenhauerean view in *Proust* of the possibilities of music where "music is the Idea itself, unaware of the phenomena, existing ideally outside the universe, apprehended not in Space but in Time only, and consequently untouched by the teleological hypothesis" (*Proust* 92). To bring words to the level of music would then be to rid words of their relation to phenomena, to bring them out of time, and therefore remove them from the will-to-live. Unfortunately words may approach this state, but, to approach is not necessarily to reach, so, at the close of the play, Opener and Voice are still urging "come on" as it is "*nearly*. . . this time. . . it's the right one. . . finish. . . no more stories. . ." (304). Although Opener can be seen as a mediating figure, he does lay claim to a relation between himself and the text of the play. In response to those who say, "That is not his life, he does not live on that," Opener contends, "I have lived on it. . . till I'm old. / Old enough. / Listen" (300). This suggests Opener is rather less a figure of mediation than a figure of translation. The "life" (rather like Fox's twin) is translated into the artistic medium (the story of Woburn), yet that process of translation necessarily means the story will not transcend the will-in-time.

The examples of *Not I, Rough for Radio II* and *Cascando* all suggest that aesthetic reproduction refuses to forego its potency, no matter how much the artist wishes to bring that reproduction out of the will-in-time through failure and impotence. Once the voice is broached, being cannot be avoided. In Beckett's final play, *What Where*, a note of regrettable resignation to the potency of aesthetic creation can be detected. The play opens with a voice, once again, which then creates a world as if out of nothing, in a parody of the God of Genesis creating light: "I switch on... Not good" (*CDW* 470). A space is thereby illuminated through which four figures (Bam, Bem, Bim, and Bom) come and go. There comings and goings are then repeated, "now with words," (472) at which point it becomes apparent that the sole purpose of their activities is to torture a figure into speech:

Bam: You gave him the works?
Bom: Yes.
Bam: And he didn't say anything?
Bom: No.
Bam: He wept?
Bom: Yes.
Bam: Screamed?
Bom: Yes.
Bam: Begged for mercy?
Bom: Yes.
Bam: But didn't say anything?
Bom: No. (473)

Bom is not believed and so is tortured in turn by Bim, who is in turn tortured by Bem and so on, until only Bam is left onstage. The confession that is sought is never forthcoming. This roundabout of pointless torture, which only results in gathering screams and tears, seems as if it will never end as Bem has not yet returned from his torturing of Bim at the close of the play, at which point Bam and his voice over a megaphone are left to conclude: "I am alone/ In the present as were I still. / It is Winter. / Without journey. / Time passes. / Make sense who may. / I switch off" (476). Many of the elements that this chapter has discussed are here in a skeletal form: a generating voice of uncertain origin, suffering beings engendered in an enclosed space and then tortured (unsuccessfully) into speech, a final renunciation and close. The names of the torturers and tortured, Bam, Bem, Bim, and Bom, are reminiscent not only of *How It Is* but also of the Clinch twins of *Murphy* and are therefore suggestive of the play as a form of summation of Beckett's works. Largely interchangeable figures are each brought into being to act as torturer and victim in a fruitless search for "what where," which, once known, will end the sadistic series. As each victim lapses into unconsciousness because of the pain inflicted, the "what where" cannot be forthcoming. Although the end of the play might only be a passing respite, this idea of passing into unconsciousness suggests another way in which the sadistic cycle can be broken: one can refuse to enter into speech at all and embrace the quiescence of unconsciousness. If the potency of aesthetic creation is such that speech inevitably engenders suffering it might certainly be better just to "switch off" (*CDW* 476).

Conclusion

Beckett's career is marked by a paradox of diversity and coherence. Few writers in the twentieth century have ranged across genres to the degree that Beckett has. From essays to poetry to prose and drama, he has apparently restlessly moved from genre to genre, challenged the traditions of those genres, and often blurred the lines between them. One must of course add to this the fact that Beckett was for most of his career shuttling between two languages (and, with the addition of German, into which he also translated his work in his later career, one might argue three) not only between works, but within the works themselves, so that there are at least two *Endgame*s, two *Godot*s, two *Molloy*s. Yet, despite this diversity, Beckett's signature across the oeuvre is unmistakable, so it is not out of place, and is indeed common, to think of Beckett's career as following an unwavering arc of development, with the artist honing and cutting his resources to the point of abstraction or pure expression: an ending that can be envisaged, one might argue, even in his earliest prose. Such a characterization might be debatable, but, then, the feeling of a family likeness between the Speaker of *A Piece of Monologue* and Molloy, for example, allows us, without too much hesitation, to speak of the "Beckett character," the "Beckett bum," or even "Beckettian man"; a figure already discernible in Belacqua of *Dream of Fair to Middling Women*.

This coherence in diversity might be explained by a further constant in his work: the regrettable and suffering nature of being. From *Proust* onwards, the refrain has been that it is better not to exist, that being born is a calamity, a sin for which one cannot atone. It is a refrain that Beckett found within pre-Socratic thought, in the theology of Augustine, in the pessimism of Schopenhauer, in the pages of Proust, in the theories of Otto Rank, and elsewhere. This is never more clear than in the manner in which Beckett dealt with sex and sexuality over his career. I have argued that what appears to be an almost instinctive, and certainly Swiftian, disgust with sex in the early prose is more a reaction against the reproductive possibilities of sexual intercourse. Nonreproductive sexual activity—be it masturbation, anal penetration, or homoerotic forms of sexual expression—persist throughout the work in what might amount to a surprising degree of sex within Beckett's oeuvre. The exploration of sexual forms has also been seen to have a disruptive effect in terms of the social mores within which Beckett was enmeshed, particularly in respect of his native Ireland. But sexual expression does more than just challenge the supposed prudery of the Irish Free State. The turn into nonreproductive forms of sexual expression, including possible same-sex relations, refuses to ally social identity within sexual preference. Rather than championing a "queer" sexuality in counterpoint to the "normal," and thereby restricting the queer within the parameters it might seek to question, Beckett's ambiguous use of nonreproductive sexuality severs the link between the sex object and the identification of the subject that approaches it. More often than not, Beckett's characters are indifferent to the niceties of sexual choice and the identity politics that plays around that choice, and merely seek a means to scratch the itch of sexual desire, no matter how feeble that desire might be. In this respect, Molloy, who has quite a full sexual history, can serve as an example. He is not too concerned which orifice is involved in sex as long as there is the "unction of a little mucous membrane..." (*M* 57).

The need to scratch the itch of sex, however, indicates the tenacity of sexual desire, and, therefore, the tenacity of the will-to-live. Beckett's indebtedness to Schopenhauer is never more clear than in this shared belief in the link between desire, procreation, and the creation of further suffering beings as momentary phenomena of the ever-living, and ever-demanding, will-to-live. Accepting that the will-to-live and procreation are the means by which suffering enters the world (and, as we have seen, the same point is made in different terms by St. Augustine and Mani) is one thing; how to then avoid perpetuating suffering is quite another. So, Beckett's aesthetic creation is shadowed by natural forms of procreation, and all the attendant horrors. Although Beckett attempts to turn away from paradigms of creativity that are informed by, or predicated on, natural procreation, the result still remains the same: the creation of a suffering being. This is compounded by the fact that Beckett, as author, must elicit speech and possibly even meaning from this new suffering being; and the means to that end are further suffering. In such a way, artistic creation is implicated within the same ethical considerations as sexual reproduction. No matter how abstract his prose or drama become, Beckett's works—so often a question of beginning again out of nothing—are unable to attain a pure form of creation that is not in some way based upon the paradigm of sexual reproduction, or infected by it. Art, then, is still seen to be held within the field of the will-to-live and unable to escape. It is on this point that Beckett breaks with Schopenhauer and the Romantic notion of surpassing the will through aesthetic means. Beckett does not see art as any consolation for life, but as implicated within the suffering of life.

The regrettable potency of aesthetic creation has been implied by many of the arguments in this book. It is a potency with which Beckett struggled throughout most of his career. This is to suggest that Beckett's so-called aesthetics of failure is not a description of his work, but an aim his works fail to reach; an aspiration of failure, not an actuality. This, one might suggest, derives from the nature of aesthetic creation itself, for, in the words of Otto Rank, the "root of the problem of art [...] is finally a *problem of form*. As it appears to us, all 'form' goes back to the primal form of the maternal vessel..."[1] In these terms, Beckett's restless cross-genre explorations were always doomed to fail if the hope was to find a form free from the implications of birth. No matter what technical means were adopted, the return to the site of the womb as a site of creation, which also entails expulsion, was inevitable. Paradoxically, the more Beckett tried to avoid traditional forms, the more the presence of the "maternal vessel" was felt. So, the more abstract Beckett's work grew, the clearer the "primal form" became, and with it the inevitability of replicating aspects of actual birth on the aesthetic plane. The "meremost minimum" of the late prose and plays was still drawn to the emergence of a suffering and often dismembered body within a confined space. A body in a place seem to be the minimum of Beckett's art, and they are not minimal enough.

Of course, one play dispenses with this meremost minimum: *Breath*. The curtain opens on a stage empty but for scattered rubbish. The cry of an infant being born is heard, immediately followed by an intake of breath as the lights grow to their brightest. Silence. The breath is let out as the lights lessen to their dimmest. The cry of the infant is heard once more. Silence. The curtain closes. These simple elements combine to form an image of the troubled relation between sexual and aesthetic reproduction that has formed the core of this book. The stage, as Rank implies, is a womb-like space, already filled with the detritus of life. The first, brief, faint vagitus of the child is at once a being entering into the world and entering into suffering. It barely matters whether the cry is because of expulsion from the womb or the demand for food and comfort, for both speak to the same process: one is expelled into desire, want, and, hence, suffering. The inspiration and exhalation of breath, coupled with the image of the rubbish strewn across the stage, suggest that while there is life, there is waste and the discarded;

a world of scraps and remnants rather than fullness or plenitude. The second infant's cry suggests a common Beckettian notion: that one is born astride the grave, or that death is to be born again through the "great cunt of existence" (*MD* 114). One can argue over the details of these moments and how they are juxtaposed, but one thing, I would suggest, is clear: that at this most abstract point of Beckett's art, modes of aesthetic and sexual reproduction coalesce. The stage might be clear of actual human form, but the necessity for a space—a womb—remains. The cry we hear may not be embodied, but it is a cry in response to the space we see on stage; a cry of suffering as the child is expelled into life. The cry is repeated at the close, as if in death. Procreation, birth, suffering, and death are here paralleled by the business of the theater. The curtain opens, "life," as if out of nothing, is revealed on the stage, and the suffering action ensues at the prompting of a voice the audience cannot hear—the voice of the text. Thus, even in so abstract a play, Beckett's art is still doing *too much*. As soon as aesthetic creation is entered into, a world is created—the womb-like stage—and a suffering being associated with that world is also brought into life. It seems as if Beckett cannot rid his art of the unfortunate implication that aesthetic creation means bringing beings into a world, and, because they are in a world, making them suffer.

As my argument has progressed, one question has repeatedly emerged, and it is a question for which I have no answer. If I am correct, and Beckett never freed his art from the ethical implications of an aesthetic creation infected by paradigms of sexual reproduction and so continued to create suffering beings on the aesthetic plane, why did he not take the only possible option open to him? Why, almost to his deathbed, did Beckett keep creating? Why did he not just stop?

Notes

Introduction

1. Samuel Beckett, "Waiting for Godot" in *Samuel Beckett: The Complete Dramatic Works* (London: Faber and Faber, 1990), 18. Hereafter all Beckett plays, except *Eleutheria,* are cited in the body of the text as *CDW.*
2. Frederick Simoons, *Plants of Life, Plants of Death* (Madison: University of Wisconsin Press, 1998); see especially Chapter 4, "Mandrake, a Root Human in Form."
3. William Shakespeare, *Henry VI, Part 2,* Act III, sc. 2, l.314, *The Complete Oxford Shakespeare I: Histories,* eds. Stanley Wells and Gary Taylor, (Oxford: Oxford University Press, 1987).
4. Hugo Rahner, *Greek Myths and Christian Mastery* (New York: Biblio and Tannen, 1971), 257–8.
5. Jonathan Dollimore, *Death, Desire and Loss in Western Culture* (Harmondsworth: Allen Lane, Penguin, 1998), 46.
6. Ibid., 44.
7. St. Augustine, *Confessions,* 8.1, trans. R. S. Pine-Coffin (Harmondsworth: Penguin, 1961), 158. Cited by Beckett in *Beckett's Dream Notebook* (Reading, PA: Beckett International Foundation, 1999), 20. Beckett used the 1907 Everyman library edition, translated by E. B. Pusey.
8. St. Augustine, *Concerning The City of God against the Pagans,* trans. Henry Bettenson (Harmondsworth, Penguin, 2003), 591.
9. Ibid., 577.
10. Ibid., 524.
11. Ibid., 515.
12. Ibid., 523.
13. *Malone Dies,* (London: Faber and Faber, 2010), 114. Hereafter cited in the body of the text as *MD.*
14. James Knowlson, *Light and Darkness in the Theatre of Samuel Beckett* (London: Turret Books, 1972). Although Manichaeism is in some senses a Gnostic religion, I prefer that the terms are separated, not least because certain forms of Christian Gnosticism were attacked for promiscuity, whereas Manichaeism

advocated and practiced extreme asceticism for the *perfectus* of the religion. Similarly, the Gnostic reverence for the female Sophia (knowledge) does not sit well with Beckett's occasionally virulent misogyny. For Gnosticism and Manichaeism, see Yuri Stoyanov, *The Other God: Dualist Religions from Antiquity to the Cathar Heresy* (New Haven, CT: Yale University Press, 2000).

15. M/S Reading 1396/4/16. XV, 45. Reprinted in Knowlson, *Light and Darkness in the Theatre of Samuel Beckett.*

16. S. E. Gontarski, *The Intent of Undoing in Samuel Beckett's Dramatic Texts* (Bloomington: Indiana University Press, 1985). Gontarski notes how Manichaean thought segues well with that of Schopenhauer to such a degree that he feels able to move from Manichaean to Schopenhauerean terminology when discussing *Krapp's Last Tape.* (In particular cf. 60.)

17. "Proust" in *Proust and the Three Dialogues with Georges Duthuit,* (London: Calder, 1987), 67. Hereafter cited in the body of the text as *Proust.*

18. Calderón de la Barca, *La Vida es Sueño,* I,i, 111–2, ed. Albert Solomon (Manchester: Manchester University Press, 1961); "To have been born is mankind's greatest sin," in *Life is a Dream,* trans. William E. Colford (New York: Barron's 1958).

19. Arthur Schopenhauer, *World as Will and Representation,* Vol. I, trans E. F. J. Payne, (New York: Dover, 1969), §51, 254.

20. Arthur Schopenhauer, *Essays and Aphorisms,* trans. R. J. Hollingdale (Harmondsworth: Penguin, 2004), 63.

21. Arthur Schopenhauer, *World as Will and Representation,* Vol. II, trans E. F. J. Payne, (New York: Dover, 19 69),13–14.

22. Schopenhauer, *World as Will and Representation,* Vol. I, § 60, 328.

23. Schopenhauer, *Essays and Aphorisms,* 47–8.

24. Gottfried Büttner, "Beckett and Schopenhauer," *Samuel Beckett: Endlessness in the Year 2000, Samuel Beckett Today/Aujourd'hui* 11 (2002): 116.

25. Schopenhauer, *World as Will and Representation,* Vol. I, §68, 390.

26. Ibid., §57, 314.

27. Ibid., §34, 178–9.

28. Ibid., § 27, 152.

29. Ibid., § 60, 327.

30. Ibid., § 62, 334.

31. Ibid., § 36, 185.

32. Ibid., § 37, 195.

33. Ibid., § 52, 267.

34. Alan Goldman, "Plain Sex," in *The Philosophy of Sex: Contemporary Readings,* eds. Alan Soble and Nicholas Power (Lanham, MD: Rowman and Littlefield, 2007), 56.

35. Robert Solomon, "Sex and Perversion," in *Philosophy and Sex,* eds. Robert Baker and Frederick Elliston (Buffalo, NY: Prometheus Books, 1975), 279.

36. Roger Scruton, *Sexual Desire: A Philosophical Investigation* (London: Continuum, 2006), 14.

37. Alan Soble, "Masturbation Again," in *The Philosophy of Sex: Contemporary Readings*, ed. Alan Soble and Alan Nicholas Power (Lanham, MD: Rowman and Littlefield, 2007), 75–98.
38. Christopher Hamilton, "Sex," in *The Philosophy of Sex: Contemporary Readings*, 103.
39. Ibid.
40. Ludwig Wittgenstein, *Philosophical Investigations I*, trans. G. E. M. Anscombe (Oxford: Blackwell, 1983), § 66.
41. Samuel Beckett, *How It Is*, (London: Faber and Faber, 2009), 66. Hereafter cited in the body of the text as *HII*.

1 A Rump Sexuality: The Recurrence of Defecating Horses in Beckett's Oeuvre

1. Author's comment to Eoin O'Brien, Introduction to *Dream of Fair to Middling Women* (Dublin: Black Cat Press, 1992), x.
2. John Pilling ed., *Beckett's Dream Notebook* (Reading: Beckett International Foundation, 1999), 47–57; 59–69.
3. Samuel Beckett, *Dream of Fair to Middling Women* (Dublin: Black Cat Press, 1992), 1. Hereafter cited in the body of the text as *Dream*.
4. John Pilling, *A Companion to* Dream of Fair to Middling Women (Tallahassee, FL: Journal of Beckett Studies Books, 2004), 17.
5. Marcel Proust, *In Search of Lost Time Vol. 1 Swann's Way*, trans. C. K. Scott Moncrieff and Terence Kilmartin, ed. D. J. Enright (London: Vintage, 1996), 164.
6. *Ibid.*, 164–168.
7. Samuel Beckett, *Molloy*, (London: Faber and Faber, 2009), 12. Hereafter cited in the body of the text as *M*.
8. Hugh Kenner, *Samuel Beckett: A Critical Study* (London: John Calder, 1962), 124.
9. Ibid., 123.
10. C. J. Ackerley rightly asserts in conversation that the inclusion of the horn allows for Wagnerian overtones at the end of Molloy's narrative. The manuscript evidence supports this. However, once the horn is inserted into the text and the possibilities of its presence are explored by Beckett, a Wagnerian resonance does not preclude those of a different nature, such as the sexualized reading offered here.
11. Samuel Beckett, *Mercier and Camier* (London: Faber and Faber, 2010), 70. Hereafter cited in the body of the text as *MC*.
12. Janet Menzies, "Beckett's Bicycles," *The Journal of Beckett Studies* No. 6 (1980): 101.
13. Ibid., 99.
14. Jake Kennedy, "Modernist (Im)mobilities: Marcel Duchamp, Samuel Beckett and the Avant-Garde Bike," *Tout-fait: The Marcel Duchamp Studies On-Line Journal* (2005): 1, www.toutfait.com/online_journal_details.php?postid=4331.

15. Gilles Deleuze and Félix Guattari, *Anti-Oedipus: Capitalism and Schizophrenia,* trans. Robert Hurley, Mark Seem, and Helen R. Lane (London: Athlone Press, 1984), 2.
16. Pilling, *A Companion to* Dream of Fair to Middling Women, 18.
17. Sigmund Freud, *Case Histories I: "Dora" and "Little Hans,"* The Penguin Freud Library Vol. 8, trans. Alix and James Strachey, ed. Angela Richards (London: Penguin, 1983), 283.
18. Ibid., 284.
19. Ibid., 264.
20. Ibid., 286.
21. Sigmund Freud, "The Sexual Theories of Children," in *On Sexuality: Three Essays on the Theory of Sexuality and Other Works, The Penguin Freud Library* Vol. 7. trans James Strachey, ed. Angela Richards (London: Penguin, 1991), 197. The emphasis is Freud's.
22. Freud, *Case Histories I,* 239.
23. Ibid., 217.
24. Beckett, *The Unnamable,* (London: Faber and Faber, 2010, 45. Hereafter cited in the body of the text as *U.*
25. Freud, *Case Histories I,* 285.
26. Ibid., 197.
27. Ibid., 290.
28. A homophonic pun on the French for mother.
29. Letter to Nuala Costello, February 27, 1934, in *The Letters of Samuel Beckett: 1929–1940,* eds. Martha Dow Feshenfeld and Lois More Overbeck (Cambridge: Cambridge University Press, 2009), 187–188.
30. Ibid., 188.
31. Ibid., 192.
32. The offspring of a female donkey and a male horse.
33. C.f. Mary Bryden, *Samuel Beckett and the Idea of God* (London: Palgrave, 1998), 109, where she points out the Greek for hinny, *ginnos,* is not to be found in the original Biblical accounts of the entry into Jerusalem. If it is Maddy's own mistake, this only further personalizes the issue.
34. Psalm 145:14. The King James Bible.

2   The Horror of Sex

1. Jeri L. Kroll, "Belacqua as artist and lover: 'What a Misfortune,'" *The Journal of Beckett Studies,* Vol. 3 (1978): 11.
2. Yoshiki Tajiri, "The Mechanization of Sexuality in Beckett's Early Work," *Samuel Beckett Today/ Aujourd'hui* Vol 12 (2002): 195.
3. Matthew Feldman, *Beckett's Books: A Cultural History of Samuel Beckett's "Interwar Notes"* (London: Continuum, 2006), 148–9.
4. John Fletcher, *Samuel Beckett's Art* (London: Chatto and Windus, 1967), 129.

5. Samuel Beckett, *Murphy* (London: Faber and Faber, 2010), 71. Hereafter cited in the body of the text as *Murphy*.

6. Within Murphy's first zone of mind "the pleasure was reprisal, the pleasure of reversing the physical experience. Here the kick that the physical Murphy received, the mental Murphy gave. It was the same kick, but corrected as to direction." (71)

7. Letter to Thomas McGreevy, 12 September 1931, *The Letters of Samuel Beckett 1029-1940* ed. Feshenfeld and Overbeck (Cambridge: Cambridge University Press), 87.

8. Thomas W. Laqueur, *Solitary Sex: A Cultural History of Masturbation* (Cambridge, MA: Zone Books, 2003).

9. Ruby Cohn, ed., "MacGreevy on Yeats," in *Disjecta: Miscellaneous Writings and a Dramatic Fragment* (London: Calder, 1983), 95.

10. Samuel Beckett, *Collected Poems 1930–1978* (London: Calder, 1986), 16.

11. Lawrence E. Harvey, *Samuel Beckett: Poet and Critic* (Princeton, NJ: Princeton University Press, 1970), 260.

12. Ibid., 76.

13. David Green, "Beckett's *Dream:* More Niente than Bel," *The Journal of Beckett Studies,* Vol. 5 Pt. 1&2 (1995): 70.

14. Ibid., 77

15. St. Augustine, *Confessions* VIII, 7, trans. R. S. Pine-Coffin (Harmondsworth: Penguin, 1961), 169.

16. Samuel Beckett, *More Pricks than Kicks* (London: Faber and Faber, 2010), 17. Hereafter cited in the body of the text as *MPTK*.

17. Kroll, "Belacqua as Artist and Lover," 37.

18. Voltaire, *Candide, or Optimism*, trans. Henry Morley (1922), introduction and notes Gita May (New York: Barnes and Noble Classics, 2003), 45.

19. Kroll, "Belacqua as Artist and Lover," 50.

20. Sigmund Freud, "Three Essays on Sexuality," in *On Sexuality*, 70.

21. Ibid., 69–70.

22. John Fletcher, *The Faithful Shepherdess,* ed. F. W. Moorman (London: Dent, 1972).

23. Andrew Gibson, "Afterword: Beckett, Ireland and Elsewhere," in *Beckett and Ireland,* ed. Sean Kennedy (Cambridge: Cambridge UP, 2010), 184.

24. C. J. Ackerley, *Demented Particulars: The Annotated Murphy* (Tallahassee, FL: Journal of Beckett Studies Books, 1998), 130.

25. The evidence that Miss Counihan may be a prostitute is slight, but somewhat compelling. When Wylie decamps to London, we are told that Miss Counihan's attractions begin to pall and that "It was only in Dublin, where the profession had gone to the dogs, that Miss Counihan could stand out as the object of desire of a man of taste." (*Murphy* 123) The profession is clearly implied to be prostitution, although this does not quite amount to saying that Miss Counihan was actually a prostitute, although her financial motivations throughout the novel seem stronger than her emotional ones. One might add to this that Neary asks Murphy to "define let us say [his] *commerce* with this Miss

Counihan..." (6. Emphasis added.) At the least, there is undoubtedly a strong association between Miss Counihan and financial gain through love.

26. John Pilling, "*Proust* and Schopenhauer: Music and Shadows" in *Beckett and Music,* ed. Mary Bryden (Oxford: Oxford University Press, 1998), 174.

27. Again Beckett departs from Schopenhauer in his condemnation of opera. The latter is much more relaxed about the role of the librettist. See Pilling above.

28. Greene, *Menaphon,* in *The Dramatic and Poetical Works of Robert Greene and George Peele,* ed. Rev. Alexander Dyce (London: Routledge, 1861), 286–291.

29. Peele, "The Hunting Cupid", in *The Dramatic and Poetical Works of Robert Greene and George Peele,* ed. Rev. Alexander Dyce (London: Routledge, 1861), 603.

30. Ackerely, *Demented Particulars,* 184. It is Ackerley who first identified the source of the songs.

31. Jennifer M. Jeffers, *Beckett's Masculinity* (New York: Palgrave Macmillan, 2009), 47–50.

32. David Hatch, "Samuel Beckett's 'Che Sciagura' and the Subversion of Irish Moral Convention," *All Sturm and No Drang: Beckett and Romanticism/Beckett at Reading 2006, Samuel Beckett Today / Aujourd'hui* 18 (2007): 242.

33. Ibid., 254.

34. Ibid., 252.

35. Ibid., 253.

36. 1 Cor.7:1–2, The King James Bible.

37. St. Augustine, *On Marriage and Concupiscence,* Bk I, ch. 5, trans. Philip Schaff (Whitefish, MT: Kessinger, 2010), 265.

38. Ibid., 270.

39. Ibid., 271.

40. "Resolutions from 1930," Lambert Conference, http://www.lambethconference. org/resolutions/1930/1930-15.cfm.

41. Pater Marin, *Censorship in the Two Irelands 1922–1939* (Dublin: Irish Academic Press, 2006), 81.

42. Ibid., 60, 62.

43. Cited in Diarmaid Ferriter, *Occasions of Sin: Sex and Society in Modern Ireland* (London: Profile, 2009), 188.

44. Mary Louise Roberts, *Civilization without Sexes: Reconstructing Gender in Postwar France, 1917–-27* (Chicago: University of Chicago Press, 1994), 94.

45. Cited in Ferriter, *Occasions of Sin,* 191.

46. Angus McLaren, *Twentieth-Century Sexuality: A History* (Oxford: Blackwell, 1999), 4.

47. George Bernard Shaw, "The Censorship," *Irish Statesman* 11 (1928), reprinted in *Banned in Ireland: Censorship and the Irish Writer,* ed. Julia Carlson (Athens: University of Georgia Press), 134.

48. Ibid., 136.

49. McLaren, *Twentieth-Century Sexuality,* 67.

50. William B. Yeats, "The Censorship and St. Thomas Aquinas," *Irish Statesman* 11 (1928), reprinted in *Banned in Ireland,* 130–133.

51. "The Irish Censorship," *The American Spectator* 1 (November 1932), reprinted in *Banned in Ireland*, 141.
52. "The Mart of Ideas," *Bell* 4 (June 1942), reprinted in *Banned in Ireland*, 149.
53. Ferriter, *Occasions of Sin*, 2.
54. Quoted in Terence Brown, *Ireland: A Social and Cultural History, 1922–1985* (London: Fontana, 1987), 146.
55. Ferriter, *Occasions of Sin*, 141.
56. Cited in Ferriter, *Occasions of Sin*, 108.
57. *Irish Times*, February 6, 1935, quoted in Marin, *Censorship in the Two Irelands*, 206.
58. Evidence to the Committee of Euan Duffy, October 30, 1930, cited in Ferriter, *Occasions of Sin*, 142.
59. Ackerley, *Demented Particulars*, 10.
60. J. C .C. Mays, "Young Beckett's Irish Roots," *Irish University Review: A Journal of Irish Studies*, 14 (1984): 23.
61. Rina Kim, "Severing Connections with Ireland: Women and the Irish Free State in Beckett's Writing," *Historicising Beckett / Issues of Performance, Samuel Beckett Today / Aujourd'hui*, 15 (2005): 62.
62. Ackerley, *Demented Particulars*, 10.
63. "The Censorship of Publications Act, 1929." Part I, Preliminary paragraph 2: Definitions. The Irish Statute Book. http://www.irishstatutebook.ie/1929/en/act/pub/0021/print.html#sec2.
64. Sigmund Freud, "'Civilized' Sexual Morality and Modern Nervous Illness," in *Civilization, Society and Religion: The Penguin Freud Library*, vol. 12, ed. James Strachey and Albert Dickson (London: Penguin, 1985), 46.
65. McLaren, *Twentieth-Century Sexuality*, 113.
66. Quoted in Terence Brown, *Ireland: A Social and Cultural History, 1922–1985*, 146.
67. Quoted in Ferriter, *Occasions of Sin*, 111.

3   The Horrors of Reproduction

1. Samuel Beckett, *The Expelled, The Calmative, The End, First Love* (London: Faber and Faber, 2009), 80; Hereafter cited in the body of the text as *ECEFL*.
2. Phil Baker, *Beckett and the Mythology of Psychoanalysis* (London: Macmillan, 1997), 93.
3. Sigmund Freud, *Case Histories II: The Penguin Freud Library* Vol. 9, trans. James Strachey (London: Penguin, 1990), 317.
4. J. D. O'Hara, *Samuel Beckett's Hidden Drives: Structural Uses of Depth Psychology* (Gainesville: University Press of Florida, 1997), 75.
5. Baker, *Beckett and the Mythology of Psychoanalysis*, 95.
6. Freud, *Case Histories II*, 322.
7. Ibid, 340.
8. Ibid., 341.

9. Otto Rank, *The Trauma of Birth* (1929; repr., New York: Dover, 1993), 29.
10. Ibid., 47.
11. For subtle uses of Rankian motifs, see Feldman, *Beckett's Books*, 31; 114–115.
12. Baker, *Beckett and the Mythology of Psychoanalysis*, 96.
13. Rank, *The Trauma of Birth*, 35.
14. Ibid., 47–48.
15. Ibid., 28.
16. Ibid., 85.
17. The "Whoroscope Notebook" cited by Feldman, *Beckett's Books*, 64.
18. Friedrich Nietzsche "Philosophy during the Tragic Age of the Greeks," in Rank, *The Trauma of Birth*, 169.
19. Susan Brienza, "Clods, Whores, and Bitches: Misogyny in Beckett's Early Fiction," in *Beckett's Women,* ed. Linda Ben-Zvi (Urbana and Chicago: University of Illinois Press, 1990), 101.
20. Mary Bryden, *Women in Samuel Beckett's Prose and Drama: Her Own Other* (Lanham, MD: Barnes & Noble, 1993), 7.
21. Rubin Rabinovitz, "Stereoscopic or Stereotypic: Characterization in Beckett's Fiction," in *Women in Beckett: Performances and Critical Perspectives,* ed. Linda Ben-Zvi (Urbana: University of Illinois Press, 1992), 115.
22. C. J. Ackerley, "*Lassata Sed*: Samuel Beckett's Portraits of his Fair to Middling Women," *Samuel Beckett Today/Aujourd'hui* 12 (2002): 56.
23. James Acheson, "Beckett and the Heresy of Love," in *Women in Beckett*, 68.
24. Kristin Morrison, "'Meet in Paradize': Beckett's Shavian Women," in *Women in Beckett*, 82.
25. Brienza, "Clods, Whores, and Bitches," 101.
26. Bryden, *Women in Samuel Beckett's Prose and Drama*, 6.
27. Ibid., 7.
28. Ibid., 20.
29. According to Bryden, "E. M. Cioran relates in *Partisan Review* a conversation with Beckett when the latter picks out for special mention a passage from *Gulliver's Travels* in which the hero is paralysed with fear at the advance of a young female Yahoo...," *Women in Samuel Beckett's Prose and Drama,* 48.
30. John Fletcher, "Samuel Beckett and Jonathon Swift: Toward a Comparative Study" http://www.themodernword.com/beckett/paper_fletcher.html (accessed December 16, 2010): 14 (pagination according to PDF file).
31. Ibid., 13.
32. Ibid., 14.
33. Vivian Mercier, "Samuel Beckett and the Sheela-na-gig," *The Kenyon Review* XXIII (1961): 305.
34. Ibid., 323, 323–24.
35. Ibid., 308.
36. Ibid.
37. Rank, *The Trauma of Birth*, 20.
38. Ibid., 35.

39. Ibid., 188.

40. Daniella Caselli, "The Child in Beckett's Work: Introduction," *Historicising Beckett/Issue of Performance Samuel Beckett Today/Aujourd'hui* 15 (2005): 259.

41. Terence Brown, "Some Young Doom: Beckett and the Child," in *Ireland's Literature: Selected Essays* (Mullingar: Lilliput, 1988), 117.

42. Stephen Thompson, "'It's not my fault sir': The Child, Presence and Stage Space in Beckett's Theatre," *Historicising Beckett/Issues of Performance: Samuel Beckett Today/Aujourd'hui 15* (2005): 262.

43. Ibid., 261–2.

44. Terence Brown, "Some Young Doom," 119.

45. *Company* in Samuel Beckett, *Company/Ill Seen Ill Said/Worstward Ho/Stirrrings Still* (London: Faber and Faber, 2009), 6. Hereafter cited in the body of the text as *C*.

46. John Calder, *The Philosophy of Samuel Beckett* (London: Calder, 2001), 129.

47. Brown, "Some Young Doom," 125.

48. Ibid., 131.

49. St. Augustine, "On the Merits and Forgiveness of Sins, and on the Baptism of Infants," in *St Augustine Anti-Pelagian Writings: Nicene and Post-Nicene Fathers of the Christian Church* Vol. 5 (1887), trans. Philip Schaff (Whitefish, MT: Kessinger, 2004): iii, 7, 71.

50. Augustine, *Concerning the City of God against the Pagans*, trans. Henry Bettenson (Harmondsworth, Penguin, 2003), xiii, 3, 512.

51. Ibid., xiii, 6, 515.

52. Arthur Schopenhauer, *Essays and Aphorisms*, trans. R. J. Hollingdale (Harmondsworth: Penguin, 2004), 63.

53. Schopenhauer, *World as Will and Representation* I, trans. E. F. J. Payne (New York: Dover, 1969), §60, 328.

54. Ibid., §51, 254.

55. Schopenhauer, *Essays and Aphorisms*, 47.

56. Thompson, "'It's not my fault sir'", 264.

57. Lee Edelman, *No Future: Queer Theory and the Death Drive* (Durham and London: Duke University Press, 2004), 11. Edelman advocates challenging the hegemony of the child and the political framework of futurity through the figure of the *Sinthom*osexual, one who embraces negativity, one who "affirms a constant, eruptive jouissance that responds to the inarticulable Real, to the impossibility of sexual rapport or of ever being able to signify the relations between the sexes" (74). The inhumanity, marginalization, abject nature, and negativity of the *Sinthom*osexual make comparisons with Beckett's male anti-heroes tempting and suggests one possible queer reading of Beckett's works.

58. Ibid., 13.

59. Schopenhauer, *Essays and Aphorisms,* 50.

60. Ibid., 47.

61. Schopenhauer, *World as Will and Representation* Vol. I, §27, 152.

62. Sean Kennedy, "'A Lingering Dissolution': *All That Fall* and the Protestant Fears of Engulfment in the Irish Free State," *Assaph: Studies in the Theatre* 17/18, (2003): 255.

63. Schopenhauer, *Essays and Aphorisms,* 49.
64. Mary A. Doll, *Beckett and Myth: An Archetypal Approach* (Syracuse, NY: Syracuse University Press, 1988), 6.
65. C. J. Ackerley and S. E. Gontarski, *The Grove Companion to Samuel Beckett* (New York: Grove, 2004), 485: entry on Rodin.
66. Christopher Ricks, *Beckett's Dying Words* (Oxford: Oxford University Press, 1993), 78.
67. Elizabeth Barry, *Beckett and Authority: The Uses of Cliché* (London: Palgrave Macmillan, 2006), 26.
68. Mercier, "Samuel Beckett and the Sheela-Na-Gig," 324.
69. Ibid., 308.
70. Schopenhauer, *World as Will and Representation Vol. II,* 534.
71. Ibid., 546.
72. Ibid., 542–43.
73. Ibid., 543.
74. Ibid.
75. Ibid.
76. Ibid., 539.
77. Ibid., 536.
78. Schopenhauer, *World as Will and Representation* Vol I, § 60, 328.
79. Ibid., § 60, 330.
80. As set out in his unpublished article "'Explore other channels': Beckett, Homosexuality and the Politics of Fertility," as delivered at the IASIL 2005 conference, Prague, July 26. See also "'First Love': Abortion and Infanticide in Beckett and Yeats," *Samuel Beckett: Debts and Legacies, Samuel Beckett Today/Aujourd'hui* 22 (2010): 79–92.
81. Cited in Schopenhauer, *World as Will and Representation,* Vol. I, § 60, 329.
82. Schopenhauer, *World as Will and Representation* Vol. I, § 54, 277.

4 Alternating and Alternative Sexualities

1. Leo Bersani, "Sociality and Sexuality," *Critical Inquiry* Vol. 26, No. 4 (Summer 2000): 656.
2. Michel Foucault, *The History of Sexuality,* vol. 1 (Harmondsworth: Penguin, 1990), 43.
3. Schopenhauer, *World as Will and Representation,* Vol. II, 561.
4. Ibid., 567.
5. Peter Boxall, "Beckett and Homoeroticism" in *Palgrave Advances in Samuel Beckett Studies,* ed. Lois Openheim (Basingstoke: Palgrave Macmillan, 2004), 110.
6. Jeffers, *Beckett's Masculinity,* 50.
7. Ibid., 53.
8. Harold Pinter, *Betrayal* (London: Faber and Faber, 1991), 35, 41.
9. Boxall, "Beckett and Homoeroticism," 117.

10. AnJanette Brush, "The Same Old Hag: Gender and (In)difference in Samuel Beckett's Trilogy," in *Engagement and Indifference: Beckett and the Political,* eds. Henry Sussman and Christopher Devenney (Albany: State University of New York Press, 2001), 133.

11. Leo Bersani, *Homos* (Cambridge, MA: Harvard University Press, 1995), 4.

12. Ibid., 3, 5.

13. Samuel Beckett, *The Complete Short Prose* (New York: Grove Press, 1995), 186. (hereafter *CSP*)

14. Boxall, "Beckett and Homoeroticism," 114.

15. The former proposition would find support in Bersani, who argues that "if a community were ever to exist in which it would no longer seem natural to define all relations as property relations (not only my money or my land, but also my country, my wife, my lover), we would first have to imagine a new erotics" (*Homos* 128). The bartering of a kiss rather than of a material possession might suggest the erotic relation replacing the property relation.

16. Bersani, *Homos,* 10.

17. For an exemplary reading of new forms of connectedness, see Boxall, who traces the modes of connection between the body of Molloy, the landscape, and the anatomy of Ruth/Edith (Boxall, "Beckett and Homoeroticism," 122–124).

18. Bersani, *Homos,* 7.

19. Ibid., 181.

20. Calvin Thomas, "Cultural Droppings: Bersani's Beckett," *Twentieth Century Literature* 47.2 (Summer 2001): 169.

21. Leo Bersani and Ulysses Dutoit, *Acts of Impoverishment: Beckett, Rothko, Resnais* (Cambridge, MA: Harvard University Press, 1993), 26, 27.

22. Bersani, *Homos,* 101.

23. Lee Edelman, *No Future: Queer Theory and the Death Drive* (Durham and London: Duke University Press, 2003), 21.

24. Edelman, *No Future,* 29.

25. Dylan Evan, *An Introductory Dictionary of Lacanian Psychoanalysis* (London: Routledge, 1996), 189.

26. Edelman, *No Future,* 36–37.

27. Ibid., 13.

28. Ibid., 101.

29. Ibid., 25.

30. Boxall, "Beckett and Homoeroticism," 118.

31. Alain Badiou, *On Beckett,* eds. Nina Power and Alberto Toscano (Manchester: Clinamen Press, 2003), 28.

32. Ibid., 12.

33. Ibid., 11.

34. Ibid., 28.

35. Ibid., 33.

36. Leo Bersani and Ulysse Dutoit, *Acts of Impoverishment,* 62.

37. Ibid., 63.

38. Ibid., 65.
39. Sigmund Freud, "'A Child is Being Beaten' (A Contribution to the Study of the Origin of Sexual Perversion)," in *On Psychopathology: The Penguin Freud Library*, vol. 10, trans. James Strachey, (London: Penguin, 1979), 175.
40. Ibid, 180.
41. Sigmund Freud, "The Economic Problem of Masochism," (1924) in *On Metapsychology: The Penguin Freud Library*, Volume 11, ed. and trans. James Strachey and Angela Richards, (London: Penguin, 1991), 418.
42. In contrast to Freud, but via a reading of him influenced by Leplanche, Bersani argues that, "sexuality would be that which is intolerable to the structured self" and yet one actively seeks out such a self-shattering, even though it might contain the unpleasure of self-divestiture. This turn suggests that sexuality "could be thought of as a tautology for masochism" (*The Freudian Body, Psychoanalysis and Art* [New York: Columbia University Press], 38, 39).
43. Kathy Sisson, "The Cultural Formation of S/M: History and Analysis," in *Safe, Sane and Consensual: Contemporary Perspectives on Sadomasochism*, ed. Darren Langdridge and Meg Barker (London: Palgrave Macmillan, 2007), 28.
44. Sheila Jeffreys, *Unpacking Queer Politics: A Lesbian Feminist Perspective* (Oxford: Blackwell, 2003), 120.
45. Lorena Leigh Saxe, "Sadomasochism and Exclusion" in *Adventures in Lesbian Philosophy*, ed. Claudia Card (Bloomington and Indianapolis: Indiana University Press, 1995), 66.
46. Michel Foucault, "Sade, Sergeant of Sex" trans. Alan Johnson in *Aesthetics, Method, and Epistemology*, Vol.2 *Essential Works of Foucault*, ed. James D. Faubion (Hardmondsworth: Penguin, 1998). Cited in Bersani, *Homos*, 88.
47. Bersani, *Homos*, 97.
48. Gilles Deleuze, "Coldness and Cruelty" in *Masochism*, (New York: Zone Books, 1991), 40.
49. Ibid., 39.
50. As cited in Deleuze, "Coldness and Cruelty," 38–39.
51. Ibid., 28–29.
52. Ibid., 124.
53. Calvin Thomas offers an alternative anally inflected relation via the concept of *Durchfall* that suggests not only failure and collapse but also "forgetting oneself" in an involuntary emptying of the bowels: "In terms of Bersani's hostility to seriousness, success, and sociality itself, what links Beckett's self-forgetful *Durchfall*, his 'determination to fail,' with Genet's invitation to view his works of literature [as] 'cultural droppings' is precisely the abject, marginal status of both Genet himself as gay outlaw and the Beckettian figure of the hero as the outcast, the self-forgetting, the expelled" (6).
54. William Hutchings, "'Shat into Grace' or Tale of a Turd: Why it is How it is in Samuel Beckett's *How It Is*," *Papers in Language and Literature* 21 (1985): 87.
55. Ibid., 83–4.
56. Ibid., 83.

5 Sex and Aesthetics

1. *The New Oxford Dictionary of English* (Oxford: Clarendon Press, 1998).
2. Clas Zilliacus, *Beckett and Broadcasting: A Study of the Works of Samuel Beckett for and in Radio and Television* (Abo: Abo Akademi, 1976), 32.
3. Ibid., 70.
4. Schopenhauer, *World as Will and Representation*, Vol. I §8, 35.
5. Zilliacus, *Beckett and Broadcasting*, 41.
6. Bryden, *Women in Samuel Beckett's Prose and Drama*, 101.
7. Ibid., 96.
8. Mercier, "Samuel Beckett and the Sheela-Na-Gig," 323.
9. Paul Lawley, "Adoption in Endgame," in *New Casebooks: Waiting for Godot* and *Endgame*, ed. Steven Connor (Basingstoke: Macmillan, 1992), 122.
10. Zilliacus, *Beckett and Broadcasting*, 30.
11. James Knowlson and John Pilling, *Frescoes of the Skull: The Later Prose and Drama of Samuel Beckett* (London: Calder, 1979), 86. Although the book has dual authorship, Knowlson was responsible for the chapter concerning *Krapp*.
12. S. E. Gontarski, *The Intent of Undoing in Samuel Beckett's Texts* (Bloomington: Indiana University Press, 1985), 60.
13. Knowlson and Pilling, *Frescoes of the Skull*, 88.
14. Jason David BeDuhn, *The Manichaean Body in Discipline and Ritual* (Baltimore, MD: Johns Hopkins University Press, 2002), 211.
15. Henri-Charles Puech, "The Concept of Redemption in Manichaeism" in *The Mystic Vision*, ed. J. Campbell (Princeton, NJ: Princeton University Press, 1968), 265.
16. Ibid., 292.
17. Knowlson and Pilling, *Frescoes of the Skull*, 87.
18. BeDuhn, *The Manichaean Body*, 166.
19. St. Augustine, "Reply to Faustus the Manichaean" 20.13, trans. Rev. Richard Stothert in *The Anti-Manichaean Writings of St. Augustine* (Whitefish, MT: Kessinger, 2005), 258.
20. Vivian Mercier, *Beckett/Beckett* (London: Souvenir Press, 1990), 198.
21. Julie Campbell has come to a similar conclusion, albeit through a different route. Rather than an emphasis on the oppositions within the play, Campbell applies Freud on the scatological humor of the play and argues that "the strongly defined contrasts between darkness and light undergo a process of convergence." ("The Semantic Krapp in *Krapp's Last Tape*," *Samuel Beckett: Crossroads and Borderlines, Samuel Beckett Today/Aujourd'hui* 6 (1994): 70). Her scatological emphasis differs from my own in that it focuses on elimination rather than on retention of feces, as shall be seen.
22. Gontarski, *The Intent of Undoing*, 61.
23. As quoted in Gontarski, *The Intent of Undoing*, 59.
24. Pierre Chabert, "*Krapp's Last Tape*: A Ritual of Listening and Recording," in *Beckett in the Theatre*, eds. Dougald McMillan and Martha Fehsenfeld (London: John Calder, 1988), 288–89.

25. P. J. Murphy, "Reincarnations of Joyce in Beckett's Fiction," *Debts and Legacies: Samuel Beckett Today/Aujourd'hui* 22 (2010): 73.
26. James Joyce, *A Portrait of the Artist as a Young Man* (London: Penguin, 1992), 227.
27. Ibid., 240.
28. Ibid., 224.
29. Ibid., 236.
30. Ibid., 231. As will be seen later in the chapter, such Romantic notions of the aesthetic sublime—in particular those of Schiller and Schopenhauer—gave Beckett pause.
31. Schopenhauer, *The World as Will and Representation* Vol. I, § 38, 196.
32. Schopenhauer, *On the Will in Nature,* trans. E. F. J. Payne. (New York: Berg, 1992), 83.
33. Wilhelm Windelband, *A History of Philosophy* (1901; Cresskill, NJ: Paper Tiger, 2001), 601.
34. Mark Nixon, " 'Scraps of German': Samuel Beckett reading German Literature' " *Samuel Beckett Today/Aujourd'hui* 16 (2006): 260–282.
35. James Knowlson, *Damned to Fame: The Life of Samuel Beckett.* (London: Bloomsbury, 1996), 242.
36. Ibid., 477.
37. Erik Tonning, *Samuel Beckett's Abstract Drama: Works for Stage and Screen 1962–1985* (Oxford, Bern, etc: Peter Lang, 2007), 183.
38. Feldman, *Beckett's Books*, 49, citing TCD MS 10967/248, and v. 253.
39. H. Porter Abbott, *Beckett Writing Beckett: The Author in the Autograph* (Ithaca, NY: Cornell University Press, 1996), 58.
40. Friedrich von Schiller, "Letters on the Aesthetic Education of Man," trans. Elizabeth M. Wilkinson and L. A. Willoughby in *Essays,* eds. Walter Hindered and Daniel O. Dahlstrom (London: Continuum, 1993), 173.
41. Ibid., 172.
42. Ibid.
43. Knowlson, *Damned to Fame,* 39,47.
44. Ibid., 457.
45. Schiller, "Letters," 169.
46. Friedrich von Schiller, "The Stage as a Moral Institution," trans. Jane Bannard Greene in *Essays on German Theater,* ed. Margaret Herzfeld-Sander (New York: Continuum, 1985), 33.
47. Mathew Feldman, *Beckett's Books,* 50, citing TCD MS 10967/252.1.
48. Schopenhauer, *World as Will and Representation* Vol. I, § 36, 185.
49. Ibid., § 60, 328.
50. Ibid.
51. C. G. Jung, *Dream Analysis: Notes of the Seminar Given in 1928–1930 by C. G. Jung,* ed. William McGuire (London: Routledge and Kegan Paul, 1984), 429.
52. Schopenhauer, *World as Will and Representation* Vol. I, § 36, 185.
53. Erik Tonning, *Samuel Beckett's Abstract Drama,* 39.
54. Nixon, "Scraps of German," 278.

55. C. J. Ackerley, *Obscure Locks, Simple Keys: The Annotated Watt* (Tallahassee, FL: Journal of Beckett Studies Books, 2005), 108.

6 Aesthetic Reproduction across the Oeuvre

1. Ulrika Maude, *Beckett, Technology and the Body* (Cambridge: Cambridge University Press, 2009), 10.
2. Abbott, *Beckett Writing Beckett*, 93.
3. Ibid., 92.
4. See Paul Stewart, *Zone of Evaporation: Samuel Beckett's Disjunctions* (New York and Amsterdam: Rodopi, 2006), 140–145.
5. Hugh Kenner, *Flaubert, Joyce and Beckett: The Stoic Comedians* (1962) (Normal and London: Dalkey Archive Press, 2005) 87.
6. Maurice Blanchot, "Where Now? Who Now?" *Evergreen Review* 2, 7 (Winter 1959), reprinted in *On Beckett: Essays and Criticism*, ed. S. E. Gontarski (New York: Grove Press, 1986), 144.
7. J. E. Dearlove, "The Voice and Its Words: *How It Is*" in *On Beckett: Essays and Criticism,* ed. S. E. Gontarski (New York: Grove Press, 1986), 156.
8. H. Porter Abbott suggests that "Beckett, in his reprocessing of the two epic subjects—how it is and how it began—abolishes the traditional structure and thematics of the former, subsuming the entire subject of 'how it its' into an ontology of new beginnings." (*Beckett Writing Beckett,* 99) My focus on the invocation of the muse necessarily engages with the nature of this ontology.
9. John Milton, *Paradise Lost,* ed. Alastair Fowler (London and New York: Longman, 1990), ll. 19–26.
10. Coetzee, J. M., "Murphy" in *Doubling the Point: Essays and Interviews*, ed. David Atwell (Cambridge, MA: Harvard University Press, 1992), 31.
11. To "fail better" is, of course, a repeated refrain in *Worstward Ho*: "Ever failed. No matter. Try again. Fail Again. Fail Better." (*C* 81).
12. Otto Rank, *The Trauma of Birth,* 156.
13. Ibid., 147.
14. Ibid., 189.
15. Ibid., 158.
16. Abbott, *Beckett Writing Beckett,* 1–22.
17. According to James Knowlson, Beckett's own intrauterine memories "were associated more often with feelings of being trapped and unable to escape, imprisoned and in pain." *Damned to Fame:,* 2.
18. Knowlson, *Frescoes of the Skull,* 138.
19. Samuel Taylor Coleridge, *Biographia Literaria–Or Biographical Sketches of My Literary Life and Opinions* (1817) (London: Read Books, 2006), 167.
20. Daniela Caselli, "Tiny Little Things in Beckett's *Company*" in *Samuel Beckett Today/Aujourd'hui* 15 (2005), 273–274.
21. Anthony Cronin, *Samuel Beckett: The Last Modernist* (London: Flamingo, 1997), 15.
22. James Knowlson, *Damned to Fame: The Life of Samuel Beckett,* 652; 652–3.

23. Ibid., 652.
24. Abbott, *Beckett Writing Beckett,* 11.
25. Ibid.
26. Ibid., 15.
27. Ibid., 19.
28. Steven Connor, *Samuel Beckett: Repetition, Theory and Text* (Oxford: Basil Blackwell, 1988), 126.
29. Stanton B. Garner Jr., *The Absent Voice: Narrative Comprehension in the Theater* (Urbana and Chicago: University of Chicago Press), xiv.
30. Walter D. Asmus, "Practical Aspects of Theatre, Radio and Television: Rehearsal Notes of the German Premiere of Beckett's *That Time* and *Footfalls* at the Schiller-Theatre Werkstatt, Berlin," *The Journal of Beckett Studies,* Vol. 2 (Summer, 1977): 82–96.
31. Mel Gussow (ed.), *Conversations with and about Beckett,* (New York: Grove Press, 1996), 89.
32. Connor, *Samuel Beckett: Repetition, Theory and Text,* 185.
33. Ibid., 192.
34. Ibid., 193.
35. James Knowlson, *Damned to Fame,* 590.
36. Considering the evidence for and against the play being written *for* Whitelaw, Knowlson judges that "it would be truer to say that he wrote the play *for the occasion,* believing at that time that Irene Worth was going to play it." (*Damned to Fame,* 663)
37. *Conversations with and about Beckett,* 85.
38. Ibid., 86.
39. Connor suggests that Mouth "performs the function [...] of a miniaturized stage." (*Samuel Beckett: Repetition, Theory and Text,* 162).
40. Knowlson, *Frescoes of the Skull,* 200.
41. Ann Wilson, "'Her Lips Moving': The Castrated Voice of *Not I,*" in *Women in Beckett: Performance and Critical Perspectives,* ed. Linda Ben-Zvi (Urbana and Chicago: University of Illinois Press, 1992), 198–199. Interestingly, in the essay which follows Wilson's, Dina Sherzer argues that *Not I* demonstrates Beckett's "uncanny sense of what it means to be on the margins and to be female" ("Portrait of a Woman: The Experience of Marginality in *Not I*". [206]). Connor points out that the image of the mouth "with its teeth and tongue includes phallic fullness and vaginal hollowness..." (*Samuel Beckett: Repetition, Theory and Text,* 163).
42. Wilson, "Her Lips Moving," 192.
43. Keir Elam, "*Not I:* Beckett's Mouth and the Ars(e) Rhetorica, " in *Beckett at 80 / Beckett in Context,* ed. Enoch Brater (Oxford: University of Oxford Press, 1986), 124–48.
44. Knowlson, *Frescoes of the Skull,* 203.
45. Simon Critchley, *Very Little...Almost Nothing: Death, Philosophy, Literature* (London: Routledge, 1997), 175.
46. James Knowlson, *Damned to Fame,* 590.

47. Knowlson, *Frescoes of the Skull*, 197, adapting Enoch Brater "Dada, Surrealism and the Genesis of *Not I*," *Modern Drama* XVIII, no. 1, (March 1975): 57. Steven Connor also makes use of the anecdote in *Repetition, Theory and Text*. "Failure to understand is the essence of the play, the gesture seems to say, and one cannot comprehend or interpret this failure from the outside; all one can do is replicate it" (189).

48. Martin Esslin, "Samuel Beckett and the Art of Radio," in *On Beckett: Essays and Criticism*, ed. S. E. Gontarski (New York: Grove Press, 1986), 381.

49. Martin Esslin, "What Beckett Teaches Me: His Minimalist Approach to Ethics," *Beckett in the 1990s: Samuel Beckett Today / Aujourd'hui* 2 (1993): 15.

50. Michael Robinson, *The Long Sonata of the Dead* (New York: Grove, 1969), 298.

51. Paul Lawley, "The Difficult Birth: An Image of Utterance in Beckett," in *Make Sense Who May: Essays on Samuel Beckett's Later Works,* eds. Robin J. Davies and Lance St. John Butler (Gerrards Cross: Colin Smythe, 1989), 3 and 10.

52. Ibid., 3.

53. Zilliacus, *Beckett and Broadcasting*, 134.

54. Ibid., 136.

Conclusion

1. Rank, *The Trauma of Birth*, 160.

Bibliography

Works by Samuel Beckett

"Che Sciagura." In *TCD: A College Miscellany* 36 (14 Nov. 1929), 42.

Company, Ill Seen Ill Said, Worstward Ho, Stirrings Still. London: Faber and Faber, 2009.

The Complete Dramatic Works. London: Faber and Faber, 1990.

The Complete Short Prose. New York: Grove Press, 1995.

Disjecta: Miscellaneous Writings and a Dramatic Fragment. Edited by Ruby Cohn. London: Calder, 1983.

Dream of Fair to Middling Women (Dublin: Black Cat Press, 1992).

Eleutheria. Translated by Barbara Wright. London: Faber and Faber, 1996.

The Expelled, The Calmative, The End, First Love. London: Faber and Faber, 2009.

How It Is. London: Faber and Faber, 2009.

The Letters of Samuel Beckett 1929-1940. Edited by Martha Dow Feshenfeld and Lois More Overbeck. Cambridge: Cambridge University Press, 2009.

Malone Dies. London: Faber and Faber, 2010.

Mercier and Camier. London: Faber and Faber, 2010.

Molloy. London: Faber and Faber, 2009.

More Pricks Than Kicks. London: Faber and Faber, 2010.

Murphy. London: Faber and Faber, 2009.

Proust and the Three Dialogues with Georges Duthuit. London: Calder, 1987.

Selected Poems: 1930–1989. London: Faber and Faber, 2009.

The Unnamable. London: Faber and Faber, 2010.

Watt. London: Faber and Faber, 2009.

Other Works

Abbott, H. Porter. *Beckett Writing Beckett: The Author in the Autograph.* Ithaca, NY: Cornell University Press, 1996.

Acheson, James. "Beckett and the Heresy of Love." In *Beckett's Women.* Edited by Linda Ben-Zvi. Urbana and Chicago: University of Illinois Press, 1990.

Ackerley, C. J. *Demented Particulars: The Annotated Murphy*. Tallahassee, FL: Journal of Beckett Studies Books, 1998.

——— "Lassata Sed: Samuel Beckett's Portraits of his Fair to Middling Women." *Samuel Beckett Today/Aujourd'hui* 12 (2002): 56–69.

——— *Obscure Locks, Simple Keys: The Annotated Watt*. Tallahassee, FL: Journal of Beckett Studies Books, 2005.

Ackerley, C. J. and S. E. Gontarski. *The Grove Companion to Samuel Beckett*. New York: Grove, 2004.

Asmus, Walter D. "Practical Aspects of Theatre, Radio and Television: Rehearsal Notes of the German Premiere of Beckett's *That Time* and *Footfalls* at the Schiller-Theatre Werkstatt, Berlin." *The Journal of Beckett Studies* 2 (Summer, 1977): 82–96.

Augustine, *The Anti-Manichaean Writings of St. Augustine*. Translated by Philip Schaff. Whitefish MT: Kessinger, 2005.

——— *Concerning the City of God against the Pagans*. Translated by Henry Bettenson. Harmondsworth, Penguin, 2003.

——— *Confessions*. Translated by R. S. Pine-Coffin. Harmondsworth: Penguin, 1961.

——— *On Marriage and Concupiscence*. Translated by Phillip Schaff. Whitefish MT: Kessinger, 2010.

——— "On the Merits and Forgiveness of Sins, and on the Baptism of Infants." In *St Augustine Anti-Pelagian Writings: Nicene and Post-Nicene Fathers of the Christian Church Vol. 5* (1887). Translated by Philip Schaff. Whitefish, MT: Kessinger 2004.

Badiou, Alain. *On Beckett*. Edited by Nina Power and Alberto Toscano. Manchester: Clinamen Press, 2003.

Baker, Phil. *Beckett and the Mythology of Psychoanalysis*. Basingstoke: Macmillan, 1997.

Barca, Calderón de la. *La Vida es Sueño*. Edited by Albert Solomon. Manchester: Manchester University Press, 1961.

Barry, Elizabeth. *Beckett and Authority: The Uses of Cliché*. London: Palgrave Macmillam, 2006.

BeDuhn, Jason David. *The Manichaean Body in Discipline and Ritual*. Baltimore: Johns Hopkins University Press, 2002.

Bersani, Leo. *The Freudian Body, Psychoanalysis and Art*. New York: Columbia University Press.

——— *Homos*. Cambridge, Mass.: Harvard University Press, 1995.

——— "Sociality and Sexuality." *Critical Inquiry* 26, no. 4 (Summer, 2000): 641–656.

Bersani, Leo, and Ulysses Dutoit. *Acts of Impoverishment: Beckett, Rothko, Resnais*. Cambridge, MA: Harvard University Press, 1993.

Blanchot, Maurice. "Where Now? Who Now?" *Evergreen Review* 2 (Winter 1959). Reprinted in *On Beckett: Essays and Criticism*. Edited by S. E. Gontarski. New York: Grove Press, 1986.

Boxall, Peter. "Beckett and Homoeroticism." In *Palgrave Advances in Samuel Beckett Studies*. Edited by Lois Openheim. Basingstoke: Palgrave Macmillan, 2004.

Brater, Enoch. "Dada, Surrealism and the Genesis of *Not I*." *Modern Drama* XVIII, no.1, (1975): 49–59.

Brienza, Susan. "Clods, Whore, and Bitches: Misogyny in Beckett's Early Fiction." In *Beckett's Women*. Edited by Linda Ben-Zvi. Urbana and Chicago: University of Illinois Press, 1990.

Brown, Terence. *Ireland: A Social and Cultural History, 1922–1985*. London: Fontana, 1987.

———— "Some Young Doom: Beckett and The Child." In *Ireland's Literature: Selected Essays*, Mullingar: Lilliput, 1988.

Brush, AnJanette. "The Same Old Hag: Gender and (In)difference in Samuel Beckett's Trilogy." In *Engagement and Indifference: Beckett and the Political*. Edited by Henry Sussman and Christopher Devenney. Albany: State University of New York Press, 2001.

Bryden, Mary. *Samuel Beckett and the Idea of God*. London: Palgrave, 1998.

———— *Women in Samuel Beckett's Prose and Drama: Her Own Other*. Lanham, MD: Barnes & Noble, 1993.

Büttner, Gottfried. "Beckett and Schopenhauer." *Samuel Beckett: Endlessness in the Year 2000, Samuel Beckett Today/Aujourd'hui* 11 (2002): 114–112.

Calder, John. *The Philosophy of Samuel Beckett*. London: Calder, 2001.

Campbell, Julie. "The Semantic Krapp in *Krapp's Last Tape*." *Samuel Beckett: Crossroads and Borderlines, Samuel Beckett Today/Aujourd'hui* 6 (1994): 63–86.

Carlson, Julia. *Banned in Ireland: Censorship and the Irish Writer*. Athens: University of Georgia Press.

Caselli, Daniella. "The Child in Beckett's Work: Introduction." *Historicising Beckett/ Issues of Performance, Samuel Beckett Today/Aujourd'hui* 15 (2005): 259–260.

———— "Tiny Little Things in Beckett's Company." *Historicising Beckett/Issues of Performance, Samuel Beckett Today/Aujourd'hui* 15 (2005): 271–280.

Chabert, Pierre. "*Krapp's Last Tape*: A Ritual of Listening and Recording." In *Beckett in the Theatre*. Edited by Dougald McMillan and Martha Fehsenfeld. London: John Calder, 1988.

Coetzee, J. M. "*Murphy*." In *Doubling the Point: Essays and Interviews*. Edited by David Atwell. Cambridge, MA: Harvard University Press, 1992.

Coleridge, Samuel Taylor. *Biographia Literaria———— Or Biographical Sketches of My Literary Life and Opinions*. (1817) London: Read Books, 2006.

Connor, Steven. *Samuel Beckett: Repetition, Theory and Text*. Oxford: Basil Blackwell, 1988.

Critchley, Simon. *Very Little…Almost Nothing: Death, Philosophy, Literature*. London: Routledge, 1997.

Cronin, Anthony. *Samuel Beckett: The Last Modernist*. London: Flamingo, 1997.

Dearlove, J. E. "The Voice and Its Words: *How It Is*." In *On Beckett: Essays and Criticism*. Edited by S. E. Gontarski. New York: Grove Press, 1986.

Deleuze, Gilles. "Coldness and Cruelty." In *Masochism*. New York: Zone Books, 1991.

Deleuze, Gilles, and Félix Guattari. *Anti-Oedipus: Capitalism and Schizophrenia*. Translated by Robert Hurley, Mark Seem, and Helen R. Lane. London: Athlone Press, 1984.

Doll, Mary A. *Beckett and Myth: An Archetypal Approach*. Syracuse, NY: Syracuse University Press, 1988.

Dollimore, Jonathan. *Death, Desire and Loss in Western Culture*. Harmondsworth: Allen Lane, Penguin, 1998.

Dyce, Alexander, Rev. (ed.). *The Dramatic and Poetical Works of Robert Greene and George Peele*. London: Routledge, 1861.

Elam, Keir. *"Not I:* Beckett's Mouth and the Ars(e) Rhetorica." In *Beckett at 80/ Beckett in Context*. Edited by Enoch Brater. Oxford: University of Oxford Press, 1986.

Edelman, Lee. *No Future: Queer Theory and the Death Drive*. Durham and London: Duke University Press, 2004.

Esslin, Martin. "Samuel Beckett and the Art of Radio." In *On Beckett: Essays and Criticism*. Edited by S. E. Gontarski.New York: Grove Press, 1986.

———"What Beckett Teaches Me: His Minimalist Approach to Ethics." *Beckett in the 1990s: Samuel Beckett Today/Aujourd'hui* 2 (1993): 13–20.

Evan, Dylan. *An Introductory Dictionary of Lacanian Psychoanalysis*. London: Routledge, 1996.

Feldman, Matthew. *Beckett's Books: A Cultural History of Samuel Beckett's "Interwar Notes."* London: Continuum, 2006.

Ferriter, Diarmaid. *Occasions of Sin: Sex and Society in Modern Ireland*. London: Profile, 2009.

Fletcher, John. *The Faithful Shepherdess*. Edited by F. W. Moorman. London: Dent, 1972.

Fletcher, John. *Samuel Beckett's Art*. London: Chatto and Windus, 1967.

———. "Samuel Beckett and Jonathon Swift: Toward a Comparative Study." http://www.themodernword.com/beckett/paper_fletcher.html (accessed December 16, 2010).

Foucault, Michel. *The History of Sexuality, vol. 1*. Translated by Robert Hurley. Harmondsworth: Penguin, 1990.

——— *The History of Sexuality vol. 2: The Use of Pleasure*. Translated by Robert Hurley. Harmondsworth: Penguin, 1992.

——— "Sade, Sergeant of Sex." Translated by Alan Johnson. In *Aesthetics, Method, and Epistemology, Essential Works of Foucault, vol.2*. Edited by James D. Faubion. Hardmondsworth: Penguin, 1998.

Freud, Sigmund. *Case Histories I, "Dora" and "Little Hans": The Penguin Freud Library*, vol. 8. Translated by Alix and James Strachey. Edited by Angela Richards. London: Penguin, 1983.

———*Case Histories II. The Penguin Freud Library*, vol. 9. Edited and translated by James Strachey and Angela Richards London: Penguin, 1990.

———*Civilization, Society and Religion. The Penguin Freud Library*, vol. 12. Edited and translated by James Strachey and Albert Dickson. London: Penguin, 1985.

——— *On Metapsychology: The Penguin Freud Library*, vol. 11. Edited and translated by James Strachey and Angela Richards. London: Penguin, 1991.

——— *On Psychopathology: The Penguin Freud Library*, vol.10. Edited and translated by James Strachey and Angela Richards. London: Penguin, 1979.

———— *On Sexuality: Three Essays on the Theory of Sexuality and Other Works, The Penguin Freud Library,* vol. 7. Translated by James Strachey. Edited by Angela Richards. London: Penguin, 1991.

Garner Jr., Stanton B. *The Absent Voice: Narrative Comprehension in the Theater.* Urbana and Chicago: University of Chicago Press.

Gibson, Andrew. "Afterword: Beckett, Ireland and Elsewhere." In *Beckett and Ireland*. Edited by Sean Kennedy. Cambridge: Cambridge University Press, 2010.

Goldman, Alan. "Plain Sex." In *The Philosophy of Sex: Contemporary Readings.* Edited by Alan Soble and Alan Nicholas Power. Lanham, MD: Rowman and Littlefield, 2007.

Gontarski, S. E. *The Intent of Undoing in Samuel Beckett's Dramatic Texts.* Bloomington: Indiana University Press, 1985.

Green, David. "Beckett's Dream: More Niente than Bel." *The Journal of Beckett Studies* 5 Pt. 1&2 (1995): 67–80.

Gussow, Mel (ed.). *Conversations with and about Beckett.* New York: Grove Press, 1999.

Hamilton, Christopher. "Sex." In *The Philosophy of Sex: Contemporary Readings.* Edited by Alan Soble and Alan Nicholas Power. Lanham, MD: Rowman and Littlefield, 2007.

Harvey, Lawrence E. *Samuel Beckett: Poet and Critic.* Princeton: Princeton University Press, 1970.

Hatch, David. "Samuel Beckett's 'Che Sciagura' and the Subversion of Irish Moral Convention." *All Sturm and No Drang: Beckett and Romanticism/Beckett at Reading 2006, Samuel Beckett Today/Aujourd'hui* 18 (2007): 241–256.

Hutchings, William. " 'Shat into Grace' or Tale of a Turd: Why it is How it is in Samuel Beckett's *How It Is.*" *Papers in Language and Literature* 21 (1985): 64–87.

Jeffers, Jennifer M. *Beckett's Masculinity.* New York: Palgrave Macmillan, 2009.

Jeffreys, Sheila. *Unpacking Queer Politics: A Lesbian Feminist Perspective.* Oxford: Blackwell, 2003.

Joyce, James. *A Portrait of the Artist as a Young Man.* London: Penguin, 1992.

Jung, C. G. *Dream Analysis: Notes of the Seminar given in 1928-1930 by C. G. Jung.* Edited by William McGuire. London: Routledge and Kegan Paul, 1984.

Kennedy, Jake. "Modernist (Im)mobilities: Marcel Duchamp, Samuel Beckett and the Avant-Garde Bike." *Tout-fait: The Marcel Duchamp Studies On-Line Journal* (2005), 1. www.toutfait.com/online_journal_details.php?postid=4331 (Accessed February 21, 2006).

Kennedy, Sean. " 'First Love': Abortion and Infanticide in Beckett and Yeats." *Samuel Beckett: Debts and Legacies, Samuel Beckett Today/Aujourd'hui* 22 (2010): 79–92.

———— " 'A Lingering Dissolution': All That Fall and the Protestant Fears of Engulfment in the Irish Free State." *Assaph: Studies in the Theatre* 17/18 (2003): 247–262.

Kenner, Hugh. *Flaubert, Joyce and Beckett: The Stoic Comedians.* (1962) Normal and London: Dalkey Archive Press, 2005.

————. *Samuel Beckett: A Critical Study*. London: John Calder, 1962.

Kim, Rina. "Severing Connections with Ireland: Women and the Irish Free State in Beckett's Writing." *Historicising Beckett/Issues of Performance, Samuel Beckett Today/Aujourd'hui* 15, (2005): 57–69.

Knowlson, James. *Damned to Fame: The Life of Samuel Beckett*. London: Bloomsbury, 1996.

————. *Light and Darkness in the Theatre of Samuel Beckett*. London: Turret Books, 1972.

Knowlson, James, and John Pilling. *Frescoes of the Skull: The Later Prose and Drama of Samuel Beckett*. London: John Calder, 1979.

Kroll, Jeri L. "Belacqua as artist and lover: 'What a Misfortune.'" *The Journal of Beckett Studies*, Vol 3 (1978): 10–39.

Laqueur. Thomas W. *Solitary Sex: A Cultural History of Masturbation*. Cambridge, MA: Zone Books, 2003.

Lawley, Paul. "Adoption in *Endgame*." In *New Casebooks: Waiting for Godot and Endgame*. Edited by Steven Connor. Basingstoke: Macmillan, 1992.

————. "The Difficult Birth: An Image of Utterance in Beckett." In *Make Sense Who May: Essays on Samuel Beckett's Later Works*. Edited by Robin J. Davies and Lance St. John Butler. Gerrards Cross: Colin Smythe, 1989.

Leigh Saxe, Lorena. "Sadomasochism and Exclusion." In *Adventures in Lesbian Philosophy*. Edited by Claudia Card. Bloomington and Indianapolis: Indiana University Press, 1995.

Marin, Pater. *Censorship in the Two Irelands 1922-1939*. Dublin: Irish Academic Press, 2006.

Maude, Ulrika. *Beckett, Technology and the Body*. Cambridge: Cambridge University Press, 2009.

Mays, J. C. C. "Young Beckett's Irish Roots." *Irish University Review: A Journal of Irish Studies*, 14 (1984): 18–33.

McLaren, Angus. *Twentieth-Century Sexuality: A History*. Oxford: Blackwell, 1999.

Menzies, Janet. "Beckett's Bicycles." *The Journal of Beckett Studies* No. 6 (1980): 97–105.

Mercier, Vivian. *Beckett/Beckett*. London: Souvenir Press, 1990.

————. "Samuel Beckett and the Sheela-na-gig." *The Kenyon Review* XXIII (1961): 299–324.

Milton, John, *Paradise Lost*. Edited by Alastair Fowler. London and New York: Longman, 1990.

Morrison, Kristin. "'Meet in Paradize': Beckett's Shavian Women." In *Women in Beckett: Performance and Critical Perspectives*. Edited by Linda Ben-Zvi. Urbana and Chicago: University of Illinois Press, 1992.

Murphy, P. J. "Reincarnations of Joyce in Beckett's Fiction." *Debts and Legacies; Samuel Beckett Today/Aujourd'hui* 22 (2010): 67–78.

Nixon, Mark. "'Scraps of German': Samuel Beckett reading German Literature." *Samuel Beckett Today/Aujourd'hui 16* (2006): 259–282.

O'Hara, J. D. *Samuel Beckett's Hidden Drives: Structural Uses of Depth Psychology*. Gainesville: University Press of Florida, 1997.

Pilling, John (ed). *Beckett's Dream Notebook*. Reading: Beckett International Foundation, 1999.

——— *A Companion to Dream of Fair to Middling Women*. Tallahassee: Journal of Beckett Studies Books, 2004.

——— "*Proust* and Schopenhauer: Music and Shadows." In *Beckett and Music*. Edited by Mary Bryden. Oxford: Oxford University Press, 1998.

Pinter, Harold. *Betrayal*. London: Faber and Faber, 1991.

Proust, Marcel. *In Search of Lost Time Vol 1 Swann's Way*. Translated by C. K. Scott Moncrieff and Terence Kilmartin. Revised by D. J. Enright. London: Vintage, 1996.

Puech, Henri-Charles. "The Concept of Redemption in Manichaeism." In *The Mystic Vision*. Edited by J. Campbell. Princeton, NJ: Princeton University Press, 1968.

Rabinovitz, Rubin. "Stereoscopic or Stereotypic: Characterization in Beckett's Fiction." In *Women in Beckett: Performances and Critical Perspectives*. Edited by Linda Ben-Zvi. Urbana: University of Illinois Press, 1992.

Rahner, Hugo. *Greek Myths and Christian Mastery*. New York: Biblio and Tannen, 1971.

Rank, Otto. *The Trauma of Birth*. (1929) New York: Dover, 1993.

Ricks, Christopher. *Beckett's Dying Words*. Oxford: Oxford University Press, 1993.

Roberts, Mary Louise. *Civilization without Sexes: Reconstructing Gender in Postwar France, 1917–27*. Chicago: University of Chicago Press, 1994.

Robinson, Michael. *The Long Sonata of the Dead*. New York: Grove, 1969.

Rout, Ettie. *Safe Marriage: A Return to Sanity*. London: Heineman, 1922.

Schiller, Friedrich von. "Letters on the Aesthetic Education of Man." Translated by Elizabeth M. Wilkinson and L. A. Willoughby. In *Essays*. Edited by Walter Hindered and Daniel O. Dahlstrom. London: Continuum, 1993.

——— "The Stage as a Moral Institution." Translated by Jane Bannard Greene. In *Essays on German Theater*. Edited by Margaret Herzfeld-Sander. New York: Continuum, 1985.

Schopenhauer, Arthur. *Essays and Aphorisms*. Translated by R. J. Hollingdale. Harmondsworth: Penguin, 2004.

——— *On the Will in Nature*. Translated E. F. J. Payne. New York: Berg, 1992.

——— *The World as Will and Representation*, Vols. I and II. Translated by E. F. J. Payne. New York: Dover, 1969.

Scruton, Roger. *Sexual Desire: A Philosophical Investigation*. London: Continuum, 2006.

Shakespeare, William. *Henry VI, Part 2*. In *The Complete Oxford Shakespeare I: Histories*. Edited by Stanley Wells and Gary Taylor. Oxford: Oxford University Press, 1987.

Simoons, Frederick. *Plants of Life, Plants of Death*. Madison: University of Wisconsin Press, 1998.

Sisson, Kathy. "The Cultural Formation of S/M: History and Analysis." In *Safe, Sane and Consensual: Contemporary Perspectives on Sadomasochism*. Edited by Darren Langdridge and Meg Barker. London: Palgrave Macmillan, 2007.

Soble, Alan. "Masturbation Again." In *The Philosophy of Sex: Contemporary Readings.* Edited by Alan Soble and Alan Nicholas Power. Lanham, MD: Rowman and Littlefield, 2007.

Solomon, Robert. "Sex and Perversion." In *Philosophy and Sex.* Edited by Robert Baker and Frederick Elliston. Buffalo, NY: Prometheus Books, 1975.

Stewart, Paul. *Zone of Evaporation: Samuel Beckett's Disjunctions.* New York and Amsterdam: Rodopi, 2006.

Stopes, Marie. *Enduring Passion.* Toronto: McClelland and Stewart, 1928.

Stoyanov, Yuri. *The Other God: Dualist Religions from Antiquity to the Cathar Heresy.* New Haven, CT: Yale University Press, 2000.

Tajiri, Yoshiki "The Mechanization of Sexuality in Beckett's Early Work." *Samuel Beckett Today/Aujourd'hui* 12 (2002).

——— *Samuel Beckett and the Prosthetic Body: The Organs and Senses in Modernism.* London: Palgrave Macmillan, 2007.

Thomas, Calvin. "Cultural Droppings: Bersani's Beckett." *Twentieth Century Literature* 47.2 (Summer 2001): 169–196.

Thompson, Stephen, "'It's not my fault sir': The Child, Presence and Stage Space in Beckett's Theatre." *Historicising Beckett/Issues of Performance, Samuel Beckett Today/Aujourd'hui* 15 (2005): 261–270.

Tonning, Erik. *Samuel Beckett's Abstract Drama: Works for Stage and Screen 1962–1985.* Oxford, Bern, etc: Peter Lang, 2007.

van de Velde, Theodore. *Ideal Marriage: Its Psychology and Technique.* (1926) New York: Random House, 1957.

Voltaire. *Candide, or Optimism.* Translated by Henry Morley (1922), Introduction and notes by Gita May. New York: Barnes and Noble Classics, 2003.

Wilson, Ann. "'Her Lips Moving': The Castrated Voice of Not I." In *Women in Beckett: Performance and Critical Perspectives.* Edited by Linda Ben-Zvi–. Urbana and Chicago: University of Illinois Press, 1992.

Windelband, Wilhelm. *A History of Philosophy.* (1901) Cresskill, NJ: Paper Tiger, 2001.

Wittgenstein, Ludwig. *Philosophical Investigations I.* Translated by. G. E. M. Anscombe. Oxford: Blackwell, 1983.

Zilliacus, Clas. *Beckett and Broadcasting: A Study of the Works of Samuel Beckett for and in Radio and Television.* Abo: Abo Akademi, 1976.

Index

Works by Samuel Beckett are listed under individual titles. Information found in the notes are denoted by n. (eg., Campbell, Julie, n. 211)